Ranji

Ranji

PRINCE OF CRICKETERS

ALAN ROSS

COLLINS

8 Grafton Street London W1

1983

William Collins Sons and Co. Ltd.
London · Glasgow · Sydney · Auckland
Toronto · Johannesburg

British Library Cataloguing in Publication Data

Ross, Alan
 Ranji.
 1. Ranjitsinhji   2. Cricket players—India—
 Biography
 I. Title
 796.35'8'0924   GV915.R/

ISBN 0—00—217075—2

First published 1983
© Alan Ross 1983
Set in Garamond
Made and Printed in Great Britain by
William Collins Sons & Co Ltd, Glasgow

For Michael Davie and Bill Purkiss
in memory of A. F. Wensley

'Who will ever forget the cricket ground at Hove in those days, salt tang in the air, and the deck chairs full, and a stand in progress between Ranji and Fry? East and West twain for hours, the occult and the rational.'

Neville Cardus

'He was an ambassador of cooperation, friendship and good will between the two races. When he had succeeded to the great responsibility of rulership he never wearied of working for the advancement and welfare of his people. A great ruler and a great gentleman, a tried and trusted personal friend.'

Lord Willingdon, Viceroy of India

CONTENTS

CONTENTS

ILLUSTRATIONS

ILLUSTRATIONS

Preface

The year 1983 is the fiftieth anniversary of the death of K. S. Ranjitsinhji, an English cricketer and an Indian prince. As the former he was unique, as the latter enlightened.

To someone like myself, born in India and brought up in Sussex, Ranji has special meaning. The Sussex–India connection is more than sentimental, as it was for Ranji and, in due course, for his remarkable nephew Duleepsinhji. Ranji began a Sussex link with the sub-continent that has continued to this day.

Ranji played for Sussex, missing only the season of 1898, between 1895 and 1904. He played again, though rather less often, in 1908 and 1912. In 1920, aged 48, he played four innings. K. S. Duleepsinhji played for Sussex from 1926 to 1932. Since the war Indians and Pakistanis who have played for Sussex include the Nawab of Pataudi, Javed Miandad and Imran Khan.

The writing of this book is in the nature of a return for the pleasure and involvement Sussex cricket has given me. I came to live in Sussex during Duleep's last season when Sussex, but for the illness that ended his career, might well have won the championship. In the five innings I saw him play his grace and his frailty were equally apparent. In the spring of the next year Ranji died.

I had little idea until I began this book of the complexity of Ranji's character or of the twists and turns of his career. The Indian part of his life – from 1907 when he became Jam Saheb of Nawanagar, 'the prince of a little State, but the king of a great game', to his death on 2 April 1933 – would make a long enough book on its own. The Lytton papers in the India Office Library contain four boxes of documents dealing with the vexed problem of the Nawanagar ports alone.

I have tried to avoid going too deeply into local issues that, however absorbing to Ranji at the time, are of relatively little interest now. Ranji's life was almost equally divided between cricket and affairs of State. His own wish that the former should not take precedence over the latter extended to the appointing of a biographer, Roland Wild, who had little interest in and scant knowledge of cricket.

That was fifty years ago. Today it is Ranjitsinhji the legendary cricketer who concerns us, rather than the Prince. The ruler has his due place in these pages, nevertheless, for Ranji not only pulled Jamnagar into the twentieth century, proving himself an imaginative, conscientious and progressive administrator but, in the League of Nations at Geneva and in the Chamber of Princes at Delhi, he was involved in some of the historic events of his time. His legacy can be seen in the streets of his capital today.

Among those who have been of assistance to me in the writing of this book I must first put the present Jam Saheb and Ranji's great nephew, Prince Satrusalyasinhji. A talented performer for Sussex Club and Ground himself, and unlucky not to play for the county, he put at my disposal the splendid Pratap Vilas Palace for as long as I wanted. Also, he arranged for us to see – sometimes driven by him, sometimes not – every place that had significance in Ranji's life, both in Jamnagar and in the outlying country: his birthplace at Sarodar, his hunting lodge at Kileshwar, his summer house at Balachari. We visited with him the ports of Bedi and Rozi, the development of which was close to Ranji's heart. He could not have been more generous of both time and hospitality. Moreover he made available, from the long-neglected accumulation of albums in the Jam Palace, many of the photographs that are in this book.

Also in India, my thanks are due to Mr Peter Rogerson, Headmaster of Rajkumar College, Rajkot, for his kindness and hospitality. Mr J. P. Vara, of Jamnagar, the son of Ranji's own photographer, has been immensely helpful over photographs, as has Mr Clive Finn, in relation to photographs at Hove.

I should like, also, to thank the staff in the libraries of the India

Office, *The Times* and the *Daily Mail* for their courteous assistance; Mr H. A. Osborne, the Librarian at the County Ground, Hove; Mr Stephen Green, the Curator at Lord's; Mr Arthur Dumbrell, Honorary Secretary of the Sussex Cricket Society; Mr Nicholas Sharp and Mr Humphrey Brooke. I am particularly grateful to Dr E. W. Prosser Thomas, of Seaford, the Jam Saheb's personal physician during the last years of his life. Mr J. W. McKenzie generously loaned me numerous volumes of *Wisden*, which made my work that much easier. George Cox, whose years in the Sussex eleven briefly overlapped with Duleep's, and Bill Purkiss have been helpful in a variety of ways. It was with the latter, one of the best schoolboy cricketers of his time, that I initially heard at first hand of Ranji, for our years in the eleven at Haileybury coincided with the arrival as coach of Bert Wensley of Sussex, and subsequently of Nawanagar.

The manuscript was typed for me by Liz Claridge, who accompanied me on my travels in India and Ireland, and whose suggestions on the Indian sections have been invaluable. Without her this quest for Ranji would have been a far less enjoyable task than it has been.

Alan Ross

PART ONE

K S Ranjitsinhji

ONE

The Rajput Inheritance

A less likely place than Sarodar for the birth of a great cricketer would be hard to imagine. Such green as there is derives from a handful of palm trees, the flutter of parrots. Cricket in memory is essentially greenness, the moist, changing greens of England, the harder green of Australia and South Africa, the tropical lush green of the West Indies. All the watering in the world can only raise the faintest of green tidemarks to the cricket fields of India and these briefly. Sarodar, a small village in the western province of Kathiawar, where Ranjitsinhji was born on 10 September 1872, is even by Indian standards the antithesis of green. As far as the eye can see the earth, thickened with thorn-bush and scrub, is camel-coloured. The landscape has a parched, biblical air, stony and glinting. Early in the day a desert freshness makes movement possible, and again, at dusk, the colourless siphonated blue turns saffron.

Photographs, showing a jumbled sprawl of agricultural build-ings, do Sarodar little justice. It is, in its way, a kind of paradise, a low-walled encampment flung over a hill, its towers and turrets commanding the plain. Its magic is of site and the imagination, scarcely of facilities. A century later it remains almost unchanged, a place of shepherds and animals, of wood smoke and wandering bullocks, virtually as inaccessible and remote. It has acquired water and neatly cultivated squares the size of cricket fields; corn, cotton, alfalfa spread from it. There is, perhaps, a poetic rightness about its charm as a birthplace for Ranji, but he himself, as Brad-man did to Bowral, extracted and adapted its poetry to cricket.

Cricket often runs in families, the childhood of cricketers seem-ing in retrospect entirely in keeping, an inheritance of blood, ritual and environment that made distinction inevitable. Ranji had no such luck. Within a day's ride of Sarodar at the time of his birth there were scarcely twenty-two yards of flat ground, let alone a blade of grass. Cricket did become for him – through the skills of his nephew, the great Duleep (and the by no means negligible achievements of the present Jam Saheb) – a family affair, but he was the first of the line. In this, at any rate; for in other respects Ranji's lineage, stemming as it did from Krishna, the deified hero of the Mahabharat and ruler of nearby Dwarka over three thousand years ago, was of the grandest. He was justly proud of it. His ancestors included both soldiers and statesmen of renown, and, less commonly, noted humanists. At a time when Indian princes were noted largely for corruption, idleness and self-indulgence, Ranji's forebears were responsible in their own states for crucial economic reforms and the removal of prevailing social abuses, most particularly slavery, suttee and infanticide.

Ranji's own clan, the Jadejas, were Rajput warriors and long-time rulers of Sind. They claimed descendancy from the Persian Emperor Jamshed, deriving from him their title. Leaving Sind, the Jadejas moved down to Cutch, from where, as the result of a dream, Jam Rawal, founder of the present house, set forth to Jamnagar in 1535.

It would be absurd to suggest that succession through the dozen or so generations that separated Ranji from Jam Rawal was in any way orderly. Sometimes it was as a result of family treachery, by which rightful heirs were killed off, more often as consequence of a whole series of retaliatory murders. What E. M. Forster, secretary to the Maharajah of Dewas, wrote in our own time: 'hidden in this vast domestic hot-bed there was always the possibility of poison' was even truer in earlier and more bloodthirsty centuries. In his book *The Last Maharajas* Jacques Pouchepadass observed: 'Every royal child had to be closely protected from this risk [of poisoning], generally engendered by a multiplicity of wives and concubines, each of whom wanted the throne for her own offspring and fought with the others for the favour of the reigning prince. The bitterness of the deserted wives and the antipathy inherent in the Indian family structure between the dowager and her daughter-in-law, led to the formation of various factions within the court, which the prince found difficult to balance against each other, and which had considerable influence on the course of public affairs.'

Of nothing was this truer than of the circumstances in which Ranji was first adopted heir to the *gadi* (throne) of Nawanagar and then disinherited.

Jam Rawal, having been told in his dream to leave the Moghul-threatened deserts of Cutch, cross the seas, and establish himself in Kathiawar, set off with a small army into the territory of Jam Tamachi, who had been responsible for the murder of his own father. A series of bloody encounters took place, at the end of which, by deeds of great valour and some treachery, Jam Rawal became undisputed master of the whole of Kathiawar.

Taking advice from his astrologers on the site – a few miles from the sea and between two rivers, the Rangmati and the Nagmati – Jam Rawal established his capital, calling it Nawanagar, or 'new town'.

Nearly sixty years later, in 1590, the Moghuls, much humbled by a series of defeats at the hands of the Jadejas, mounted a vast attack at Bhucharmori. One of the legendary battles in Rajput history was fought, the Moghuls, despite having their own army decimated, finally routing the Jadejas and occupying Nawanagar.

From the time of the Moghul occupancy to the arrival of the British into the area, early in the nineteenth century, Nawanagar was the scene successively of conspiracies, dictatorships, assassinations and civil wars. When the Moghul Emperor, Aurangzeb, died in 1707, the Jadejas under Raysinhji were able to recapture their old capital, now called Islamnagar, and rename it Jamnagar.

As Moghul influence faded in western India, the power of the Khawas increased. The Khawas, household slaves in Rajput families, often acquired great influence over their masters, as much through their proximity and cunning as through their devotion. One of the most notable of them, Meru, so enslaved the young Jam Lakhaji that he virtually ruled in his stead. He had the Jam's wife assassinated for trying to get rid of him and when Jam Lakhaji died in 1768 Meru continued to rule in the name of

Lakhaji's eldest son Jasoji. When neighbouring Maharajahs sent forces to drive Meru out he defeated them. In due course Jasoji rebelled against his enforced impotence and Meru imprisoned him. He had meanwhile fortified Jamnagar, completely encircling the city with white walls, towers and gates. Sporadic attempts by Cutch troops to take Jamnagar were easily beaten off.

For half a century Meru Khawas was the virtual ruler of Jamnagar. Only when he died in 1800 was Jam Jasoji able to reassert his rightful powers. By then the British Government, through their Residents, had begun to act as mediators in land disputes. There were to be no more rovings by the Jadejas, but no more invasions or exploitations either.

Nevertheless, Jasoji had his own ideas of what properly belonged to him, and he was unwise enough to dispute the fortress of Kandorna, which Colonel Walker, Resident at Baroda, demanded be handed back to Porbandar. Colonel Walker, with the help of Maratha troops from Baroda, stormed the fortress and returned it. Jasoji had better luck in 1813 when Fateh Mahomed, a Moslem general at the head of a Cutch army, invaded Jamnagar but was halted by the British. A year later, after forty-six years on the throne, most of them purely nominal, Jasoji died. While recognising his brother Sataji, an opium addict, as his successor, Jasoji took the precaution of appointing a prime minister, Jagjiwan Derji, with the authority of a regent.

In 1820 Sataji died, being succeeded by the adopted son of Jasoji's widow, Ranmalji, son of the Jadeja lord of Sarodar. The curious shortage of male heirs has continued to this day.

Ranmalji, however, proved to be a gift from the gods, an inspired and creative ruler with a social sense and a developer's eye. He excavated the main lake, the Jamsarovar, round which Nawanagar elegantly curves, and built the fortified palaces that grace the causeway across it. He was, in addition, an enthusiastic and skilful hunter of the lions and panthers that prowled between the Barda Hills and the city. Of all his predecessors it was to Ranmalji that Ranji seems to have been closest in character and inclination.

Of Ranmalji's seven sons all save one, Vibhaji, had died before he did. In 1852, five years before the Mutiny, Vibhaji succeeded his father. The comparative peace and plenty of his inheritance were shattered by events not directly connected with the Mutiny, but affected by it. The Waghers from the district of Okhamandal rose against the Baroda Marathas to whom, at a recent settlement of the Kathiawar peninsula, they had been assigned. The Gaekwad's troops failed to contain the Waghers, as did the British when they were called in. The Waghers began to extend their ambitions to Jamnagar itself and a showdown took place in the Barda Hills. From this Jam Vibhaji emerged victorious. Outstanding in the battle was Jadeja Jhalamsinhji, an officer from Sarodar and a nephew of Jam Ranmalji.

Vibhaji, aware of precedent and wishing to take no risks over the succession, acquired fourteen wives. But even these proved inadequate for the provision of a male heir.

Vibhaji, no less than his father, was a loved and humanitarian ruler, an excellent sportsman. On presenting the Order of KCSI to him in 1878, Sir J. B. Peile, Political Agent of Kathiawar, remarked in his address: 'The race of His Highness the Jam was long regarded with special veneration as the foremost Hindu dynasty of this peninsula, stout in fight with the Viceroys of Akbar; generous to fallen greatness in Muzuffar; bold in aggressive warfare on Mendarda and Jeytpur.' He might have added that this warlike ancestry was less relevant to the well-being of his subjects than his commercial enterprise and provisions for education and social welfare.

Unfortunately Vibhaji's judgment in affairs of state deserted him in his relationships with women. His roving eye was responsible for two disastrous enterprises only remedied by an act of God.

In the first instance Vibhaji, already past middle age and having failed to produce a son, despite having fourteen wives, became involved with a Sindi labourer and part-time prostitute, Dhanbai, whom he saw at work one day on the shore of the Jamsarovar Lake. Declining his invitation to enter his zenana, Dhanbai agreed to come to him only if he married her and allowed her three sisters to accompany her. Vibhaji, for whom any official marriage to a

Muslim was out of the question, managed to get resurrected an obsolete form of ritual. Dhanbai became a kind of morganatic wife. The three sisters entered the zenana.

In 1872 the son, allegedly born of that union some years before, was declared presumptive heir to the throne of Jamnagar. It was rumoured that the boy, Kalobha, was not only not Vibhaji's son but that Dhanbai was already pregnant when Vibhaji first set eyes on her. Nevertheless Vibhaji, having given up all hope of his Rajput queens, was disinclined to question it.

It was a vanity he came to regret. Some years later an attempt to poison Jam Vibhaji's food was discovered and traced to Kalobha. The boy was disinherited and banished. Astonishingly, his mother and her three sisters, each of them apparently attractive, remained.

Vibhaji now had to look about for another heir. He decided to ask Jhalamsinhji of Sarodar, the hero of Barda, for one of his sons. Umedsingi was adopted, and re-named Raysinhji. Within a year he was dead, poisoned either by Dhanbai herself or on her orders.

It was to Sarodar that Vibhaji turned again. The choice this time fell on Ranjitsinhji, seven-year-old grandson of Jhalam-sinhji, and second son of Jiwantsinhji, that 'ideal of a Rajput gentleman' in the words of Fitzgerald, the austere Agent to the Governor of Bombay. Vibhaji, taking no chances, entrusted Ranjitsinhji to the care of the political agent, Colonel Barton, with the instruction that he be brought up well away from Jamnagar.

The solemn ceremony of adoption, totally binding in Hindu law, took place in the temple of Dwarki Puri, a mile from Jamnagar. 'An hour before dawn,' Roland Wild wrote, 'a slow-moving cavalcade left Jamnagar. Both the Jam Saheb and Ranjitsinhji travelled in *sigrans*, the closed carts commonly used for purdah ladies. A circuitous route was taken, and the escort was formed of eighty lancers. The boy's father and grandfather watched the ceremony which was officially recorded by the India Office, the Government of India, and the Bombay Government.'

Ranjitsinhji remained at Sarodar and in due course was sent to Rajkot. It was while he was there that Janbai, one of Dhanbai's sisters, gave birth to a child which she announced was Vibhaji's.

Almost certainly Janbai's child had been brought into the zenana from outside, but Vibhaji, threatened by the four women, was prevailed upon to request the Bombay Government to reverse the recognition of Ranjitsinhji and to accept Janbai's son as heir apparent.

The request was refused; Janbai was neither a legal Rani nor even a 'morganatic' wife. It seemed the end of the matter.

Vibhaji, pestered still further by the sisters, was, however, driven to seeking the intervention of the Viceroy, Lord Ripon. The latter, aware of Vibhaji's services to the state and anxious to have a chance of showing friendship to a prince in return, agreed to indulge what seemed to him a harmless whim. He overruled the Bombay Government. Jaswantsinhji was accepted as being the son of one Vibhaji's Ranis and therefore heir to the *gadi* of Jamnagar.

About Jaswantsinhji Charles Kincaid, Judge of the Court of Judicature at Bombay and long-serving officer in Kathiawar, observed no doubt accurately but certainly with prejudice: 'He was an unattractive figure. He had had every advantage – an English tutor, education at the Rajkumar College, constant coaching at cricket, tennis, polo, pigsticking, hockey, shooting. Yet he never learnt to play any game properly. Nor did he ever show the least interest in sport. I, as an agency official, attended the ceremony of installation. I well remember my disgust when I saw the loutish bastard of a lowborn concubine seated on the throne of Jam Rawal; while my unfortunate friend, the lawful heir, had not even been invited to the investiture.'

Jaswantsinhji, however little he may have been related to Vibhaji, who died in 1894, seemed to share at least one disability with him. Though served by five wives he, too, failed to produce a son. Before that defect could be remedied Jam Jaswantsinhji died, supposedly of typhoid, in 1906. He had been Jam for barely three years.

The way seemed, at last, to be open for Ranjitsinhji, though even now he did not succeed without opposition. On 16 November 1906, soon after the death of Jaswantsinhji, a letter appeared in *The Times* in reply to an article on the Nawanagar succession. It was from Holman, Birchwood of 50 Lime Street, London EC1, solicitors to K. S. Lakhubba, son of the Kalobha who had been disinherited for trying to poison Vibhaji: 'On legal and customary points alone it cannot be contended that K. S. Lakhubba was disinherited forever, and received from his uncle a grant of *giras* in the form and amount previously given only to heirs presumptive to the *gadi*.' The objection, however, seemed more technical than wholehearted and not much more was heard of it.

Vibhaji, from the moment of his first adoption of Ranjitsinhji, never saw him again. He had been dead thirteen years when Ranjitsinhji, at the age of thirty-five, returned to his capital.

TWO

Rajkumar College
and England

It was fortunate, in more ways than one, that Ranjitsinhji was spared a childhood among the intrigues of the zenana. Soon after his formal adoption he was taken to stay with his uncle, the Rajah of Dhrangadhra, returning to Sarodar only for short visits. He was never allowed remotely near Jamnagar.

In December 1870, two years before Ranjitsinhji's birth, the Rajkumar College for the sons of princes had been opened at Rajkot, an agreeable and unusually airy town that is the road and rail centre of Saurashtra. Gandhi, born on the coast at Porbandar, spent most of his childhood there, his father being for many years Dewan (Chief Minister). The town was also the headquarters of the British Resident for the Western States of India. Auto-rickshaws, tongas, bullock carts and the brightly decorated Public Carriers nowadays compete for supremacy along the wide, tree-lined boulevards, but the place, though bustling, has a genial, disciplined air proper to a former provincial military and political headquarters. Small streets, their narrow houses either balconied with wooden balustrades or with wrought-iron verandahs painted pale olive, lead off a series of main roads that soon reach open country. Just off centre the old polo grounds form a grassless, dusty *maidan* that in Ranjitsinhji's childhood must have echoed to the rattling of horses' hooves and the clack of polo sticks. There are handsome jasmine and hibiscus-filled gardens, a few remnants of colonial architecture and the usual bulbous public buildings. Gandhi's old home, the Kaba Gandhino Delo, holds a permanent exhibition, there is a large Government Milk Dairy run with the help of Unicef just outside the town, and the Lal Pari Lake on the horizon is a pleasant picnic spot for town people and boys alike.

27

If, a century after its foundation, the Rajkumar College has lost ground to similar foundations in the hill country further north, it is mainly because of its urban situation and the heat.

Although the school, begun with only a handful of pupils and regarded, especially by the Ranis, with much initial suspicion, was broadly organised along the lines of an English public school, it did not affect to turn Indians into Englishmen. Its proper aims were well stated in a speech day address of 1900 by Lord Curzon, Viceroy and Governor-General in India:

> If this College were to emancipate its students from old-fashioned prejudices or superstitions at the cost of denationalisation I, for one, should think the price too heavy. The Anglicised Indian is not a more attractive spectacle in my eyes than the Indianised Englishman. Both are hybrids of an unnatural type. No – we want the young Chiefs who are educated here to learn the English language, and to become sufficiently familiar with English customs, literature, science, modes of thought, standards of truth and honour, and, I may add, with manly English sports and games, to be able to hold their own in the world in which their lot will be cast, without appearing to be dullards or clowns, and to give to their people, if they subsequently become Rulers, the benefit of enlightened and pure administration. Beyond that we do not press them to go. After all, those Kumars who become Chiefs are called upon to rule, not an English but an Indian people; and as a Prince who is to have any influence and to justify his own existence, must be one with his own subjects, it is clear that it is not by English models alone, but by an adaption of Eastern prescriptions to the Western standard, that he can hope to succeed. Chiefs are not, as is sometimes imagined, a privileged body of persons. God Almighty has not presented them with a 'sanad' to do nothing in perpetuity. The State is not their private property; its revenues are not their privy purse. They are intended by Providence to be the working-bees and not the drones of the hive. They exist for the benefit of their people; their people do not exist for them. They are intended to be types and leaders

and examples. A Chief at whom any one of his subjects can point the finger of scorn is not fit to be a Chief. If these views are correct it is clear that this College has a great and responsible work devolved upon it; since it ought to be not merely a school of men, but a nursery of statesmen; and that the worst way of discharging its trust would be to rob its pupils of their surest claim to the confidence of their countrymen – which is this, that, though educated in a Western curriculum, they should still remain Indians, true to their own beliefs, their own traditions, and their own people.

As it happened, the idea, long nursed by British administrators, took on. The boys, removed from the unhealthy atmosphere of a court life both corrupt and dominated by women, thrived. Their physical condition, to which much necessary attention was given, greatly improved.

It was, however, a radical change in every aspect of a prince's upbringing. For instead of the customary princely pursuits, lolling on horseback or comfortably installed for the shooting of large animals, the boys were encouraged actually to take exercise themselves. They were required to do athletics and gymnastics, to play cricket, football, tennis and racquets. They were given military instruction. At that time many Maharajahs were exceedingly plump and unhealthy and their children, if not frail, showed every signs of emulating them.

The boys, especially in the early days, were heavily guarded, each pupil's personal retinue being in constant proximity to classroom and dormitory. Ranjitsinhji himself, during the months he spent as a seven-year-old in a bungalow at Rajkot before entering the school, was attended by a staff of seventeen, ranging from a tutor in Gujerati to a barber doubling up as torchbearer, a coachman and a water-carrier. All this was paid for by Jam Vibhaji, as were the wages of the two troopers and six footmen permanently on guard.

On 11 June, aged eight, Ranjitsinhji entered the Rajkumar College of thirty-seven boys. His first appearance in the records is in the report of speech day, 1880, where he is listed as 'No. 35.

Ranjitsinhji of Nawanagar', a member of the sixth class. His schoolfellows that day bear such names as Gagubha of Shapur, Kala Vala of Lumi, the Nawab of Janjira, the Raja of Bansda. Today only a small proportion of the pupils of Rajkumar College come from ex-ruling families. In Ranjitsinhji's day, in the school's infancy, all of them were potential rulers.

The Principal of Rajkumar College when Ranjitsinhji arrived was Chester Macnaghten, a remarkable man of thirty-seven to whom Ranjitsinhji came to owe a great deal. Macnaghten had long-standing links with India, for his grandfather, Sir Francis Macnaghten, had been a Judge in Calcutta and his father, Elliot, an officer of the Supreme Court at Calcutta, a Director of the East India Company and a Member of the Council of the Secretary of State for India. As a child, asthma prevented Macnaghten from going to Harrow; instead he was brought up by Edmund Venables, Canon of Lincoln. He went up to Trinity, Cambridge, in 1862 and after a spell in India recovering from illness took his degree in Classics in 1866. He immediately returned to India as tutor and companion to the Maharajah of Darbhanga, a role in which E. M. Forster and J. R. Ackerley succeeded him elsewhere. Ackerley's *Hindoo Holiday*, especially, gives an astringent, affectionate account of some of the duties involved.

Rajkumar College, for the first twenty-five years of its existence, was created in the benevolent and understanding image of Macnaghten. When the Roscoe Mullins statue of Macnaghten – a standing figure in grey Sicilian marble on a red Aberdeen granite pedestal – that now stands before the main entrance to the College was unveiled in 1898, Lord Sandhurst in his speech compared the influence of Macnaghten on Indian education with that of Arnold of Rugby and Jowett of Balliol in England.

It seems to have been no idle reference. for in the records of the college – its crest, an elephant argent, trunk or, on wreath of sable and gules; its arms, two rampant lions – compiled forty years later by a former pupil, His Highness Sir Bharsinhji KCSI, Maharajah of Bhavnagar, the testimonies to the all-round qualities of Macnaghten are remarkable. Macnaghten, who is buried in Christchurch Cemetery, Rajkot, died in 1896, the year in which his most famous pupil scored 2,780 runs, at that time the highest aggregate ever made in an English summer.

Ranjitsinhji's progress at Rajkumar was steady rather than scintillating. At the age of thirteen, however, he won the Fergusson Gold Medal for English speaking, reciting 'Young Lochinvar', a poem which, with other similar hardy annuals, he seems to have performed at regular intervals throughout his school career. The same year he won the gymnastics prize.

Even while Ranjitsinhji was there the school changed rapidly. Macnaghten had persuaded the parents that a single servant was all that was necessary for their son's safety and comfort so, instead of the young kumars being vastly outnumbered wherever they were by arrays of bloodthirsty-looking and mutually suspicious attendants, the atmosphere began gradually to approach that of an ordinary school. In due course Ranjitsinhji worked his way up; by the time he was sixteen he had proved himself by far the best cricketer, as well as racquets and tennis player. He was also second headboy.

The scorecard printed on page 32, and taken more or less at random, is typical of many. The match was in Ranjitsinhji's last year and the visitors were a reputedly strong team brought by Kumar Shri Madarsinhji of Sayla.

The main cricket ground at Rajkumar is a large, grassless and dusty oval. Bullocks, hens and peacocks amble round the boundary meditatively. The noise of trucks and rickshaws drifts across from the surrounding streets.

It has, nevertheless, atmosphere, and the boys playing today do so with a technical correctness and enthusiasm that compares favourably with any equivalent school in England. It is not an easy ground to field on and Ranjitsinhji, writing years later, tried to explain why they had been so good at it: 'It is difficult to see why our fielding at the Rajkumar College should have been so far superior to the batting and bowling, unless it was due to the prevailing idea that fielding was just as important as batting or bowling, and to the fact that a high degree of skill is most easily attained in fielding. I am quite sure that the fielding of this school from the year 1882 to 1888 was superior to that of an average

English public school eleven. Yet there was no one to teach us much, and no fine fields to excite in us a desire to excel. Perhaps one reason was that we had no net practice. Whenever we played it was a game. Very often there were fifteen boys on each side, so if the fielding side wanted an innings the same day they had to hold every catch and save all the runs they could.'

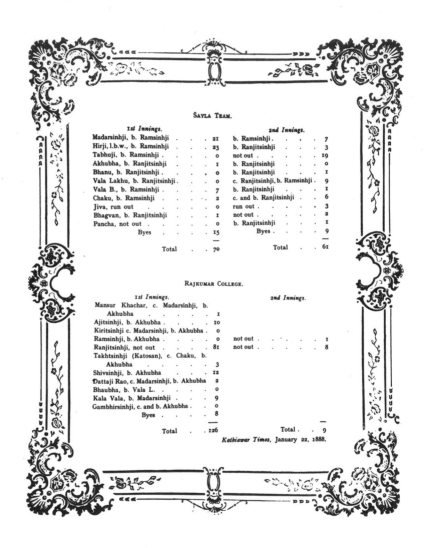

SAYLA TEAM.

1st Innings.		*2nd Innings.*	
Madarsinhji, b. Ramsinhji	21	b. Ramsinhji	7
Hirji, l.b.w., b. Ramsinhji	23	b. Ranjitsinhji	3
Tabhuji, b. Ramsinhji	0	not out	19
Akhubha, b. Ranjitsinhji	1	b. Ranjitsinhji	0
Bhanu, b. Ranjitsinhji	0	b. Ranjitsinhji	1
Vala Lakhu, b. Ranjitsinhji	0	c. Ranjitsinhji, b. Ramsinhji	9
Vala B., b. Ramsinhji	7	b. Ranjitsinhji	1
Chaku, b. Ramsinhji	2	c. and b. Ranjitsinhji	6
Jiva, run out	0	run out	3
Bhagvan, b. Ranjitsinhji	1	not out	2
Pancha, not out	0	b. Ranjitsinhji	1
Byes	15	Byes	9
Total	70	Total	61

RAJKUMAR COLLEGE.

1st Innings.		*2nd Innings.*	
Mansur Khachar, c. Madarsinhji, b. Akhubha	1		
Ajitsinhji, b. Akhubha	10		
Kiritsinhji c. Madarsinhji, b. Akhubha	0		
Ramsinhji, b. Akhubha	0	not out	1
Ranjitsinhji, not out	81	not out	8
Takhtsinhji (Katosan), c. Chaku, b. Akhubha	3		
Shivsinhji, b. Akhubha	12		
Dattaji Rao, c. Madarsinhji, b. Akhubha	2		
Bhaubha, b. Vala L.	0		
Kala Vala, b. Madarsinhji	9		
Gambhirsinhji, c. and b. Akhubha	0		
Byes	8		
Total	126	Total	9

Kathiawar Times, January 22, 1888.

Rajkumar College, a handsome, double-storeyed gothic building that in those early days formed only three sides of the present quadrangle, undoubtedly developed in Ranjitsinhji most of the qualities – except perhaps the extravagance – for which he was later renowned. He took to the school and the school took to him. Long after he had left he continued to lavish presents upon it: cups for athletics and racquets, money for a swimming pool.

Not surprisingly, when it was decided, in 1888, to take three kumars to England for further education, Ranjitsinhji was selected to be one of them. Chester Macnaghten decided to accompany the three boys, Ranjitsinhji, Ramsinhji of Sihor, and Mansur Khachar of Jashan, himself.

In a farewell speech Chester Macnaghten remarked of Ranjitsinhji: '. . . a better or manlier boy has never resided within this College . . . disappointments and troubles come to us all, and he has had his, and has borne them bravely. Recollecting his College career, I think he may look back without regret. I speak of him because he has taken so marked a lead in the College that he will be specially remembered.'

By this time Ranjitsinhji had, of course, learned of the developments at Jamnagar. 'After the speeches on that last day,' the *Kathiawar Times* reported on 4 March 1888, 'the boys, staff and visitors adjourned to the garden which had been decorated with clusters of tumbler lights. All the kumars, one by one, put garlands round the necks of their guests and showered flowers on them. Cheers were given for the Macnaghtens and for the three kumars who were leaving for England to compete for the Civil Service and for the Bar.'

When Ranjitsinhji walked through the quadrangle with its central gol-mohur tree and neat flowerbeds for the last time as a pupil, he was not quite sixteen years old. His education was still being underwritten by the Agency at Rajkot into whose hands he had been entrusted, and at various times relatives, neighbouring maharajahs, and wealthy businessmen chipped in. But there was no more money to be had from the official state purse. Ranjitsinhji, for many years to come, was to be acutely short of money, a fact not immediately apparent from his style of living.

If Ranjitsinhji arrived at Rajkumar College an intelligent, alert but unsophisticated country boy from Sarodar, he left it an accomplished all-round athlete in the British tradition. The desert life, with its princely hunting and shooting rituals, had been exchanged for expert tuition in the sports habitual to English army officers and country gentlemen. Chester Macnaghten was not a cricket Blue but he was a useful cricketer and a devoted coach. At some comparatively early stage he must have realised that he had in his charge a boy of quite outstanding promise. How that promise would develop in English conditions was another matter. Ranjitsinhji, born the son of a Bhayat, a Rajput landowner, had come to Rajkumar as the heir to the throne of Nawanagar. He was leaving the school with no particular prospects and few tangible assets except his skill as a cricketer. What had produced in the boy with no cricketing blood in his veins a talent so close to genius was a mystery, but then genius, in anything, has rarely an identifiable lineage.

Most, though not all, of the greatest players reveal their class as schoolboys. In Ranjitsinhji's case standards for comparison were missing. It is one thing to be the best in a team of adolescent Indian kumars none of whom was remotely bred to the game: quite another to suggest that, in the English climate and in vastly more competitive company, the skills would survive to any memorable degree.

Ranjitsinhji remarked in the passage quoted that there were no nets and little teaching at Rajkumar. If that were really the case it may have been to his advantage in the developing of techniques that initially owed little to orthodoxy. As Ranjitsinhji acquired greater experience he learned how to adapt to circumstances; but while he batted, as every good player must necessarily do, with proper regard for correct principles, he enriched them with an imaginative brilliance unlike anyone else's. At Rajkot, if not at Sarodar, he must have picked up a bat and used it as if it was an extension of himself, as if hitting a cricket ball was the most natural thing in the world. In later life he revealed himself master of all the princely skills, too, but after Australian fast bowling they must have seemed comparatively tame accomplishments.

In March 1888 Ranjitsinhji made the first of what were to be scores of journeys between Kathiawar and England. In later years he was to use his private train for the Bombay part of the trip but on this occasion, with his companions Ramsinhji and Mansur Khachar, and escorted by Macnaghten, he travelled less grandly. In the course of time he must have grown to know the country in both directions like the back of his hand – the north-easterly curve of line through the flat plains up to Viramgam and Ahmedabad, the red, stony emptiness dotted here and there with mudwalled villages or broken up with patches of silvery sugar cane, the ruined forts and palaces, deserted mosques, just discernible among clusters of palm trees. Over all this land Rajput princes, Moghul emperors nawabs and sultans had fought their long, wearying wars. Always in the middle distance, through the train windows, women in vivid saris, pink, turquoise, orange, gold, were to be seen stooped over in the blinding heat or swaying along causeways over the salt pans, brass pots on their heads.

After the plains come the wide banyan-lined rivers with women pounding their washing and egrets stalking the reeds by the lakes. Buffaloes wade in the shallows and hugely-laden bullock carts trail clouds of dust as the line veers south-east to Baroda, a city whose Maharajah was to play some part in Ranjitsinhji's life.

Between Baroda and Bombay the line runs more or less parallel to the coast. The Indo-Saracen extravagances of Ahmedabad, the riverside gardens ringing the walled lake city of Baroda, give way to richly cultivated farm country, the shell-pink fluff of cotton, the dusty yellow of alfalfa. Nearer to Bombay lies Surat, the milk-white domes of the Swami Narayan temple, its cluster of mosques, mills and fire-temples seeming to float out of the surrounding green. All down this coast, successively ruled by the Dutch, Portuguese and British, rivers curve under the railway to flow into the Gulf of Cambay. For Ranjitsinhji, crossing the Mahim cause-way for the last run into Bombay Central, it was the start of a great adventure. What went on in the zenanas of Jamnagar no longer concerned him. The old and ailing Jam Vibhaji had made his decision and it was the six-year-old Jaswantsinhji, whatever his real origins, who would in due course inherit the *gadi* that had been promised to Ranjitsinhji. At the age of sixteen it may well have seemed a less exciting prospect than what England might offer.

THREE

Cambridge

Ranjitsinhji spent the wet summer of 1888 with the Macnaghtens in London. The Australians under P. S. McDonnell were in England. So, too, was Gandhi, bearing a letter of introduction to Ranjitsinhji, his neighbour in India. At Lord's, in the first Test of a low-scoring series, England were bowled out by Ferris and Turner for 53 and 62, losing in two days by 61 runs. W. G. Grace made 24 in the second innings, the top score on either side. At the Oval a month later England took their revenge, winning comprehensively by an innings and 137 runs. William Barnes made 62 in England's innings and took 7 for 50 in the match. Surrey, the champion county, provided five of the England side on their home ground.

The final Test, played at Old Trafford in the last days of August, was a punishing victory for England by an innings and 21. The Australians, caught on a sticky dog, were bowled out, mainly by Peel, for 81 and 70, the match being all over before lunch on the second day. The England team at Lord's, the first one Ranjitsinhji was to see in action, batted in order: W. G. Grace, R. Abel, W. Barnes, G. A. Lohmann, W. W. Read, T. C. O'Brien, R. Peel, A. G. Steel (captain), W. Gunn, J. Briggs, M. Sherwin. How astonished he would have been to learn that, eight years later, he would be playing his first Test match in the company of three of these – Grace, Abel and Briggs.

There were indications, before this summer, that Ranjitsinhji's first love was lawn tennis. He was already a player of considerable ability. But the atmosphere and excitement of a Test match changed his priorities; henceforth, though at different times in his life tennis, shooting, fishing and billiards captured his attention, cricket was what mattered. To everything he did Ranjitsinhji brought a perfectionist's scruple, a scientific concern with probability. What he saw on the cricket grounds of England during the summer of 1888 made him determined to put his own talent to the test. Unlike those of his nephew, Duleepsinhji, nearly forty years later, Ranjitsinhji's gifts at that stage were rough and untutored. Whereas Duleepsinhji came to Cambridge with a technique matured by years of coaching at Cheltenham, Ranjitsinhji relied mainly on wrist and eye. He had, according to R. S. Goodchild, the Headmaster of St Faith's, Cambridge, where Ranjitsinhji played his cricket while preparing for the entrance to Trinity, virtually no orthodox defence at all.

It was to be five years before Ranjitsinhji's cricket was given a properly competitive context. In 1892 he passed into Trinity. Most of his time since Macnaghten's return to India, had been spent in Chaucer Road, Cambridge, where he, and his fellow kumar Ramsinhji, had been placed in the care of the Reverend Louis Borissow, Chaplain of Trinity. Borissow, responsible both for Ranjitsinhji's moral welfare and his academic study, was more confident of success in the former role than in the latter. For some months he had real doubts about whether his pupil would ever settle sufficiently to any one thing, work or play. When not playing cricket at St Faith's on the Trumpington Road, Ranjitsinhji was on the tennis court. Evenings were spent either at the billiard table or fiddling about in the Borissow's boxroom which he had converted into a photographic studio. Ranjitsinhji's passion for photography had plenty of scope in later life when few of either his or his friends' activities went unrecorded. Taking each other's pictures, or having them taken by court photographers in front of slain tigers or dressed up in a variety of ceremonial costumes, appropriately bejewelled, on state visits, was always a favourite occupation of maharajahs. Ranjitsinhji was no exception and though, after the loss of his right eye, he was careful to show only his left profile, the pictures in this book reveal the obvious pleasure he took in dressing up for the camera.

In relation to what happened after Ranjitsinhji's departure from

Cambridge and his throwing in his lot with Sussex, his performances for the University were more notable for their quality than
their quantity. In 1893 he got his Blue, but his progress towards
it, in the years 1890–92, was not spectacular. The fact that he was
an Indian, from an obscure and small school with no cricketing
credentials, meant that he was at first a curiosity, not someone to
be taken seriously in competition with star recruits from famous
public schools. The casual passer-by, observing him in 1890 laying
about him for Fitzwilliam Hall or the Cassandra Club, would have
been more likely to have assessed him an intuitive entertainer than
a future batsman of classical proportions. Ranjitsinhji, however,
was never slow to learn from watching others and, innings by
innings, he adjusted and refined his technique.

In due course he progressed from Parker's Piece cricket to
Fenner's, reputedly scoring three centuries in one day on the
former. It seems hard to credit the circumstances, even on a ground
where as many matches are played simultaneously as on a *maidan*,
but Ranjitsinhji himself vouched for the truth of the story. He
made his first hundred before lunch for his original team, then,
wandering over to an adjacent game where they were a man short,
scored another. Returning to his own game at tea-time, he found
his side still batting, strolled off again and, coming across another
team in trouble, helped them out with a third hundred.

By now Ranjitsinhji, ever one to do things in the grand manner,
was engaging the professional coaches at Fenner's for his own
purposes. Richardson, Lockwood, Watts, and Jack Hearne were
among those required to bowl to him for hours on end.

There are numerous instances of Ranjitsinhji's reputedly
unorthodox approach to batting, but Sir Stanley Jackson's surprise at seeing him 'nearly going down on his knees to pull a ball
to leg' seems odd. Many good batsmen have done precisely that,
Rohan Kanhai among them. More serious, perhaps, was his
inability to keep his right leg still. Ranjitsinhji recalls in the Batting
chapter of *The Jubilee Book of Cricket*: 'I had to have my right leg
pegged down during my first two years at serious cricket. I did not
learn to stand still when I was a small boy, so I had to start learning
how to do it after having contracted bad habits.'

To this pegging of the right foot has been attributed the origin of Ranjitsinhji's famous leg-glance or glide. Over the years, he gave many versions of how this stroke came into being, none of them particularly convincing. Pegging the right foot – a constricting and crude method at the best of times – did, however, enable the leg-stump ball to be played back or deflected with the wicket more or less covered. The variation induced by Ranjitsinhji turned an essentially defensive stroke into a profitable one. It is difficult to believe that no one ever glanced a ball before Ranjitsinhji. What seems certain, though, is that the suppleness of his wrists and his speed of eye allowed him to exploit the stroke to an unique degree.

Although Ranjitsinhji came to Cambridge without fanfare or repute, he did not arrive friendless. The Borissows gave him exactly the kind of family background calculated to bring him out. Whether out of deference to his guardian's calling or not, Ranjitsinhji took to studying the Bible and reading aloud from it. He was not without religious feeling and despite the apparent worldliness of his later life, its superficial westernisation, he reverted, particularly at moments of stress, to the orthodox Hindu practices, rituals, and superstitions of a Rajput.

With remarkable rapidity Ranjitsinhji began to assume the colourings of an English country gentleman. Gandhi was doing the same in London, prowling the West End in morning coat and tophat. Not only did Ranjitsinhji engage professional cricket coaches – one August taking Tom Hayward with him to Bournemouth – and billiard markers but he rented fishing rights and shoots, the latter initially in Norfolk. He got off to an unpropitious start by shooting pheasants on a September partridge shoot in Hampshire, his Indian background having left him unprepared for such niceties as close seasons. But he was already a good enough shot and an engaging enough guest never to lack invitations.

After passing into Trinity in 1892 Ranjitsinhji moved out of the Borissow's house into 22 Sidney Street, renting two floors above the bakery of his landlord, George Barnes. Here he established himself in comfort, acquiring a parrot from a neighbouring pub to keep him company. Popsey, already thought to be in her fifties, rarely left Ranjitsinhji's side, and she was still comparatively strong, though bald, at his death.

Ranjitsinhji's college tutor was the mathematician and astronomer, Dr Glaisher; the Master of Trinity, Dr H. M. Butler. Had he shown much interest in academic matters, he could scarcely have been in better hands. As it was, he appeared content to get by on no more study than was strictly necessary. All his excess energies went into sport. Unlike some natural athletes Ranjitsinhji was always a theorist, meticulously taking to pieces the machinery of whatever game he was playing. He was quick to recognise weaknesses in his own technique and his single-minded application to rectifying them with hours of practice was as much responsible for his success as his natural gifts.

It is difficult, at this distance, to judge precisely what Ranjitsinhji had to contend with in terms of racialism and social prejudice at Cambridge. That his cricket was not immediately taken seriously is scarcely surprising. But there is little doubt that Ranjitsinhji, one of the very first of his countrymen to go to the university, was often lonely. It is not fanciful to connect his later extravagant hospitality and generosity, as well as his determination to succeed as a cricketer, with his eagerness to break down social barriers. He was a prince, certainly, but to the average insular middle-class undergraduate of the 1890s such rank was probably not to be compared with British birth. Ranjitsinhji was the first of his kind, and as such it was up to him to make the best of a situation without precedent.

There is only one entry in the Council minutes of Trinity College that concerns Ranjitsinhji. The date is 22 November 1889, and under the heading Tutorial Applications it reads: 'Kumar Shri Ramsinhji and Kumar Shri Ranjitsinhji (one having passed the whole of the Previous Examination and the other Part I and the additional subjects), two Indian "youths of position" to be allowed to enter the College without passing the entrance examination and to reside throughout their course with Mr Borissow.'

Ranjitsinhji, though he never graduated, was in residence at Cambridge from Michaelmas Term 1889 to the Easter Term of

1893. It is really only that last term that is of much relevance.

In his previous years at Cambridge, Ranjitsinhji had performed well, but not outstandingly, in non-collegiate cricket. For Fitzwilliam Hall in 1889 he averaged 33, which included one century, and he made a double century the next year for the Cassandra Club, for whom he usually played when not appearing for Fitzwilliam Hall. But while his run-making in club cricket brought him local renown, the opposition was not usually of the quality for it to count in circles that mattered.

In 1892, however, he played regularly for Trinity, finishing second in their batting with an average of 44, including an un-beaten century. F. S. Jackson was the only one above him. He played in the Seniors match and for the 'Next Sixteen' against the First Twelve, scoring 3, 29 not out, 0 and 58. It was not quite enough, in a strong year, to get him his Blue. Years later Sir Stanley Jackson recalled that, as Cambridge captain, he never even considered Ranjitsinhji that year and had he not subse-quently visited India with Lord Hawke, who took a team there during the following winter, Ranjitsinhji might not have inter-ested him in 1893. Jackson had, however, seen Ranjitsinhji bat in 1892. He described one occasion thus: 'One day in 1892 on my way up to Fenner's I noticed a match in progress on Parker's Piece, and seeing a rather unusually large crowd of spectators I stopped to watch. As luck would have it Ranji was at the wicket. After a short exhibition of brilliant and certainly unorthodox strokes I thought Ranji was stumped, but much to the satisfaction of the crowd, the umpire decided in his favour. I left the scene not particularly impressed.'

Jackson, in his second year as captain, had a strong hand of eight old Blues and several talented Seniors to sort out, among them J. Douglas, P. H. Latham, A. J. L. Hill, E. C. Streatfield, C. M. Wells, the wicket-keeper L. H. Gay, and H. E. Bromley-Davenport. There was little room for newcomers, however talented. On 8 May 1893, Ranjitsinhji, having made 8 and 32 in the Seniors' match, played his first game at Fenner's for the University, against C. L. Thornton's eleven. It was, he confessed later, the only occasion in his cricketing career when he actually felt nervous. In an easy Cambridge victory Ranjitsinhji made 18 against a useful attack which included Mold.

From that innings onwards Ranjitsinhji never looked like losing his place. It was as much the manner in which he batted as the runs he made that confirmed him as a player of quality; his fielding too, usually at slip, had endeared him to the Cambridge bowlers.

Ranjitsinhji's scores during the next few weeks included 40 and 11 not out against the Gentlemen of England, 17 against Yorkshire, 55 against MCC, 38 and 0 against Surrey. He had batted coolly against such bowlers as J. T. Hearne and S. M. J. Woods, Lockwood and Richardson. It was against the Australians, however, that he fully established himself. The Australians, captained in 1893 by J. McC. Blackham, their wicket-keeper, drew two Tests and lost one that summer, but they had a powerful attack consisting of Turner, Trumble, Bruce, Trott, Giffen and McLeod. Ranjitsinhji made top score in both Cambridge innings, 58 and 37 not out, the University being bowled out in their second innings for 108 on a difficult pitch.

The University match, the 59th between the two universities, was played at Lord's on July 3 and 4. Ranjitsinhji, having made, since his feats against the Australians, 40 against Sussex at Brighton and 54 against MCC at Lord's, was down to bat at No. 4.

Cambridge batted first, F. S. Jackson opening the innings with Douglas, and getting them off to a good start. Jackson, incidentally, was to get his first Test cap at Lord's two weeks later and make 91. In the second Test at the Oval, which England, captained by W. G. Grace, won by an innings and 43, Jackson made top score of 103 going in at seven. Yorkshire declined to release him for the third Test.

Once Jackson and Douglas were out Cambridge lost wickets steadily to the left-arm medium pace of G. F. H. Berkeley, later to become the author of the standard work on the Emperor Menelik. Berkeley finished with the remarkable figures of 5 for 38 in 30 overs, bowling Ranjitsinhji, who much admired him, for 9. C. B. Fry, coming on third change, took 2 for 27 and Cambridge were all out for 182.

Oxford, apart from 32 by their captain, the elegant L. C. H. Palairet, could make little of Wells's bowling. They were put out for 106, Wells taking 5 for 35 in 34 overs, 19 of them being maidens. Ranjitsinhji took two catches at short slip, C. B. Fry observing in his autobiography, *Life Worth Living*, that he 'fielded marvellously'.

When Cambridge batted a second time, Jackson and Latham got fifties and though the middle order collapsed for the second time Perkins and Gay propped up the tail. Cambridge were all out for 254, leaving Oxford to make 330 to win. Ranjitsinhji was caught off Bathurst for 0.

Oxford made no show at all, only two of their batsmen reaching double figures. Of their total of 64, C. B. Fry made 31.

Ranjitsinhji's failure in the University match was, inevitably, a disappointment. Another, at the Oval a month later, was his early dismissal in both innings for the Gentlemen against the Players. His final match involving the University was for a Combined Past and Present University side against the Australians on the United Services ground at Portsmouth. The match was drawn, not an uncommon occurrence on the kind of wicket batsmen dream about. Ranjitsinhji made 44, top score, but three of the Australians, Bruce, Bannerman and Trumble, scored hundreds against non-descript bowling. The Australians' total of 843 was the highest score for a first-class match at that time.

In terms of Ranjitsinhji's career his Cambridge figures were nothing special: 386 runs for an average of 29.9. Nevertheless, he was third in the Cambridge batting averages, and had established himself as a slip catcher – 'something of a wonder', as H. S. Altham described him – of remarkable quickness and anticipation.

Ranjitsinhji's last summer at Cambridge saw him finally accepted, not only as a leading sportsman, but as someone with a recognisable social credibility. He was elected to the exclusive Hawks Club – the Cambridge equivalent of Vincent's at Oxford – the first Indian to become a member. His general expansiveness, added to his prowess at cricket, had resulted in his rooms in Sidney Street becoming the regular scene of supper-parties, games of poker, and sing-songs. Ranjitsinhji, though frugal in his own habits – at least as far as food and drink were concerned – was lavish in his provision of entertainment and presents for his guests. It was not surprising, therefore, that he was soon in financial difficulties.

Money was to be a recurrent worry for Ranjitsinhji throughout his life. His State was never to be a rich one, and at this stage he was merely living on an annual grant, comfortable but not limitless. But even at Cambridge he pursued the notion, prevalent enough among Indian maharajahs, that extravagant hospitality was in itself a symbol of grandeur. Such a concept led in most instances to ostentation of the most vulgar sort. With Ranjitsinhji a kind of natural innocence seems to have saved him. He simply behaved as he thought a Rajput prince should behave, despite the fact that, in his case, he had neither been brought up at court nor was in a direct line of succession. Such factors did not deter him. He was justly conscious of his ancestry and of the obligations that he felt it entailed. At Cambridge, no less than at his house in Staines in later years, Ranjitsinhji became the victim of his own sociability.

He also had an instinctive feeling for the outward trappings of caste and position. Once installed as the Jam Saheb he was able to indulge his love of finery to his heart's content. At Cambridge, inevitably, it had to take more modest forms, but this still did not preclude him from acquiring the first motorcar ever to be observed coughing its way along the streets of the city. His early passion for motorcars was never to leave him.

The same was true of his love of clothes and jewellery, which always had to be of the best. Not only did Ranjitsinhji equip himself handsomely for every conceivable social occasion in terms of suits and shoes, but he dispensed expensive watches and rings to all and sundry, as well as building up a sizeable collection of such objects for himself.

It was not only his fellow undergraduates whom Ranjitsinhji, on the evenings when he was not playing billiards at the Liberal Club, entertained at all hours. He was wise enough to include in his Sidney Street *soirées* and shooting and fishing expeditions,

the proprietors of the establishments he so lavishly patronised, so
that when he went down, owing large sums of money all round,
they were in the main content to wait upon payment. They were
not let down. In due course, they were all paid with interest.
Moreover Ranjitsinhji, long after he had become Jam Saheb and
a celebrity, continued to use their services. About one of these
friends, the Bridge Street photographer Harry Stearn, Fry later
wrote:

> He was a keen sportsman with a gun, and always had at least
> fifty pounds in notes in his pocket. That was no reason to blow
> a hole through a fir tree about a yard above my head, shooting
> at the hen pheasant which got up in front of me. I gave him the
> shooting volume in the 'Fur and Feather' series, with certain
> passages marked. Ranji told me that Harry Stearn took this as
> a great compliment, and put the book on his drawing-room
> table, but never opened it.

'Country Vicar', the well-known essayist of the time, writing
about Ranjitsinhji much later, observed: 'He was different from
the other Cambridge cricketers of my time and aroused different
feelings. The others I respected and admired, but Ranji I loved.'
    H. S. Altham described Ranjitsinhji as 'underrated' by his
contemporaries at Cambridge as a batsman. 'Country Vicar',
watching him bat on his return to England after an interval of four
years in 1912 – now stout and almost forty – recalled the undergraduate figure of his own youth. 'What the majority of the
spectators saw in him I do not know – perhaps merely an Indian
potentate, nearly forty years of age, playing England's national
game extraordinarily well. All must have been aware that they
were watching a master batsman.
    'I saw someone quite different – a young man, dark of face, very
slight, with a fluttering silk shirt, buttoned at the wrists – a figure
the embodiment of grace, agile as a panther. Memories – un-
forgettable memories – were revived.
    'The breathless hush when a defeated batsman had vanished
into the black doorway of the pavilion – the tense expectancy with
which we awaited his successor. The glimpse of a cap of Cambridge

Blue, crowning a lissom form; and at that appearance, a ripple of applause – breaking out faintly at first, but gathering strength until it burst into a roar of welcome which grew and grew in volume. The public were greeting one who was little short of an idol . . . To me, in 1912, it was not the Jam Saheb batting; it was still K. S. Ranjitsinhji – the Ranji of my youth. I had visions of what had been in what was.'

If, statistically, Ranjitsinhji plays only a modest part in the annals of Cambridge cricket, the fact that he could inspire such touching recollections years later must allow that he was, indeed, already someone out of the ordinary.

FOUR

The First
Sussex Season

Ranjitsinhji spent only one season, that of 1893, playing for Cambridge, going down from Trinity on the death of Jam Vibhaji the following spring. Overtures were made on Ranjit- sinhji's behalf for him to succeed, but they never looked like coming to anything. The Viceroy had granted Jam Vibhaji's wishes in the matter and that was all there was to it. Since Jassaji – the name taken for the new Jam Saheb – was under age the British took an even closer hand in administration of state affairs than customary, but there was to be no reversal of policy in relation to the succession. Ranjitsinhji was left to his own devices, his income much reduced.

He was now known to everyone as 'Ranji'. *Punch* had once referred to him as 'Run-get Sinhji' and his Cambridge colleagues habitually called him Smith, but by the end of the 1893 season it had become Ranji. Ranji it stayed.

There had been approaches, before he left Cambridge, by Surrey for Ranji to join them. He had, after all, been on close terms with Tom Hayward, only a year his senior, and under whose critical scrutiny he had batted in the nets for hundreds of hours.

But Ranji had other ideas. It was generally assumed that his reasons for wanting to settle down with Sussex were that they were a comparatively weak side, in which Ranji would be certain of a place, not necessarily the case with Surrey. Ranji himself put it rather differently to Percy Cross Standing, author of *Ranjitsinhji, Prince of Cricket*, (published in 1903 at the price of one shilling): 'There would have been no honour and glory in assisting (say) Surrey to win matches, seeing that in 1894 they had Abel, Walter Read, K. J. Key, Maurice Read, Brockwell, Lockwood, Hayward and Richardson all at their best.'

48

That may have been partly the case, but not only Surrey were after Ranji. His real motive seems to have been the wish to join C. B. Fry, who, the same age as Ranji, played his first match for Sussex in 1894, after coming down from Oxford. Ranji and Fry had opposed each other in the university match and struck up an immediate friendship. Ranji had made 40 for Cambridge against Sussex at Hove and had taken a liking to the place and the players. Brighton, with its Regency architecture and raffish crowds, its racegoers and rakes, gamblers and bucks, its sparkling sea air, seems absolutely right as a background for Ranji and one feels that he must have sensed it. The elegance and oriental extravagance of the Pavilion, the art of Nash and Ranjitsinhji's genius were at one. The Prince Regent's style was much after Ranji's heart.

The hefty Australian, W. L. Murdoch, was the Sussex captain when Ranji first played at Hove. It was his first year as captain and he remained in charge until sharing the job with Ranji in 1899. Murdoch, who had first played for Australia as long ago as 1876, had captained the side at the Oval in 1880 when England, under Lord Harris, won by five wickets. Grace made 152 in England's first innings, a score Murdoch himself topped by one in Australia's second innings.

Murdoch, whom Fry described as being of 'medium height, but rather round all over, with a round black moustache, round black eyes, and a round tanned face . . . the most sanguine, dark-complexioned man of my era' had one of the oddest of careers. Having left Australia at the age of 34 he came to England and kept wicket in a Test match against South Africa at Cape Town in 1892. As late as 1904, in his fiftieth year, he made 140 for the Gentlemen at the Oval.

At the time of Ranji's arrival, Murdoch was forty, known to be in Billy Newham's words 'a mighty man at shifting licquor', and on certain occasions observed as walking to the wicket circuitously. Generally, however, he liked to put himself on view in front of the pavilion at lunchtime with only a glass of water in his hand.

Before Ranji could play for the county, he had to qualify. Accordingly he based himself at Brighton, confining his first-class cricket necessarily to MCC matches and Festival games. In August he went on tour with his old club, the Cassandra.

The wet summer of 1894, therefore, was a season of slight lull for Ranji. In all he played only sixteen first-class innings, making 387 runs at an average of 32. He played for MCC against both universities, making 94 against Cambridge at Lord's under W. G. Grace's captaincy, and being bowled for 0 first ball by Fry in the Oxford match. Ranji and Grace batted together at Lord's for the first time, putting on 200 in two hours, Grace's 196 being his highest score at Lord's in thirty years of playing there.

For the South against the North at Scarborough, Ranji made 42 and 52 not out. In addition, in matches not regarded as first-class, he made 53 and 146 not out against a South African touring side at Portsmouth, and 137 not out at Lord's against a Dutch eleven, his first hundred there.

If, for Ranji, this was essentially a period of marking time, he was nevertheless learning and widening his experience. When not playing himself, he was able to watch and study the methods of the leading batsmen and bowlers, particularly on rain-affected pitches. Mold, Richardson and Jack Hearne each took over 200 wickets that summer, which was, on the whole, a lean one for batsmen, though Brockwell, Abel, Grace, Jackson and William Gunn all had their moments.

If the Brighton of the 1890s in which Ranji settled was not quite the exuberant town familiar to Mrs Thrale, Lady Jersey and Mrs Fitzherbert, it was not essentially different. It was still a place where people – the gentry and the riff-raff, equally with East Enders – went to have a good time. It had vitality and style, the eighteenth century not lost to view under modern development. Moreover, there has always been a whiff of the Orient about Brighton, not only about the Pavilion, but about the town as a whole, its pleasure gardens and parades.

To the young Ranjitsinhji the domes and balconies of Brighton must have conjured up visions of India, an India momentarily lost to him, but there in memory, not beyond recall. In its piers and bathing-machines, the bulging bow windows and verandahs of its lodging houses, its fish markets and steep streets, its palatial hotels and ordered crescents, there was that mingling of the grand and the earthy, the dashing and the classic, which was part of Ranjitsinhji's own make-up. Its element of pure fantasy was akin to his own.

As Thackeray observed in *The Newcomes*: 'Here, for the sum of twopence, you can go out to sea and pace this vast deck without need of a steward with a basin.' Such an idea would have appealed to Ranji, who hated going on the sea as much as he liked looking at it.

When Ranji arrived at Hove the present Eaton Road ground had been in use twenty-three years, since, in fact, the year of his birth. It was the fourth site Sussex had taken up in a century. Ireland's Gardens was the county ground from 1791–1847; Lillywhite's Ground (now Montpelier Crescent) for a short period from 1834–44; Brunswick Ground, almost on the beach between Third and Fourth Avenue, between 1848 and 1871. Billy Newham, who had preceded Murdoch as captain, was Secretary, as he was to be for twenty years, all told. Newham was one of those great county characters who for almost their whole lifetime seem to be the bones and heart of the club. He must have been a batsman somewhat in the manner of the young George Cox, a ruthless cutter of fast bowling, very quick on his feet, and he was a fine fielder in the covers or the deep. Throughout the 1880s he was Sussex's most consistent batsman, touring Australia, as did his county colleague Brann, with Shrewsbury's side in 1887. In 1902 he and Ranji put on 344 for the seventh wicket at Leyton, a world record until 1954/55 when Atkinson and Depeiza scored 347 together at Bridgetown for West Indies against Australia. Ranji at Leyton made 230, Newham 153.

On the playing side Sussex, in the 1890s, were no great shakes. The oldest of the county teams, the county of Tom Box and John Wisden, Charles Taylor, 'the most graceful of them all', and the Lillywhites, it was going through one of its worst periods. Between 1876 and 1880 Sussex had won only two matches out of twenty-seven. Ten years later, with modest success in between,

Sussex lost sixteen matches out of eighteen. In 1892, the year Ranji played for Trinity but failed to get his Blue, Sussex lost fifteen out of twenty matches. They finished bottom in the championship in 1888, 1889, 1890, 1892 and 1896.

They were not without 'characters'. In 1887 and 1890, for example, the captain had been C. A. 'round-the-corner' Smith, in his late sixties and seventies a Hollywood star and the epitome of British India.

That great all-rounder Albert Relf, two years younger than Ranji, was to join them in 1900, but in the same season that Ranji played his first match Alfred Shaw, the former Nottinghamshire and England bowler, now in his fifties and coaching at Hove, was prevailed upon to turn out, so short of talent, bowling in particular, were Sussex.

A letter from Ranji in his own hand.

Immediate though Ranji's impact was, and though Fred Tate, father of Maurice, was in his prime, it was only at the very end of the nineties – in the last year of the century – that Sussex moved from the lowest reaches of the championship up to fifth.

Having devoted as much of the winter of 1894/95 as he could to shooting – undeterred by mounting debts, he rented shoots at various places round Cambridge as well as one at Methwold in Norfolk – Ranji took advantage of an exceptionally mild spring to spend several weeks in the nets at Cambridge.

By the time he had returned to Brighton for the start of the season and taken up his headquarters in the Norfolk Hotel on the front he was already in good form. It was, though, by no means certain at this stage how long Ranji would hold his place in a side that, weak though it was in bowling and deplorable in the field, had no shortage of batsmen.

His first match for Sussex against MCC at Lord's put the matter beyond doubt. MCC won on the third evening by 19 runs, but not before Ranji, 'playing in a fashion which beggars description', had made 77 not out and 150, taken six wickets and made two catches. For MCC, W. G. Grace, then in his forty-eighth year, scored 103 in MCC's second innings. Altogether 1,227 runs were made in the match.

Triumphant entries of this kind into new areas of experience – Test matches here and in Australia – were to become habitual to Ranji. They were in the nature of a shot across the bows, a signal of intent. 'Anything finer than his hitting,' wrote C. W. Alcock, 'has never been seen at Lord's . . . the first of that marvellous series of performances which stamped Mr Grace and Ranjitsinhji as *the* two batsmen of 1895.' Another comment, one that seems strikingly apt, was 'the ball flows from his bat like water rushes down a hill.'

What was Ranji like, at this brilliant start to his decade of glory, *the* Golden Age? The text to the Spy cartoon in *Vanity Fair*, published in 1897, describes him thus:

He is no great scholar, but he is an agreeable lad who dabbles a little in history. He mostly lives at Brighton; though he thinks

Lord's is the best cricket ground he knows . . . He is a slim, exceedingly lithe fellow, whose action in the field sometimes reminds you of a panther; and a genial and very casual person, who generally forgets an uncricketing engagement. He does not smoke or drink, and though he can give very cheery parties he professes to keep himself always fit . . . He is very good English company and he speaks unaccented English. When he is travelling he asks at every station what is the sport of the place; he is exceedingly generous, he is always at home, he has a quaint way of telling a good story, he is full of unassuming pluck, and he may be known a mile off by the elasticity of his walk. He has a violent temper, which he generally controls with marked ability; and the people idolise him.

Curiously the next cricketer to be dealt with in *Vanity Fair* was the opinionated Captain Edward Wynyard, captain of Hampshire and a captain in the Welsh Regiment who had seen service in Burma. The caption to his cartoon ends: 'He can speak his mind; and he is supposed to think less of K. S. Ranjitsinhji than some of the public do', a reference to an argument with Ranji at dinner one night. Wynyard customarily wore an I Zingari cap at a rakish angle, strapped under the chin.

Before Ranji's career was over almost every writer of stature, and many of little, had a go at describing his methods. One of the best accounts of what he actually looked like at the wicket comes from an article in the *Daily News* by the well-known essayist of the time, A. G. Gardiner. Although written on Ranji's retirement it focuses on the basic characteristic of his technique.

There is extraordinarily little display in his methods. He combines an Oriental calm with an Oriental swiftness – the stillness of the panther with the suddenness of its spring. He has none of the fine flourishes of our own stylists, but a quite startling economy of action . . . He stands moveless as the bowler approaches the wicket. He remains moveless as the ball is delivered. It seems to be upon him before he takes action. Then, without any preliminary flourish, the bat flashes to the ball, and the stroke is over. The body seems never to have changed its position, the feet are unmoved, the bat is as before . . . If the supreme art is to achieve the maximum result with the minimum expenditure of effort, the Jam Saheb, as a batsman, is in a class by himself . . . It is the art of the great etcher who with a line reveals infinity . . . The typical batsman performs a series of intricate evolutions in playing the ball; the Jam Saheb flicks his wrist and the ball bounds to the ropes. It is not jugglery, or magic; it is simply the perfect economy of a means to an end.

Sussex moved north, after Lord's, to play Nottinghamshire and Lancashire. At Trent Bridge, Nottinghamshire pounded the Sussex attack to make 726, for about two months the highest score ever made by a county. William Gunn made 219, after which Sussex, caught on a drying wicket, were bowled out twice in a day by Attewell. At Old Trafford Sussex were well beaten by seven wickets, again on a difficult pitch.

On the return journey down to Brighton Ranji can have had no illusions about the nature of Sussex's problems. He, himself, had shown remarkable technique on pitches ideal for bowlers. His four innings, 29 and 27 against Nottinghamshire, 35 and 46 against Mold and Briggs at Old Trafford, were early indications that he was not going to be merely a fair-weather batsman.

As yet, his home crowd had not properly seen him, except perhaps looking out at the sea from his Norfolk Hotel sitting room.

Their first glimpse, in the match against Gloucestershire, must have been a disappointment, Ranji managing only 19 and 9, and Gloucestershire having much the best of it. Later in the week, though, they had their reward, Ranji making 95 and 57 in a high-scoring drawn match against Somerset. Sussex made 518 in their first innings, Ranji and Marlow putting on 226 for the second wicket, but Sammy Woods got 215 for Somerset and there was never any hope of a result. The next match, against Middlesex, was also drawn, Ranji contributing 22 and 64. Each week that went by emphasised the moderateness of the Sussex bowling, its limitations not concealed by the appalling number of catches that went down. For most of the summer Sussex were not to be short of runs, but their attack lacked both pace and variety and they necessarily had to be reconciled to long days in the field.

This was the start, though, of a golden time for Ranji: 38 and
137 not out against Oxford at Hove, 30 and 58 against Kent at
Catford, 59 and 74 against Yorkshire at Hastings, 83 and 41
against Hampshire at Hove, 110 and 72 at Lord's in the return
match against Middlesex, 4 and 100 at Hove against Nottinghamshire.

In the Oxford match Fry made 125 for the University, though
at this stage Ranji was critical of his technique: 'He often cramped
the limited number of strokes he possessed by overcaution and
perhaps by diffidence. Further, he handicapped himself by assum-
ing all kinds of impossible attitudes to make them.' He was to
write very differently about him ten years later. Whether the vast
improvement in Fry's play was due mainly to batting opposite
Ranji is a matter for conjecture, though Fry, rather touchily, wrote
many years later: 'I evolved such cricket as I achieved from
watching Lionel Palairet play, and from my own inner nature.
Mostly, the latter, because I was a driver with a full swing, and
not a modulated lunger in the stylish manner of Palairet . . . The
yarn that I had a miserable talent for batting until I met Ranjitsinhji in the Sussex eleven is probably due to my being a fast
bowler as well.'

It was not until 1898, in fact, that Fry was able to play a full
season for Sussex, hitherto having to limit himself to what he
called 'the August fag-end' of the season. The development was
dramatic, Fry scoring 1,788 runs with an average of 54. Although
they had batted together for the first time in the Middlesex match
at Lords in 1895 – putting on 117 in 70 minutes, Fry making 43 –
it was not until Fry began to play the whole season for Sussex that
their association really blossomed.

That first summer of Ranji's, Sussex beat Middlesex at Lord's by
two wickets, and Kent by nine wickets, Ranji's contributions
being crucial each time. Yorkshire and Nottinghamshire beat
them, though had Ranji had anything like proper support on
either occasion they would not have done so.

After his hundred against Nottinghamshire Ranji had a comparatively lean period, particularly in the west country. At the
Oval, just before Sussex set out for Bristol, Ranji made 21 and 31,

but against Gloucestershire he managed only 17 and 2, and in the next match, at Taunton, only 1 and 7.

Back on the south coast in mid-August he finished off the season, if not as spectacularly as he had begun it, satisfactorily enough: 4 and 41 against Lancashire at Hove, 6 and 41 against Hampshire at Southampton, 51 and 53 not out against Kent and 19 and 36 against Surrey, both at Hove. Invited to play for the Gentlemen, a match conflicting with one of the Hampshire matches, Ranji declined. All the energy he had he wished to put at the disposal of Sussex.

He was not, in fact, ever very well during this first season. The blue, sea-scented air of Brighton, admirably suited to Ranji's tastes and character in so many ways, seemed to bring on his asthma. Often his bedroom light was on all night.

That May, too, was often exceptionally cold and Ranji suffered badly. Yet no one could have detected any of this from his manner of batting or his sharpness in the field. 'Everyone knows the brisk step with which he descends the pavilion steps,' wrote the correspondent of the *World*, 'and his lunging, rolling gait to the wicket . . . The Indian has the eye of the hawk and wrists like Toledo steel, and the finest of the batsman's art is his, the art of timing the ball . . . The ball leaves his blade with the swiftness of thought, as old Nyren says of Beldham's cutting.'

About Ranji's own cutting the same writer observed: 'He has a late cut which the envious gods are still practising in the Elysian Fields.' And rather more disputably: 'But just as Victor Hugo thought little of his writings and longed ever to be a painter, so does Prince Ranjitsinhji long to be a bowler rather than a bat. He practises assiduously and there are some who hold that his eager-ness to assist Tate and Bland with the ball will need no spur.'

During the Middlesex match at Lord's in July Ranji was inter-viewed by an anonymous writer for the magazine *Cricket*, 'a weekly of the game'. It cost twopence and carried under its banner a line from Byron: 'Together joined in Cricket's manly toil.' The sketch that resulted from the conversation with Ranji, conducted

after he had made a winning 72 against Hearne on an awkward
wicket, is fairly inane but it contains interesting remarks by Ranji
on the possibilities of cricket in India and the preparation of
wickets. What the article makes plain is that already, and only
three-quarters of the way through his first full season, Ranji was
considered by the best judges as just about 'the very best and most
reliable bat in the country', to quote one of them. This was the
summer, incidentally, in which Grace reached his hundredth first-
class hundred and also scored a thousand runs in May; in which
both Grace and Abel made over two thousand runs; and in which
Archie Maclaren took 424 off the Somerset bowling.

Ranji's Sussex total for the season was 1,766 at an average of
50.16. Only Grace, Abel and the Lancastrian Ward scored more
runs than Ranji; only Grace and Maclaren were above him in the
first-class averages.

The *Cricket* article quotes Ranji as replying to the question
'What grounds in England suit you best?' with, 'Fenner's at
Cambridge, Lord's, and Brighton, in the order named.' To the
question which of the bowlers he had met did he consider the best,
he replied: 'Mold and Richardson amongst the fast bowlers seem
to me most dangerous, and of slow bowlers I should unhesitatingly
say that Peel is the foremost.' His own best innings he considered,
in relation to the conditions, his 137 against Oxford and the
innings just over. 'In each case the wicket had crumbled badly.'
The photograph that accompanies the piece, taken at Cambridge
by R. H. Lord, shows Ranji in what looks like academic dress,
high-winged collar and pale tie, his moustache luxuriant but
carefully trimmed over full lips, the hair quite short but with a
wave-shaped quiff.

C. B. Fry's association with Ranji, which was to continue far
beyond the realms of cricket and to last throughout Ranji's life,
began in this late summer. Some of the most perceptive and vivid
writing about Ranji is by Fry, not least one of his earliest pieces
originally published in *Giants of the Game*. 'One would not be
surprised sometimes to see a brown curve burnt in the grass where
one of his cuts has travelled, or blue flame shiver around his bat

in the making of one of those leg-strokes.' More analytically Fry
continues:

> He tries to make every stroke a thing of beauty in itself, and he
> does mean so well by the ball while he is in . . . He starts with
> one or two enormous advantages, which he has pressed home.
> He has a wonderful power of sight which enables him to judge
> the flight of a ball in the air an appreciable fraction of a second
> sooner than any other batsman, and probably a trifle more
> accurately. He can therefore decide in better time what stroke
> is wanted, and can make sure of getting into the right position
> to make it. So he is rarely caught, as most of us are, doing two
> things at once – moving into an attitude and playing at the ball
> simultaneously . . . His desire to act and his action seem to
> coincide . . . But with far less natural quickness Ranji would
> have been a great cricketer for the simple reason that he is a
> great observer, with faculty for digesting observations and
> acting upon them. He takes nothing on trust. He sees a thing,
> makes it his own and develops it. Many of his innumerable
> strokes were originally learnt from other players, but in the
> process of being thought out and practised, have improved past
> recognition. This is partly due to his natural powers – eye,
> quickness and elasticity – and partly to his hatred of leaving
> anything he takes up before bringing it to the highest pitch of
> which he is capable. Ranji has made a science of taking liberties.
> One may fairly suspect him of regarding Tom Richardson's ball
> as bowled in the interest of cutting and driving rather than with
> a view to hitting the sticks.

Fry confirms Ranji's own statement that the famous leg-glance
derived from his trying to get out of the way of the ball, but by
moving towards point rather than towards square-leg.

> Nowadays he can place to leg within a foot of where he wishes
> almost any ball that pitches between wicket and wicket . . . He
> has a slight prejudice against forward play for forcing strokes.
> There is a moment in a forward stroke when the ball is out of
> sight and the stroke is being played on faith, so that if the ball

does anything unexpected, or the judgment is at all at fault, it is mere chance whether the stroke be good or bad . . . Why does he ever get out? Perhaps he knows himself. There may be reasons but they are not apparent.

Ranji could look back upon the first of his great seasons with some satisfaction. It is unlikely, though, that, ever the perfectionist, he did so. Nevertheless, he had made runs on all types of wickets, a century against Nottinghamshire at Hove after heavy rain, 137 against Oxford on a dusty, spinning pitch, 72 against Middlesex at Lord's on a flier. *Punch*, on 14 September, paid tribute:

> Great Grace to young Maclaren yields his place,
> And Ranjitsinhji follows after Grace.

FIVE

Test Triumph

What is remarkable about Ranji, among many other things, is how quickly he became a 'character'; before the end even of his first season he had acquired a following. Few people outside Sussex, except perhaps the regulars at Lord's, can have seen him more than half a dozen times at most, yet already he was a star. It was by no means only because he was Indian, a bloom of the tropics; not all Indian cricketers have caught the public fancy. Nor was it because, like the Aga Khan, for instance, in matters of the Turf, he was a great swell. He became that, too. But in these earliest of days it was simply because of his prowess. He batted, as he looked, like no one else. 'Prince Ranjitsinhji being now the people's darling, everyone who follows cricket can conjure up his form in the field, at point or short slip – alert and intent, ever poised ready to spring on the ball like a panther. Everyone knows how his hands find each other behind his back between the delivery of ball and ball, how the back of his gossamer shirt flutters in the wind while tremors ripple down to the wristbands which he keeps always so tightly fastened. And everyone knows how, during the interval between a wicket and "man in", no one is so keen upon the ball as the Indian Prince, no one has so many subtle ways of throwing it, or is a greater adept at catching it – now a hair's breadth almost from the Turf, now a yard above his head.'

The mannerisms, the attire, had become public knowledge, but they were merely extensions of the player. In 1896, only his second season in the first-class game, the rumour of Ranji was to become living legend.

It was, once again, an Australian summer, Harry Trott leading a side whose attack included Griffen, Jones and Trumble. Ranji

was so soon into his stride for Sussex, 30 and 74 against MCC at
Lord's, 64 and 33 against Lancashire at Old Trafford, hundreds in
successive matches against Yorkshire, Gloucestershire and Somerset, that by the beginning of June he had established himself as
the most exciting batsman in the country. In addition, at Sheffield
Park, that most lush of Sussex estates, he made 79 and 42 for Lord
Sheffield's eleven in the Australians' opening fixture.

Despite all Ranji's runs Sussex had not prospered. Lancashire,
largely through Mold's ferocity on a lively wicket, beat them
comfortably, and Yorkshire by ten wickets. Grace's double
century at Hove enabled Gloucestershire to hold out for a draw,
and Somerset in the next match were rescued by Lionel Palairet.

There was no doubt, though, that if he were considered, Ranji
must be a certainty for the first Test, to start at Lord's on 22 June.
He had made his runs, often in difficult conditions, against the
best bowlers in England.

But the circumstances of an Indian playing for England were
ones never before considered. In 1896, and it was the last year in
which this was the case, Test teams were not chosen by an independent selection committee, but by the county at whose ground
the match was to be played. Thus MCC, whose President was the
Lord Harris, six years previously Governor of Bombay, were
responsible for the team for Lord's, Lancashire for the Old
Trafford side, Surrey for the final Test at the Oval.

Lord Harris was not, in fact, in favour of playing what he called
'birds of passage', and Ranji, though asked to make himself
available, was not chosen for the Lord's Test, an omission that
resulted in public and press outcry. Some thirty years later
Duleepsinhji, Ranji's much cherished nephew and little less a
player, played in the first Test against South Africa but, objected
to by the South Africans, agreed to stand down for the rest of the
series.

The Australians, when Ranji was selected to play in the second
Test at Old Trafford three weeks later, raised no such objections.
Ranji, on being invited, insisted that the Australians should be
consulted. They were, Trott expressed his delight, and no more
was heard of the matter.

As sometimes happens when selectors miss the tide, Ranji went through an indifferent patch after his wonderful May. Indeed, between 30 May, when he made 107 in the second innings against Somerset at Hove, and 27 June, when he scored 171 not out against Oxford at Hove, Ranji batted seven times for Sussex at an average of 16. He did, however, make 7, 146 and 30 for MCC, and 47 and 51 not out for the Gentlemen. The Gentlemen v. Players match took place at Lord's immediately before the Old Trafford Test. This was Ranji's first appearance in the Lord's fixture and he entertained everyone in a crowd of ten thousand with his batting on the opening morning. 'One of the most brilliant and delightful pieces of batting seen at Lord's last season' was how *Wisden* described it. The Gentlemen, despite their weak bowling, beat the Players by seven wickets, Woods and Grace taking five wickets in the first and second innings respectively, and Ranji and Jackson making 98 and 97 in the match for once out. Ranji, incidentally, batted only ten minutes for his 47, hitting a boundary off each of the twelve balls he received except one, which he put away for three. The Players' bowling included Richardson, of whom Ranji was contemptuously dismissive, Briggs, Lohmann and Hearne. Not surprisingly the packed pavilion, then only six years old in its present form, rose to him.

After the Lord's Test, which England won by six wickets – Richardson and Lohmann bowling Australia out before lunch on the first day for 53 – Ranji came back to form for Sussex, putting together 69 and 73 against Kent at Hastings. Two and 36 against Surrey at the Oval – rarely a happy ground – was one of his quieter games, but by then he had received A. N. Hornby's invitation to take the place of William Gunn at Old Trafford. Gunn, though now thirty-eight, was a trifle unlucky to be dropped, having made 25 and 13 not out at Lord's. He played again for England against Australia three years later, on his home ground of Trent Bridge, and this time with Ranji. Jones bowled him for low scores in each innings and he was never picked for England again.

Since their defeat at Lord's the Australians had thrived. England made some odd changes, Maclaren, who had scarcely played at all,

replacing Tom Hayward, and Briggs coming in at the last moment
for Lohmann, who reported unwell on the morning of the match.

Old Trafford tends to have extremes of weather, pouring rain
or tropical heat. On this occasion it was the latter, and once Trott
had won the toss and chosen to bat, England were soon rueing the
absence of a fourth regular bowler. The Australians got off to a
good start in ideal batting conditions. Iredale, left out of the first
Test, made a handsome hundred, Giffen 80 and Trott 53. With
Australia 240 for 2 at one stage, Grace was in some trouble, calling
on seven bowlers without much success. In the end Richardson,
despite bowling 68 overs in the innings, all with the same ball as
was then the custom, found a second wind, taking the last five
wickets and finishing with 7 for 168. Australia were all out for
412, a good deal less than at one time seemed likely.

England, with weather and wicket still excellent, made a
dreadful start. Trott, surprisingly opening the bowling himself
with Jones – at Lord's it had been Jones and Giffen – had both
Grace and Stoddart stumped with only 23 on the board. Ranji,
batting at number three, took the score to 104 with Abel, but
wickets fell steadily thereafter, despite the fact that Jones strained
a muscle and could only bowl five overs. Ranji was caught by
Trott off McKibbin for 62, and only a bold 65 not out by Lilley,
going in at number eight, took England past the 200.

Ranji alone of the earlier batsmen had shown anything. His and
Lilley's efforts were not, however, enough to save the follow-on.
By the second evening England, 109 for 4, seemed to have been
cornered. Ranji was still there, but Grace had failed for the second
time in the match, Stoddart had been bowled by McKibbin for 41,
and just before close of play Giffen had removed Abel and Jackson
in quick succession.

The large crowds of the first two days, sensing an early defeat
for England, declined to part with their money a third time. England, after all, were still 72 behind and the main batting had gone.

They missed something, for although Brown was out for 19
at 132 and Maclaren for 15 at 179, Ranji, as *Wisden* put it, 'rose to
the occasion, playing an innings that could, without exaggeration,
be fairly described as marvellous.'

1 (above) Lord's 1896, First Test, from a painting by W. B. Wollen. It was in the next Test, at Old Trafford, that Ranji made his first appearance for England.

2 (below) The Parsees, at Sheffield Park, 1886. Ranji was only 14 when this party, the first of its kind, toured England.

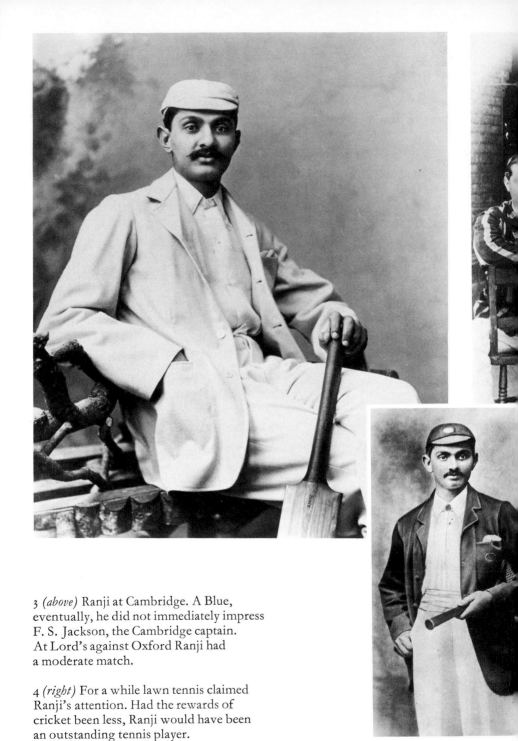

3 *(above)* Ranji at Cambridge. A Blue,
eventually, he did not immediately impress
F. S. Jackson, the Cambridge captain.
At Lord's against Oxford Ranji had
a moderate match.

4 *(right)* For a while lawn tennis claimed
Ranji's attention. Had the rewards of
cricket been less, Ranji would have been
an outstanding tennis player.

5 England, 1895. Top row: West (umpire),
K. S. Ranjitsinhji, Ward, Martin; centre row:
C. W. Wright, W. L. Murdoch, W. G. Grace (captain),
F. S. Jackson, Pougher; front row: Mold, Briggs,
Lilley

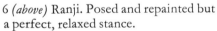

6 *(above)* Ranji. Posed and repainted but a perfect, relaxed stance.

7 *(above, right)* Fifth Test, the Oval, 1899, v. Australia. Ranji playing to the offside during his innings of 54. One of the very few pictures of Ranji in action.

8 *(right)* Ranji going through the strokes that became part of his repertoire.

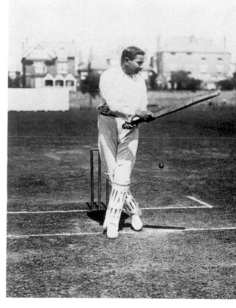

9 *(left)* Sussex under
W. L. Murdoch.

10 *(below, left)* Sussex, 1901.
Top row: Tate, Killick,
Marlow, C. L. A. Smith;
centre row: Butt, K. O. Goldie,
K. S. Ranjitsinhji, C. B. Fry,
W. Newham; front row:
Vine, Relf

1 *(above, right)* Ranji and
C. B. Fry, colleagues for
Sussex and England; also
at Geneva in 1920.

2 *(right)* On board the
Ormuz, Australia-bound.

13 *(left)* Ranji and W. G. Grace, dressed for cricket but ready for anything.

14 *(right)* Ranji at the Oval, 1912. Aged 40, and no longer the slim figure of his youth, Ranji says farewell to first-class cricket.

Wisden is not usually remarkable for other than the plainest of descriptive prose. In this instance their account rises to the occasion, too.

'Ranjitsinhji very quickly got set again, and punished the Australian bowlers in a style that, up to that period of the season, no other English batsman had approached. He repeatedly brought off his wonderful strokes on the leg-side, and for a while had the Australian bowlers quite at his mercy ... Ranjitsinhji's remarkable batting, and the prospect of the Englishmen after all running their opponents close, worked the spectators up to a high pitch of excitement, and the scene of enthusiasm was something to be remembered when the Indian cricketer completed the first hundred against the Australians ... It is safe to say that a finer or more finished display has never been seen on a great occasion, for he never gave anything like a chance, and during his long stay the worst that could be urged against him was that he made a couple of lucky snicks. He was at the wicket for three hours ten minutes, and among his hits were twenty-three 4s, five 3s and nine 2s.'

No one could write handsomer than that. Ranji carried his bat for 154, the next highest score of the innings on the last day was 19, and England were all out 305.

The Australians, needing only 125 to win, put on 20 without sign of unease. At this point Richardson, beginning a fantastic spell of fast, hostile bowling, bowled Iredale, century-maker in the first innings, for 11. Six runs later he had Darling caught at the wicket. At 28 Ranji caught Giffen off him at slip, and at 45 Trott was taken behind the wicket.

Suddenly the outcome seemed far from being a foregone conclusion, though the pitch was still playing as well as at any time in the match. Gregory and Donnan, however, inched their way forward, until at 79 Gregory was caught by Ranji at short leg off Briggs. Donnan was out at 95, Hill at 100, both to Richardson who had bowled unchanged.

With three wickets left Australia needed 25. With only nine more needed Lilley dropped Kelly off Richardson. Trumble and Kelly, however, hanging on by the skin of their teeth, saw Australia safely home. The last 25 runs, every one of which had to be fought for, took an hour to make and were made in absolute silence.

Once victorious, the Australians were given a great reception by the Manchester crowd, swelled in the sultry afternoon by a steady flow of those in the city who had picked up the signals.

If it was Ranji who initially set up the finish for one of the most dramatic of Test matches, Tom Richardson's performance was one of the greatest by a fast bowler. Altogether Richardson bowled 110 overs in the match, taking 13 wickets for 244. Neville Cardus wrote about Richardson: 'He looked the part: tall, splendidly built and proportioned, with a long – not too long – striding run culminating in a beautifully poised leap, left shoulder and side pointing down the wicket, the right arm swinging over, then finishing near or behind the left hip.'

Richardson, in his prime 'as handsome a sight as was ever seen in a cricket field, dark, black-haired, black-moustached', was famous for his break-back. Cardus wrote that when he came up to the wicket to release the ball he called to mind a great wave of the sea about to break.

This was the same Richardson, among the greatest in the long line of English fast bowlers, whom Ranji had despatched so cruelly at Lord's a week before. Richardson, in 1894/95 in Australia, had taken 69 wickets at 23.42, and in the season after this one, pounding down on the lifeless Surrey pitch, he was to take 273 wickets. He died mysteriously in the Swiss mountains – allegedly of his own volition – aged only forty-one.

After this, the next few weeks were inevitably something of an anti-climax. Ranji, in the Bank Holiday match at Hove against Middlesex, disappointed the huge seaside crowd that had come to see him bat, making only 2 and 18 in a 9-wickets Sussex defeat. He made up for this, though, in the very next match, going in at seven in the first innings against Nottinghamshire and making 52 out of 177, and in the second innings 100 not out. Sussex, as so often in the summer of 1896, failed in the first innings and then recovered so well in the second that hopeless causes were often redeemed. The innocuousness of their bowling, nevertheless, meant that though they often saved matches they rarely won them.

AUSTRALIA

F. A. Iredale	b Briggs	108	b Richardson	11
J. Darling	c Lilley b Richardson ...	27	c Lilley b Richardson	16
G. Giffen	c and b Richardson	80	c Ranjitsinhji b Richardson	6
*G. H. S. Trott...	c Brown b Lilley	53	c Lilley b Richardson	2
S. E. Gregory ...	c Stoddart b Briggs	25	c Ranjitsinhji b Briggs ...	33
H. Donnan	b Richardson	12	c Jackson b Richardson ..	15
C. Hill	c Jackson b Richardson .	9	c Lilley b Richardson	14
H. Trumble.....	b Richardson	24	not out	17
†J. J. Kelly	c Lilley b Richardson ...	27	not out	8
T. R. McKibbin .	not out	28		
E. Jones........	b Richardson	4		
Extras	(b 6, lb 8, w 1)	15	(lb 3)	3
Total	....	412	Total (7 wkts)	125

First Innings – *Fall of Wickets*
1–41, 2–172, 3–242, 4–294, 5–294, 6–314, 7–325, 8–362, 9–403, 10–412.

First Innings – *Bowling*
Richardson, 68–23–168–7; Briggs, 40–18–99–2; Jackson, 16–6–34–0; Hearne, 28–11–53–0; Grace, 7–3–11–0; Stoddart, 6–2–9–0; Lilley, 5–1–23–1.

Second Innings – *Fall of Wickets*
1–20, 2–26, 3–28, 4–45, 5–79, 6–95, 7–100.

Second Innings – *Bowling*
Richardson, 42.3–16–76–6; Briggs, 18–8–24–1; Hearne, 24–13–22–0.

ENGLAND

*W. G. Grace	st Kelly b Trott	2	c Trott b Jones	11
A. E. Stoddart ..	st Kelly b Trott	15	b McKibbin	41
K. S. Ranjitsinhji	c Trott b McKibbin	62	not out	154
R. Abel	c Trumble b McKibbin .	26	c McKibbin b Giffen.....	13
F. S. Jackson....	run out	18	c McKibbin b Giffen.....	1
J. T. Brown	c Kelly b Trumble......	22	c Iredale b Jones	19
A. C. MacLaren .	c Trumble b McKibbin .	0	c Jones b Trumble	15
†A. A. Lilley.....	not out	65	c Trott b Giffen	19
J. Briggs	b Trumble	0	st Kelly b McKibbin	16
J. T. Hearne	c Trumble b Giffen	18	c Kelly b McKibbin	9
T. Richardson...	run out	2	c Jones b Trumble	1
Extras	(b 1).................	1	(b 2, lb 3, w 1)	6
Total	....	231	Total	305

First Innings – *Fall of Wickets*
1–2, 2–23, 3–104, 4–111, 5–140, 6–140, 7–154, 8–166, 9–219, 10–213.

First Innings – *Bowling*
Jones, 5–2–11–0; Trott, 10–0–46–2; Giffen, 19–3–48–1; Trumble, 37–14–80–2; McKibbin, 19–8–45–3.

Second Innings – *Fall of Wickets*
1–33, 2–76, 3–97, 4–109, 5–132, 6–179, 7–232, 8–268, 9–304, 10–305.

Second Innings – *Bowling*
Jones, 17–0–78–2; Trott, 7–1–17–0; Giffen, 16–1–65–3; Trumble, 29.1–12–78–2; McKibbin, 21–4–61–3.

Umpires: J. Phillips, A. Chester.   * Captain   † Wicket keeper

Sussex, with Ranji's eye on fishing possibilities and the grouse season coming up, now set off on their west country tour. Ranji enjoyed himself with 38 and 54 in a losing cause at Bristol, where Grace made 301. Grace having already taken 243 not out off the Sussex bowling at Hove, every hair on his beard must have now been familiar to them. Gloucestershire only got home in the Bristol match with a quarter of an hour to spare, Ranji making them fight to the last, though with negligible support.

The match against Somerset at Taunton was a freak affair. When rain caused the match to be abandoned Sussex had made 559 and Somerset 476 for 6 wickets. Ranji scored 54, most of them in company with Fry, while the left-handed Killick batted over six hours for 191. Somerset lost an early wicket to Fred Tate, after which the Palairet brothers put on 249, both scoring over 150. A year earlier they had made hundreds in the same innings against Middlesex.

The final Test match, to be played at the Oval, allowed Ranji only one day off in between. Trouble followed the announcement of the side, five of the thirteen announced – Lohmann, Gunn, Abel, Richardson and Hayward – demanding £20, as against the £10 paid at Lord's and Old Trafford, for their services. The Surrey Committee, predictably, were in no mood to yield to so sudden an ultimatum and set about finding replacements. Two days before the match was due to start, however, Abel, Hayward and Richardson withdrew their demand.

Not everyone was in favour of their being reinstated, but the match committee, in additional hot water because of newspaper stories concerning expenses for amateurs, notably W. G. Grace's personal requirements, decided to accept them. Gunn and Lohmann were left out.

The match, rather sadly, was decided by the weather. No play was possible until five o'clock on the first day, at the end of which England were 69 for 1, Ranji having gone in at the fall of Grace's wicket just before the close.

The next day Trumble, on a disagreeable pitch, had everyone in difficulties. From being 113 for 3 England were all out 145, Trumble taking 5 for 10 in 9 overs, and altogether 6 for 59 in 40 overs.

The Australians made light of their task and, the pitch seeming to ease, reached 75 for no wicket. At this point Darling hit a ball far into the untenanted deep at the Vauxhall end and Iredale called for a fifth run. Ranji, chasing after it, produced a beautiful throw of over a hundred yards and Iredale was run out.

There was now a total collapse, the remaining nine wickets going down, six of them to Hearne, for only 44. England, with the pitch becoming increasingly spiteful, were bowled out in their second innings for 84, Trumble taking another six wickets for 30. Ranji was stumped off him for 11.

Australia, starting their innings shortly before lunch, needed 111 to win. No one appeared certain how the pitch was going to play the more it dried out. They soon learned. Darling was bowled all ends up by Hearne for 0 in the second over and in no time Australia were 25 for 9. The last pair hit about briefly but Australia, all out 44, lost by 66 runs.

It had not been a great match for Ranji, but it was a bowler's wicket from start to finish. Peel took 8 for 53, Hearne 10 for 60. The 'strikers'' contribution was mostly minimal: Richardson, hero of Old Trafford, bowled just six overs and took no wickets, Hayward had 17 hit off two overs and fell to Trumble in each innings for 0 and 13. Abel, with scores of 26 and 21, tied with F. S. Jackson for the highest scorer on the England side.

Ranji could now concentrate on Sussex in this flamboyant summer, a summer in which the Prince of Wales sought to bring back to London some of the sparkle long absent from the Court because of the Queen's prolonged mourning. In that year his horse Persimmon won both the Derby and the St Leger. He may have got himself a bad reputation, not helped by his involvement in both the Mordaunt divorce case and the Tranby Croft affair, but at least his theatre-going, race-course attendance, gambling, and sexual activity were recognisable failings in comparison with the Queen's entombment at Windsor, Balmoral and Osborne, with her whisky-drinking ghillie, John Brown, as sole companion.

In most of his pleasures the Prince of Wales was a man after Ranji's own heart. Ranji, too, was gregarious and party-giving,

attracted to all forms of sport and entertainment, especially those
that involved mastering technical skills.

During this August of 1896, however, he devoted all his
energies to cricket. Fry had re-joined Sussex, the term at Charter-
house, where he had been teaching, now over, and his friendship
with Ranji developed. Fry's own mark on the game was still
modest – in eleven innings his highest score was 92, his average
32 – but Ranji saw the month out in a blaze of glory.

The first fixture the Australians had after the Oval Test was at
Hove. They soon showed they meant business, bowling Sussex
out for 221 and 248 and winning comfortably by six wickets.
Ranji was caught off Trumble for 26 in the first innings, but in the
second he put on 123 in seventy minutes for the second wicket with
Fry. Once they were parted, Ranji being run out for 74, Trumble
ran through the rest of the Sussex batsmen.

Ranji had damaged a finger fielding and as a result went in
number seven against Lancashire in his next innings. Sussex,
making little of Mold and Briggs, were put out for 153, Ranji
scoring almost all of the last fifty. This was Eastbourne professional Joe Vine's first match and although he did not get another
for Sussex that season – despite making 36 – he much impressed
Ranji. In the seasons that followed he was to share in thirty-three
century-opening partnerships with Fry.

Lancashire declared at 345 for 4, whereupon Sussex once again
collapsed before Mold and Briggs. There seemed no hope of
saving the innings defeat, but Ranji, despite none of his partners
managing more than sixteen, scored 165 out of a total of 259 before
being stumped. The match was drawn.

It scarcely seemed possible that Ranji had anything left to
achieve in a season already grown autumnal. But he had.

Yorkshire followed their northern neighbours down to Hove
and the day after Ranji had made his 165, batted into the second
morning for 407. Jackson and Peel both got hundreds.

Sussex lost their customary quick wickets, this time to Hirst,
but no sooner had Ranji reached the crease than a typical Hove sea
drizzle set in and play had to be called off for the day.

The next morning, 22 August, Ranji set about the Yorkshire

bowlers, scoring exactly a hundred out of a total of 191 all out. Following on 216 behind, Sussex got off to one of their better starts, Fry making 42 and Marlow 30. There seemed little likelihood, though, that Sussex would keep the Yorkshire attack at bay when Ranji arrived for his second innings of the day. However, in the best of humours, he cut, drove and glanced his way to the most elegant of hundreds and in fact Sussex lost no more wickets.

Only Grace, Stoddart, Brann and Storer had scored two hundreds in the same first-class match before; no one before Ranji had ever made them on the same day.

The season ended with Sussex going north to Lord's and Nottingham, before returning for their final fixture at Hove against Surrey. The Lord's match was ruined by rain, Ranji making 28 and 42 not out. At Trent Bridge, Sussex got the worst of the wicket and were beaten by 188 runs. Ranji, at less than his best, made forties in each innings. Fry, however, had his best match for the county so far, taking five wickets in each innings and making 89 and 65, batting both times with Ranji. So much did the two Sussex innings revolve round these two that out of 184 in the first innings their share was 132, and out of 161 in the second, 106.

Against Surrey, Sussex once again got the worst of the weather. Surrey, on a lovely last day of August, made 308, after which Sussex were condemned to bat twice on pitches badly affected by rain. Lohmann took eleven of their wickets, Ranji made 38 and 10, and Surrey won by ten wickets.

It was, in its way, a bitter-sweet finish to the summer, for although Ranji, in these final matches, reached his two thousand runs for the county in the season, these last two defeats meant that Sussex ended up bottom in the championship. Out of eighteen matches they won only two and lost nine. While Ranji headed the batting with 2,113 in all Sussex matches at an average of 58.25, only Killick and Newham crept past the thousand mark. Murdoch, the captain, far from the great batsman of earlier days, averaged only 22.

It was the bowling, though, that put Sussex where they were, only Fred Tate, with 73 wickets, exceeding fifty. Too often the fielding was casual and unreliable. It needed extremes of spin or speed to bowl sides out on the genial Hove wicket, and Sussex lacked both.

Yet Ranji, packing up his gear and exchanging his Norfolk Hotel sitting room for Cambridge, could well forget his disappointments for the team. There was the prospect of good shooting on the moors, he could enjoy himself in London, and he was starting his long love affair with fishing.

Wisden, in due course, put him in the central place in their annual photograph of the Five Cricketers of the Year. Surrounding him were Lilley and Richardson, Trumble and Gregory. In their accompanying text *Wisden* remarked, after listing all Ranji's achievements, that 'as a batsman Ranjitsinhji is himself alone, being quite individual and distinctive in his style of play . . . For any ordinary player to attempt to turn good length balls off the middle stump as he does, would be futile and disastrous. To Ranjitsinhji on a fast wicket, however, everything seems possible, and if the somewhat too freely used word genius can with any propriety be employed in connection with cricket, it surely applies to the young Indian's batting.'

During the Surrey match Ranji passed Grace's record aggregate of 2,739 runs in a season, made twenty-five years earlier. Against Ranji's average of 57, however, Grace's was 78.

Ranji's full figures were 55 innings, 2,780 runs, average 57.91. He hit ten centuries. He also bowled 68 overs, taking 6 wickets for 204.

There was not only first-class cricket for Ranji during the summer of 1896. In August he played in a match at Bexhill, then being promoted as a sibling Brighton. Ranji played for a Sussex eleven against a scratch side raised by Lord de la Warr. The match would scarcely be worth mentioning had it not made such an impression on those who saw it.

The pitch was a long way below county standard and the presence of Lockwood in the home team caused some dismay. Despite agreements to the contrary Lockwood proceeded to bowl at his usual pace. The Sussex batsmen, grumbling mightily, could scarcely get themselves out quick enough.

Ranji alone appeared undeterred, indeed to be in his element. Philip Trevor, writing in his book *Cricket and Cricketers* twenty-five years later, never forgot the experience, though a certain name seems to have got oddly transposed.

I shall never forget the day when I first saw Ranji bat . . . I think I may say without fear of exaggeration that the wicket was the worst and the most dangerous on which I have seen a first-class match played. Woodcock was bowling his fastest and those who have played with and against Woodcock know, or knew, that for a few overs he could make a new ball travel about as fast as it wanted to travel. I remember that it struck me at the time that Lilley was standing nearer the bowling screen than the wicket . . . And well he might, for Woodcock's fast balls were coming from the pitch like rocketing pheasants. One of the batsmen, when he had returned to the safety of the pavilion, so I was told, said that he was glad that the wicket was as bad as it was and not a little better. As things were, Woodcock's good-length ball, pitched just clear of the leg-stump, went over his head. To the best of my recollection Sussex scored 71, of which Ranji got 49. Most men and women of my generation have, I imagine, seen Cinquevalli juggle with knives and finish his wonderful performance uncut by them. Ranji's performance that day put Cinquevalli's feats in the shade, for the ball never touched anything but the middle of his bat. He smiled quietly when it went too far over his head for him to touch at all, and when it was a shade more pitched up he did one of two things. He sprang in like a cat and drove it hard, or he whipped round and scored fours off his face. I was so amazed and enthralled that I could hardly applaud, and members of my family thought I was little short of cracked when I said 'This is the greatest ever.'

Fry, in a piece on the careful method of Archie Maclaren, mentions *en passant* that despite occasional evidence to the contrary no great batsman plays carelessly: 'Their attention is closely concentrated and their strokes quite deliberate. Ranjitsinhji appears scarcely to look at the ball or take any trouble. His electric flashes seem almost as insolently careless as they are brilliantly successful. Actually he watches the ball with feline insistence every time.'

Donald Knight, himself the most stylish of opening batsmen, wrote of Ranji's late cut: 'It was in no way a gentle tap, a stroke of the persuasive species, but, drawing himself to his full height, he slashed down on top of the seams of the ball with all the power of his wrists, which, though small and thin to look at and feel, were in reality as supple as a fine Toledo blade and as strong as bands of steel. I honestly believe that he could have gone in with an umbrella (tightly rolled), and obtained a century against the fastest bowlers in England with strokes behind the wicket, steering the ball through the slips and gliding them to leg.'

It is difficult to remember, when one reads the accounts of Ranji's batting, that he had been at the time only in his second season for Sussex. Incidentally, in connection with Philip Trevor's reminiscences, it is interesting to quote P. F. Warner on the Gentlemen v. Players match of 1904. Ranji was the last choice for the Gentlemen, only playing because A. S. Turner had to stand down. He made 5 and 121. In his book, *Lord's 1787–1945*, Warner wrote: 'It was rumoured that some of the Committee held the opinion that Ranji did not shine on a fiery wicket, and the Lord's pitches this summer were pretty lively, but if so, this was a grave error of judgment, for if ever there was a batsman who was a master when the ball was flying about it was the great Indian.'

If the cricket was over, there was still one event that autumn which required Ranji's presence. On 29 September a banquet in his honour was arranged at the Guildhall, Cambridge. The organising committee included the secretary of the Cambridgeshire Cricket Club, the Master of Peterhouse, various dons and, as honorary secretary, the journalist Newton Digby, who had been one of the very first to appreciate Ranji's talent.

The occasion, uniting the city and the university in an act of homage, brought together Ranji's friends from Cambridge and

his colleagues in the England and Sussex elevens. Among the
three hundred guests were such local luminaries as the Master of
Trinity, the Mayor, the Lord Lieutenant, the High Sheriff, and a
number of MPs. From Sussex came his captain, W. L. Murdoch,
and Billy Newham. Distinguished cricketers included F. S.
Jackson, his Cambridge captain; A. G. Steel, of Cambridge and
Lancashire; a future President of MCC, W. W. Read and Tom
Hayward. It was particularly pleasing for Ranji that the Reverend
Louis Borissow was present. Sadly, Chester Macnaghten had
died in the spring, though appropriately Dr Butler, the Master of
Trinity, was able to make reference to him in his speech.

It was an evening much like any cricket dinner, one imagines,
only more so: drink, food, toasts and speeches, anecdotes and
jokes, analogies between life and cricket, learned and ponderous
witticisms. The Guildhall had been liberally adorned with cricket
motifs, and the table decorated in the yellow, chocolate and pink
of the Cassandra Club. Dishes were named with facetious ref-
erences to events in Ranji's career. The guest of honour sat between
the Mayor and F. S. Jackson.

Unlike most such occasions this 'complimentary dinner' to
Ranji was widely reported. It is not, of course, every day that
Cambridge honours its former pupils in such fashion. But, more
relevantly, the Master of Trinity's eloquent and admiring speech,
and the newspaper comments arising from it, drew attention to
the effect of Ranji's achievement on Anglo-Indian feeling.

Replying, Ranji spoke at some length, whether in his own words
or not, it is impossible to tell. Fry remarks in his autobiography
that Ranji always preferred to have his speeches written for him,
though usually capable of having produced something better himself. Ranji referred to both Macnaghten and Borissow, as also to
Jackson and Murdoch, and confessed himself as happy at Brighton
as he had been at Cambridge. He ended up trusting that 'the wrongs
done in the past by Her Majesty's Indian subjects, and the injustice, if any, which they had suffered in days gone by, would be
forgotten, and that England and India might form one united
country, ready to show an united front to a common enemy, and
be the admiration and envy of all other nations.'

Sir Edwin Arnold, author of *The Light of Asia*, wrote next morning in the *Daily Telegraph*: 'Last night, the hearts of England and India came closer together than ever they had come before.' Sir Edwin's words, however, despite some agreeable images, today seem faintly absurd in their over-lush romanticism. While Ranji must have been happy to read that he had done 'a noble service to two continents, by bringing them together on a field which Englishmen love and understand' and that he had 'burst

MOONSHINE'S CRICKETERS.—MR. K. S. RANJITSINHJI.

COMPLIMENTARY DINNER

TO

Kumar Shri Ranjitsinhji.

| 1896.
—
For
ENGLAND
V.
AUSTRALIA
Scored
62
AND
154
NOT OUT. | | 1896.
—
For
SUSSEX
V.
YORKSHIRE
SCORED IN
ONE DAY
100
AND
125
NOT OUT. |

1896.

OBTAINED 10 "CENTURIES."

GUILDHALL, CAMBRIDGE.

29th September, 1896.

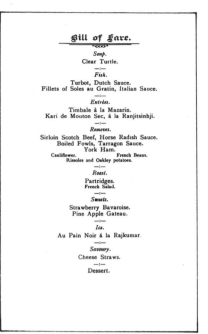

Bill of Fare.

Soup.
Clear Turtle.
—:—
Fish.
Turbot, Dutch Sauce.
Fillets of Soles au Gratin, Italian Sauce.
—:—
Entrées.
Timbale à la Mazarin.
Kari de Mouton Sec, á la Ranjitsinhji.
—:—
Removes.
Sirloin Scotch Beef, Horse Radish Sauce.
Boiled Fowls, Tarragon Sauce.
York Ham.
Cauliflower. French Beans.
Rissoles and Oakley potatoes.
—:—
Roast.
Partridges.
French Salad.
—:—
Sweets.
Strawberry Bavaroise.
Pine Apple Gateau.
—:—
Ice.
Au Pain Noir á la Rajkumar.
—:—
Savoury.
Cheese Straws.
—:—
Dessert.

upon the cricketing world like a star from the East', it is less certain how he would have reacted to being described as a 'lithe, well-built dusky hero' who 'stepped from the tent, gracefully and languidly dragging his bat'.

Once more the image of the panther was pressed into service: 'graceful as a panther in action, with lean but steely muscles under his smooth brown skin; wrists supple and tough as a creeper of the Indian jungle, and dark eyes which see every turn and twist of the bounding ball, he has adopted cricket and turned it into an Oriental poem of action.'

The *Star*, describing Ranji as 'at this moment the most popular man in England' suggested that if he had any political ambitions he would have no difficulty in securing a constituency.

In fact, what Ranji had most in mind was a rest and as many days shooting as he could manage. He got the rest but not quite in the manner he had imagined.

SIX

The Jubilee Book
of Cricket

Cold weather came unusually early during the winter of 1896/7. Ranji, shooting on the Royston estate of a friend, was caught out in a sudden snow squall. He contracted a congestion of the lungs – never a strong point with Ranji, as with many Indians in northern climates – and was put to bed. Ten weeks passed before he was on his feet again. During that period of enforced idleness – mitigated only by the reading of historical fiction, the elder Dumas being an addiction – the idea of *The Jubilee Book of Cricket* came to Ranji. 'I there and then decided to write it, and as soon as I was able to sit up I sent for a shorthand writer and dictated . . . I went through the whole game, and in the first six chapters I dealt with training and outfit, fielding, bowling, batting, captaincy and umpiring, from my own point of view, having, of course, due regard for the history and traditions of the game.'

Ranji acknowledges the help of various friends in the writing of the book – A. J. Gaston, of the *Sussex Daily News*, Fry, and Dr Butler among them – but for all that it is essentially a didactic work, a discussion of technique, it has enough agreeably personal touches for one to recognise it as at least being conceived by one person.

It is not without significance that Ranji begins with fielding, for if any county consistently threw away matches during this period it was Sussex.

'The finest exhibition of fielding it has been my good fortune to see,' Ranji writes, 'was that given at Lord's by the Oxford University eleven of 1892. They won a sensational victory, partly by good batting and good bowling, but principally by their extraordinary dash, brilliancy, and accuracy in the field. . . . M. R. Jardine was perhaps the best of the lot . . . he was perfect.'

Ranji goes on: 'With one or two brilliant exceptions the county elevens do not field nearly so well as they ought . . . On the whole the northern counties field better than the southern – probably because the spectators in the northern towns are such remorseless critics of anything like slovenliness in the field. They come not only to cheer but to jeer, and they do both with a will.'

After general remarks about fielding, Ranji takes the positions on the field one by one. What he says is clear and sensible, and every so often he illustrates a point with some personal reference. So far from being a dry and dull text book, *The Jubilee Book* remains educative and enjoyable reading even now. When such as Palairet or Agamemnon are alluded to one can detect the hand of Fry. It is particularly interesting when contemporary players are rated: for example, 'the general opinion is that Mr Blackham, the Australian, was the finest wicket-keeper the world has ever seen' or 'George Lohmann is by far the best slip I have seen.' One feels that this constant evaluation of players and expression of opinion about relative merits is more Fry's style than Ranji's.

Sussex have had many fine cover points, from, in the modern era, George Cox to Paul Parker, so it is good to see George Bean, whatever the defects of the rest of the Sussex team, singled out as the best of his time. 'He always runs a lot of batsmen out every year, many of them by throwing the wicket down.' The chapter concludes: 'A batsman may get bowled first ball, a bowler may be quilted all over the field without getting a wicket, but both can redeem themselves by good fielding, which is enough by itself to render a man worth his place on a side. A bad field is an eyesore to spectators and a millstone round the neck of his side.'

The chapter on bowling has the deductive lucidity of a philosophical treatise. Starting from general principles, Ranji goes on to analyse each kind of bowler and the ways in which the leading bowlers of his time exercised their art. Field placings for almost every kind of contingency are illustrated and the chapter concludes with an account of an imaginary cricket match in which a whole innings is analysed from the bowling angle. It opens much in the manner of Hugh de Selincourt's *The Cricket Match*: 'Stockwell and Cain leave the pavilion and are greeted with cheers appreciative

of what they have done and are going to do. Stockwell looks like
a soldier – bronzed, upright, and manly. He holds his head up
with an air that means business. Cain is a curious little fellow with
a slow, jerky gait, and a serio-comic cast of countenance. But he
is all there – a tough nut to crack, and a general favourite. He takes
block. "Does it cover 'em both, Tom? Thank you."' By the time
the side has lost all its wickets, most types of batsman and bowler,
and the adjustments in the field required, have been discussed.

In the chapter on batting Ranji naturally comes into his own.
It is his voice, rather than Fry's, that one seems to hear, though had
the book been published a few years later one might have thought
differently. No modern player, however good, could fail to
benefit from these deceptively simple analyses of the various
strokes and the deliveries against which to use or not to use them.
The masters of each stroke are mentioned and the theory behind
their play. What starts by appearing elementary develops into the
most sophisticated discussion of options.

The batting chapter, even if it had no text, would be invaluable
for its illustrations: the stances of Palairet, Dixon and Chatterton,
Ranji himself playing back, Mason playing forward, Grace playing
back, forward, half-cock and pulling, Jackson on-driving, Newham's square glance, Stoddart's forward cut, Ranji late-cutting,
and his varieties of leg-glance, Brown's short-arm hook stroke,
Hayward's forward drive, Hawke cutting – in a sense so informative are these photographs, in their demonstrations of correct
positioning of feet and hands, balance and distribution of weight,
that words are almost superfluous.

The book continues with chapters on captaincy and umpiring,
on the public schools, the universities and the counties. In a final
chapter called 'Cricket and the Victorian Era' Ranji analyses the
charm of cricket and insists upon the importance of professional-
ism and professional standards. 'If for some reason skill in cricket
suffered a sudden decline, the interest in it would wane . . . I cannot
see how cricket, as a great institution for providing popular
amusement, could, as things are now, exist without a class of
people who devote themselves entirely to it.'

Ranji, one of the first to argue against discrimination between amateur and professional, continues: 'Go to Lord's and analyse the crowd. There are all sorts and conditions of men there round the ropes – bricklayers, bank-clerks, soldiers, postmen and stock-brokers. And in the pavilion are QCs, artists, archdeacons, and leader-writers . . . It is commonplace that cricket brings the most opposite characters and the most diverse lives together. Anything that puts many very different kinds of people on common ground must promote sympathy and kind feelings.'

Ranji winds up by tracing the evolution of cricket as an art and as a spectacle, its refinements in technique and development from club to county and Test cricket.

The Jubilee Book of Cricket is, from start to finish, an immensely thoughtful and well-balanced work. If it required for its genesis that Ranji be laid low for part of a winter, then it seems to have been more than worthwhile. Reading it now, eighty years after it was first published, one is conscious of a certain piety of tone, a briskness of exhortation to the clean and healthy life. But it is not obtrusive. What matters is its depth of feeling about the game, its sane and thorough analysis of what makes for good cricket and cricketers. It was published, by Blackwood, in time for Queen Victoria's Jubilee and dedicated, 'by her gracious permission', to Her Majesty The Queen-Empress. It quickly went through several editions.

SEVEN

1897

Not surprisingly, it was some months before Ranji was properly recovered. He pottered about between Cambridge, Brighton and London, sat for his portrait to H. J. Brooks, ARA – the first of a great many over the years – and passed the evenings playing bridge and billiards. When the weather, in the early spring, improved, he got out on the moors.

What he most needed, though, was sunshine. Accordingly, he set out in March with Fry for a European jaunt. His initial intention was quite simply to head south. But somewhere along the line their plans changed. Instead of making directly for the warmth of the Riviera they moved east from Paris, into Germany first, then Austria, and finally across the Balkans into Turkey.

Here they seem to have been infected by war fever, the Turks being in the process of girding their loins for battle against the Greeks. Ranji and Fry, with some disregard for convention, determined to see what was going on. With no form of accreditation, they set out for the battle area, miraculously surviving the wrath and perplexity of Turks and Greeks alike. The Greeks had much the worst of it, which cannot have pleased Fry, though it may have Ranji.

By the time they returned to England, practice had already begun at Hove. Ranji was in much better spirits and something like his old self.

Although Sussex made another terrible start to the season, going down in their first three matches to Nottinghamshire by an innings and 74, MCC by 46, and Surrey by 279, it was soon apparent that things were going to be better. In fact, they rose from bottom place in the championship to be sixth, beating

Somerset twice, and Yorkshire, Kent and Hampshire once each.

The main reason for their improvement was the import of a Skegness-born fast bowler, Cyril Bland, who in his first season for the county took 129 wickets. Fred Tate also took a hundred wickets, the fielding and wicket-keeping was more reliable, and some of the older hands, such as Brann and Murdoch, batted with a consistency that had earlier seemed to have left them. Fry was little in evidence, but George Cox Snr made his first appearance, scoring 6 and 8, and taking 0 for 82.

Ranji, as usual, started off with a bang. After making 29 and 22 in the opening match at Trent Bridge, he scored a magnificent 260 at Lord's – his first double century – against MCC, batting only just over four hours. As well as a 6 and thirty-six 4s he hit fourteen 3s, which argues some fast and exhausting running between the wickets. Everyone was struck by the increased strength of Ranji's driving. Sussex, though making 418, actually managed to lose the match, largely due to careless fielding.

Only a week later, playing this time for MCC against Lancashire, Ranji hit 157 – 'three hours and a half's magnificent and nearly faultless cricket' was how *Wisden* described it. Considering Hearne had been among the bowlers against him in the first of these two innings and Mold and Briggs in the second, the rate of Ranji's scoring seems phenomenal. Apart from his two failures in the university match, Lord's was always a happy hunting ground for Ranji.

As far as Ranji was concerned, though, MCC matches were merely the icing on the cake. At Lord's he could show off to the top cricketing brass and entertain the gentry. The real matches, however, were the county ones and having set London by the ears once again he was happy to concentrate on these. This season, too, there was no touring side – apart from the Philadelphians – to divert attention from the championship.

Surprisingly, it was early June before Sussex played at Hove. Rain ruined the Gloucestershire match but Somerset, in an exciting, low-scoring game, were beaten by one wicket. After his fireworks at Lord's, Ranji did nothing very spectacular, and in two succeeding fixtures against the universities – Oxford beat Sussex by an innings – did not exceed 35. Kent, however, were beaten by six wickets at Tonbridge, Ranji making up for a modest 3 in the first innings with 65 not out in the second.

On 1 July Sussex played their first match ever on the Saffrons, at Eastbourne, Ranji christening the occasion with an unbeaten second innings of 129 in a drawn game against Middlesex. The Saffrons wicket has never looked back.

In the return match against Nottinghamshire Ranji made 8 and 57. Sussex then went north, to Sheffield, where Brown and Tunnicliffe put on a record 378 for the first wicket against them. Ranji did not travel with them, having been picked for the Gentlemen at Lord's. The Gentlemen had what must be one of their strongest batting sides ever – Grace, Stoddart, Mason, Dixon, Ranjitsinhji, Jackson, Ford and Jessop (who hit 67 in 35 minutes) were the first eight in the order – but they lost by 78 runs. Ranji was, unusually, bowled in each innings – by Hayward and Richardson – for single figures. Ranji rejoined the Sussex team for the Lancashire match at Old Trafford, Maclaren making a belated first appearance for Lancashire. Ranji made a dashing 87 on the first morning, but almost everyone made runs and there was never any chance of a result.

Ranji was at his silken best in the next match at Hove, taking 149 off the Hampshire attack. A week later he hit 170 off the Essex bowling.

For some weeks now Ranji had been suffering badly from recurrent bouts of asthma. He played no more long innings but, despite a succession of sleepless nights, batted consistently to the very end of August: 33 and 12 in the six-wicket defeat of Yorkshire at Hove, 3 and 33 at Lord's against Middlesex, 11 and 58 against Lancashire, 35 and 23 against Kent, and, in the last match of the season, 31 and 33 against Surrey. Although, inevitably, it was not quite as spectacular a season for Ranji as its predecessor, he still finished top of the Sussex averages, scoring 1,762 runs at an average of 45.7. He took 13 wickets, one more than Fry, in 27 fewer overs.

During August Ranji had received an invitation to join A. E. Stoddart's team to tour Australia in the coming winter. He was delighted to accept. Stoddart had led a successful expedition to Australia three years earlier, and this time he was to have the assistance of the amateurs Maclaren, Ranjitsinhji, Druce and Mason, with Richardson and Hayward from Surrey, Wainwright and Hirst from Yorkshire, Storer from Derbyshire, J. T. Hearne from Middlesex, the Lancastrian Briggs and, as second wicket-keeper, Board from Gloucestershire. It was generally reckoned to be a stronger side all-round than the one Stoddart had done so well with in 1894/95.

Before the party left, the *Sussex Daily News* organised a subscription on behalf of Ranji. In due course he received a gift of plate and a painting of himself. He had already, to celebrate the improvement in Sussex's fortunes, given each member of the team a gold medal, the Sussex emblem on one side and the player's name 'from K.S.R.' on the other. His pleasure in giving presents was always greatly to exceed his enjoyment in receiving them.

EIGHT

In Australia
1897/98

'To speak the plain truth,' *Wisden* observes, 'there has not for a very long time been anything so disappointing in connection with English cricket, as the tour of Mr Stoddart's team in Australia last winter. The team left England in September, 1897, full of hope that the triumph of three years before would be repeated, but came home a thoroughly beaten side.'

England or 'the English Team' as *Wisden* refers to them, won the first Test by nine wickets but were beaten in the remaining four, twice by an innings, once by eight wickets, and finally by six wickets. 'The Colonial players,' *Wisden* continues, 'were much more consistent in batting and far superior in bowling.'

That the Australians turned out to be the better side cannot be disputed. Several of the English party, including Stoddart himself, found no real batting form at all, while only Hearne among the bowlers caused the Australian batsmen any problems. The bowling averages make sad reading: Hirst two wickets at an average of 152, Briggs nine wickets at 53.8, Hayward four wickets at 41 each. Hearne and Richardson took twenty-two and twenty wickets respectively in the Tests, but they cost 26.90 and 35.27 runs each, ten runs a wicket more than their leading Australian counterparts. Seven Australian batsmen averaged over 35 as against three English.

There were, perhaps, extenuating circumstances for the English. Not only did several players fail to adapt properly to Australian light and pitches until the tour was almost over, but the long sea voyage was followed by an influenza epidemic among the party. Ranji himself was frequently ill. Over and above this there was serious trouble over the bowling action of Ernest Jones, the

Australian fast bowler, who was Australia's highest wicket-taker. In this, and other aspects, Stoddart's experiences were not dissimilar to Peter May's sixty years later, when a side thought to be equally strong was thoroughly defeated, at least in part through their demoralisation by a blatant thrower.

There were, nevertheless, two outstanding successes: Archie Maclaren and Ranjitsinhji. Maclaren topped the Test averages with 488 runs at 54.22, Ranji coming next with 457 runs at 50.77. For all matches Ranji had 1,157 runs and an average of 60.89, Maclaren 1,037 runs and an average of 54.57. No one else approached these figures.

During the tour Ranji kept a diary. This was published by James Bowden the following spring under the title *With Stoddart's Team in Australia* by Prince Ranjitsinhji. It went into at least four editions the same year.

It is unlikely that every word of the book was written by Ranji himself. Most probably he made notes or dictated, leaving his opinions and the general gist of events to be put into readable prose by a journalist assistant. It is a practice not unknown today.

However the book was finally concocted, it remains a consistently interesting and informative account of a cricket tour. It could hardly be called astringent, but since the book is written in the first person and Ranji is discussing his own team-mates, sharpness of comment could not fairly be expected. His observations on techniques and tactics display the same simple authority as did those in *The Jubilee Book*. There are, too, vivid impressions of the country, of travelling, and of social life. The most serious flaw derives from the fact that Ranji himself was one of the main attractions of the series and yet his own performances are passed over with little mention.

The book begins with a fulsome seventeen-page 'character sketch' of Ranji by 'Rover', but this, too, has its moments. 'To know Ranjitsinhji,' it begins, 'is to admire him, and every one who can dissociate a bat from a walking-stick knows his Ranjitsinhji.' Many of the phrases in this sketch are familiar from other writers on Ranji, but it is not always easy to discover who is appropriating what from whom. 'The *suaviter in modo* is with the Indian a far more important consideration than the *fortiter in re* . . .' is one of several such instances. Ranji on Grace is quoted: 'He founded the modern theory of batting by making forward and back play of equal importance . . . He turned its many narrow, straight channels into one great winding river.'

There are certain inaccuracies concerning Ranji's family, but in most respects 'Rover' manages to skim accurately over the main events of Ranji's life thus far.

Ranji opens his own account with a genial survey of his colleagues, somewhat in the manner of Arthur Gilligan. Thus, A. C. Maclaren: 'He is always cheerful and full of go. He imagines he is unlucky in everything, but Archie without his grumbling, as someone remarked the other day, would be like curry without chutney. He is fond of horses, and imagines he can ride, notwithstanding a slight mishap during the previous tour. In short, he is a thorough sportsman and a grand fellow.'

The narrative proper starts, 'The team sailed on the 17th September, on board the *Ormuz*, amid the good wishes of the large gathering that had assembled at Tilbury', a sentence that, for anyone who has made the same journey, must evoke memories. Ranji, as it happened, joined the ship a week later at Naples, having sensibly travelled overland to avoid the Bay of Biscay. Having some reputation for forgetfulness, Ranji reports that his skipper 'was much relieved and gratified to find me on board'.

The voyage was without incident, though Ranji suffered from asthma attacks as well as sea sickness. They stopped at Port Said, endured appalling heat in the Red Sea, and indulged in the usual shipboard pastimes. It must have been a strange feeling for Ranji watching the Malabar coast rise out of the Arabian sea. It had been nearly nine years since he had set eyes on India. The spice and land-scents, the sight of the palm-fringed beaches of western Ceylon and the steep hills of the interior could not fail to have touched him.

Their stay in Colombo was too brief for a match to be played but Ranji, enjoying a rickshaw ride round the town, was much impressed. Colombo is a more luxuriant and tropical place than

Ranji had experience of and to someone brought up on the dusty plains of Kathiawar must have appeared very exotic. 'It is one of the prettiest places man could wish to see,' he wrote. 'Big palm, coconut, and date trees, intermingled with smaller trees of other kinds, and varied plants and flowers cover the plains and surrounding hills. Fragrant herbs and cinnamon groves are to be seen on every hand.'

They were entertained by the Ceylon Club and invited to dinner at Government House. Everyone was sad to leave, most especially Ranji, deprived so long of the familiar flavours of his homeland.

The ten-day journey between Colombo and western Australia, uninterrupted by land, becomes increasingly tedious. They were unlucky with the weather, a heavy swell running most of the way and the *Ormuz* pitching and rolling. By the time the ship docked at Albany, on the extreme south-western point of Australia, not all the deck games, concerts and fancy dress balls in the world could have made them want to stay on board a minute longer.

But they were not done with the sea yet, for they had still to cross the Great Australian Bight, often as rough as the Bay of Biscay. On this occasion, however, it was on its best behaviour. When they finally left the *Ormuz* on 22 October at Largs Bay, the port of Adelaide, they had been on board five weeks.

Within four days of their arrival the team was in action, in unpleasantly cold weather, against South Australia. Several of the party were still suffering from the after-effects of 'flu or in the process of getting it. Although the match petered out in a tame draw, it was remarkable for several things: a brilliant innings of 200 by Clem Hill, made out of 408, a rejoinder of 189 by Ranji, out of 475, and the no-balling of Jones, by James Phillips, the English umpire who had travelled out with the team.

Ranji found the Adelaide wicket 'perfection itself', though was much disappointed with the pavilion and dressing rooms. The outfield, too, appeared 'very hard and bare of grass . . . much reminding one of the cricket fields of the North of England, where football plays an important part during seven months of the year.'

The South Australian innings, on a wicket where, Ranji observes, 'it was evident from the first ball bowled that the batsmen would have to get themselves out', devolved largely round Clem Hill. Ranji found him a magnificent on-side player, but short of strokes on the off, resting content 'with a square cut and a drive between cover and mid-off'.

According to *Wisden*, Ranji, though making twice as many as anyone else, was not at his best. He himself describes his innings, 'as lucky as it was useful'. With both sides making over four hundred, a draw was inevitable. They packed up early on the fourth day so as to get to Flemington in time for the Melbourne Cup.

The most notable feature of the Adelaide match, though, was Phillips's no-balling of Jones. It was an incident which brought Ranji no little trouble, and momentary unpopularity, because, commenting on it in a series of articles he was doing for the Australian *Review of Reviews*, he came down firmly on Phillips's side. Australians do not take kindly to their bowlers' actions being questioned, as I know to my cost. Seventy years later, mildly condemning Meckiff, I was only prevented from being set upon in a Melbourne bar by the protective action of Jack Fingleton.

Ranji, in his book, makes his position plain. In England, Ranji observes, Jones's action was 'at the worst, merely like some other bowlers actively engaged in English cricket – doubtful as to its fairness. Whereas now, as we saw him bowl in the first match, his action constituted in every sense a fair and square "chuck".'

This verdict was endorsed not only by all the English players but by the South Australian and in due course the Victorian public. Ranji draws a distinction between deliberate and unconscious throwing and continues: 'I have personally accused in England one bowler of throwing (and it is a curious thing that he happened to be a member of my own side, and also a personal friend), although I have not the slightest doubt, just as in this case, that he did not think that he threw. But any person unprejudiced, whether a player in Australia or in England, would see that the action of Jones or Fry constitutes in every sense a throw, inasmuch as they use, not only the wrist and shoulder, but also the elbow, which plays an important, if not leading, part in imparting the pace and projecting the ball.'

The firmness of Ranji's views made Australians suspect that Jones's bowling might not be to Ranji's liking. Jones, in fact, took seven of the English wickets for 189, felling the wicket-keeper with his first delivery. But since Ranji himself made exactly that number of runs, a fair proportion of them off Jones, it was not an aspersion that could last long, even in Australia.

Ranji goes on to make a proper case against throwing: 'mere physical or brute strength ought not to gain an advantage over the real subtleties of the art of bowling.' It was, unfortunately, a case never sufficiently heeded. In the 1950s Lock, for one, was allowed to get away with murder, and after him, Meckiff.

The Melbourne Cup, subsequently always on the MCC itinerary, safely out of the way, a close match against Victoria ended in a win for the English by two wickets. Mason on the last day made 128 not out – his one high-class innings of the tour – and Ranji 64. Ranji was much struck by the Australian fielding in both these matches and by the captaincy of Trott: 'one of the very best, if not the best, of present-day captains.' The ground at Melbourne reminded him of Old Trafford; he was pleased by the number of ladies present, and saddened by the obtuse and excessive barracking. In these two latter respects little has changed.

From Melbourne the team went by train, skirting the Riverina and Snowy Mountains, to Sydney; then, as now, an agreeable overnight journey through some of the best sheep country in Australia. In Sydney they had to attend a reception by the Mayor at the Town Hall, 'the usual number of speeches having been made and listened to, plus nine more from retiring aldermen, each one of whom impressed on us the importance of his own ward, and also the long term of years he had the honour to represent it.' That has not altered either. The cricket ground, however, delighted them – 'in no way inferior to the MCC ground.'

The New South Wales match and the Test match that followed it showed Stoddart's team at its best. The State match introduced Victor Trumper to the tourists and though he only made 5 and 0 he impressed Ranji greatly. 'He seemed to be all there, and the confidence with which he played the bowling, although it was for a very short time, makes me firmly believe that he will be a very great batsman in this country, and at no very distant date. Indeed, I have seen very few beginners play the ball so well, and show the same excellent style.' That is a remarkable judgment based on so little evidence.

After Ranji had caught Trumper off Hirst, Gregory, who opened with Trumper, was run out. Ranji observes that whereas most English batsmen are unadventurous between the wickets the Australians err in the other direction.

New South Wales were all out 311, Iredale, whom Ranji had thrown out in the Oval Test of 1896, batting beautifully for 89. He hit five fours off an over of Hirst's, each one being the result of a different stroke.

Only Maclaren and Storer made anything for the English team, Noble and McKibbin taking five wickets each. Maclaren's 142 out of 335 held the innings together, his runs coming from fierce drives, glances and late cuts. New South Wales, making 260 in their second innings, left the English needing 237 to win. Mason failed for the second time in the match, but Maclaren and Ranji put on 180 in 115 minutes. Maclaren was bowled by Noble for 100, Ranji remaining undefeated with 112, 'an innings quite without fault', according to *Wisden*.

Maclaren's feat of a hundred in each innings, the first occasion in a match of any importance that this had been achieved, augured well for the Tests. Ranji was admiring of Noble's bowling but not of his batting. A catch by Trumper on the boundary was one of the 'most brilliant bits of fielding' Ranji had ever witnessed.

Sydney at that time had a bicycle track round the perimeter of the playing area, but it was much resented and in due course dispensed with. The state captain was mercilessly barracked, for no good reason, and again Ranji was put out by it. In comparing what he had seen of Australian bowling with English, Ranji observes that the Australians 'exercised greater head power, used more dodges, and studied the batsman more than English bowlers'. The English, Ranji continues, tend to be more mechanical, relying in England on the wicket to help them. The Australians, in their own conditions, benefit from their greater adventurousness, though often sacrificing length for spin. 'I must acknowledge,' Ranji concludes, 'that I prefer the Australian method from a purely scientific cricket point of view.'

On the subject of pitches Ranji expresses agreement with the Governor of New South Wales who, at a banquet for the teams in the Hotel Australia, remarked on the imbalance of wickets in favour of batsmen, making cricket a more monotonous game than it used to be. 'The time spent in preparing Australian wickets is indeed too long, and affords the batsman an undue advantage over the bowler, who has to wait his opportunity for a night's heavy rain and a morning sun, eventualities that do not often occur in this part of the world.'

Over the weekend the English went sailing on the harbour and spent an evening pigeon shooting at the Sydney Gun Club. Stoddart came in for uninformed criticism over the question of expenses, so much so that Ranji found it necessary to go into some detail as to how such a tour is financed.

From Sydney the team moved north, playing up-country matches against Eighteen of Northern District at Newcastle and against Twenty-two of Glen Innes.

The Newcastle mosquitoes bit everyone, Ranji included. 'Hirst presented the appearance of a prickly pear. One of Mason's eyes was completely closed up, having swollen considerably, and Stoddart's face and hands were quite globular. From the discovery which the English captain made afterwards, it was not to be wondered at that he presented such a sorry picture, for the uncured skin of a large sea-bird was placed underneath his bed for drying purposes, and was the harbourer of various kinds of small insects.'

Glen Innes, in welcome contrast, they found a 'charming little place, cooled by a continual soft breeze'. At Brisbane, on the newly opened ground, a three-day fixture, not counting as first-class, was played against a combined Queensland and New South Wales side. Ranji's scores in these three matches were 47, 32, 67. He enjoyed the tropical appearance of Brisbane and a change from the monotony of 'the inevitable gum-tree'. He also had a round of golf with Lord Lamington, the Governor.

On the Sunday of the Brisbane match the government yacht took the players for a trip down Moreton Bay. The weather was cold and rough, and Ranji caught a bad chill which turned into quinsy. He was in bed for the Armidale match, in which scarcely any play was possible because of rain. So unwell was Ranji, in fact, that when the others left for Sydney on 6 December he was left behind.

Sometimes at this time of year it rains for days on end in Sydney. When it does it feels as if it will never stop. So heavy and continuous was it on this occasion, making all practice impossible, that the Sydney Trustees, without consulting either of the captains, postponed the match from the Friday to the Saturday. There was immediate outcry at this high-handed, if sensible, decision. As it turned out, the weather was so continuously foul that the match could not begin until after the weekend. For Ranji, if for no one else, the delay was a blessing in disguise. As a result, though far from fit, he was picked to play, which he certainly could not have been if the match had started on time. Stoddart, deeply upset by the sudden death of his mother, stood down, while for Australia George Giffen, though selected, declined to appear. Giffen was thirty-eight at the time and never played in a Test match again.

Maclaren, acting captain in Stoddart's place, won the toss and chose to bat, opening the innings himself with Mason. Both teams wore black crepe on their sleeves, Ranji describing the Australians as taking the field 'in their beautiful light blue colours'.

The wicket had dried out completely, the outfield remaining green and lush. Mason, for the third time running at Sydney, failed but England batted steadily against an Australian attack consisting of Jones, Trumble, McKibbin, McLeod and Trott. Maclaren made his third successive century, Tom Hayward played his first good innings of the tour and when Ranji, held back, came in towards evening England were 258 for 5. He and Hirst saw out the day, Ranji being 39 not out and confessing himself absolutely exhausted.

Next morning, after some treatment from a doctor, he continued his innings. Hirst was bowled by Jones with the score 382, after which Ranji, with only bowlers to come, took complete control. Batting in all just three hours and thirty-five minutes he was last out for 175, the highest score yet made for England in a Test. He drove with increasing power as his strength returned to him, cutting, glancing and as far as possible guiding the ball away behind the wicket. Tom Richardson who, Ranji observed, 'is not considered a bat and mostly justifies the idea' made 24 of a last wicket partnership of 74.

Jones again bowled very fast and caused a few bruises: 'He very seldom pitches a ball well up for a batsman to drive.' On this occasion Ranji considered his delivery quite fair. 'I feel sure that the unfair action he made use of in the Adelaide match was the result of trying to bowl at a greater pace than was natural to him.' By reducing his pace, too, Jones bowled a far better length and was less expensive. Ranji, however, always had his measure and the stormy atmosphere of Adelaide quickly subsided.

The Australians, reduced to 87 for 6 by some fine bowling from Hearne and Richardson, recovered to make 237. Following on, Darling got a hundred and Clem Hill 96, but although they made 408 in the second innings England needed only 96 to win. Maclaren scored 50 of these and was in at the death with Ranji.

It was a contented party that set off, in Christmas week, towards Melbourne. A day at Randwick races before leaving, an overnight stop at Melbourne, and thence from Sale by boat through the Gippsland lakes to the Kalimna Hotel at Cunningham. On the La Trobe river and during their passage through the lakes, they saw plenty of wildfowl, shooting or photographing it as the mood took them.

At the Kalimna Hotel, perched on the top of a hill with views south over farm country to the ocean, they divided their time between duck-shooting and fishing. This was just the kind of rest and change Ranji needed. The shooting party had no luck at all, though, at their first attempt, and the fishermen fared little better. The next day, travelling by steamer to look for hares, was more enjoyable, for though the hares proved elusive the team came unexpectedly on great quantities of geese, duck, coot and other wildfowl.

Ranji had his first real experience of the bush at Kalimna,

ENGLAND

J. R. Mason....	b Jones	6	b McKibbin	32
*A. C. MacLaren .	c Kelly b McLeod	109	not out	50
T. Hayward.....	c Trott b Trumble......	72		
†W. Storer.......	c and b Trott	43		
N. F. Druce.....	c Gregory b McLeod ...	20		
G. H. Hirst	b Jones	62		
K. S. Ranjitsinhji	c Gregory b McKibbin..	175	(3)not out	8
E. Wainwright ..	b Jones	10		
J. T. Hearne	c and b McLeod........	17		
J. Briggs	run out	1		
T. Richardson...	not out	24		
Extras	(lb 11, w 1)	12	(b 5, nb 1)...........	6
Total	....	551	Total (1 wkt)	96

First Innings – *Fall of Wickets*
1–26, 2–162, 3–224, 4–256, 5–258, 6–382, 7–422, 8–471, 9–477, 10–551.

First Innings – *Bowling*
McKibbins, 34–5–113–1; Jones, 50–8–130–3; McLeod, 28–12–80–3;
Trumble, 40–7–138–1; Trott, 23–2–78–1.

Second Innings – *Fall of Wickets*
1–80.

Second Innings – *Bowling*
McKibbin, 5–1–22–1; Jones, 9–1–28–0; Trumble, 14–4–40–0.

AUSTRALIA

J. Darling	c Druce b Richardson ...	7	c Druce b Briggs	101
J. J. Lyons	b Richardson	3	(7)c Hayward b Hearne ..	25
F. A. Iredale	c Druce b Hearne	25	(2)b Briggs	18
C. Hill	b Hearne..............	19	b Hearne...........	96
S. E. Gregory ...	c Mason b Hearne	46	run out	31
*G. H. S. Trott...	b Briggs	10	(8)b Richardson	27
†J. J. Kelly	b Richardson	1	(9)not out	46
H. Trumble.....	c Storer b Mason	70	(6)c Druce b Hearne	2
C. E. McLeod...	not out	50	(3)run out	26
T. R. McKibbin .	b Hearne..............	0	(11)b Hearne...........	6
E. Jones........	c Richardson b Hearne ..	0	(10)lbw b Richardson	3
Extras	(b 1, lb 1, nb 4)	6	(b 12, lb 1, w 4, nb 10)	27
Total	....	237	Total	408

First Innings – *Fall of Wickets*
1–8, 2–24, 3–56, 4–57, 5–86, 6–87, 7–138, 8–228, 9–237, 10–237.

First Innings – *Bowling*
Richardson, 27–8–71–3; Hirst, 28–7–57–0; Hearne, 20.1–7–42–5;
Briggs, 20–7–42–1; Hayward, 3–1–11–0; Mason, 2–1–8–1.

Second Innings – *Fall of Wickets*
1–37, 2–135, 3–191, 4–269, 5–271, 6–318, 7–321, 8–382, 9–390, 10–408.

Second Innings – *Bowling*
Richardson, 41–9–121–2; Hirst, 13–3–49–0; Hearne, 38–8–99–4;
Briggs, 22–3–86–2; Hayward, 5–1–16–0; Mason, 2–0–10–0.

Umpires: C. Bannerman, J. Phillips.   * Captain   † Wicket keeper setting off in a four-in-hand over rough country. They saw bell birds and mutton birds, and heard laughing jackasses. Richardson and Storer each shot a large black snake, the presence of which had caused some anxiety, and on their way home they bagged numerous snipe.

The days were warm and clear, the nights cool, and it was altogether a much refreshed team that returned to Melbourne for the second Test.

For Australia, Noble came in for Lyons. The English team was the same as for Sydney. This time Trott won the toss and with it, virtually, the match. Ranji was only passed fit at the last moment, his throat still giving him trouble. The heat, even for Melbourne, was intense. Australia, not batting particularly well but helped by dropped catches, ran up a total of 520.

Mason failed yet again and Ranji, batting at number four, came in at 60 for 2. He soon lost Maclaren, out of touch, but he and Hayward put on 59 and then he and Storer 70. Ranji was bowled by Trumble for 71. England were all out for 315 and had to follow on.

The pitch, due largely to the heat, had begun to show the cracks that are familiar to anyone who knows Melbourne. Batting was a quite different business to what it had been on the earlier days and everyone struggled in turn. Maclaren was top scorer with 38, Hayward made 33, Ranji 27. Noble finished with 6 for 49, bowling Ranji with a beauty, and Trumble with 4 for 53. Ranji, always ready to recognise flaws in the English performance, did not reckon they did badly in the circumstances. The match was lost through a combination of losing the toss, an increasingly wearing pitch, and ineffectual bowling by Hirst and Hearne. The Australian press, by and large, declined to recognise the second factor. Jones, incidentally, was again no-balled for throwing.

Everything was now nicely set up for the third Test at Adelaide ten days later. Before this, two more 'up country' matches were played, at Ballarat and Stawell. Ranji was laid low with asthma at Ballarat but recovered to enjoy some rabbit shooting on an estate at Kirkella.

Disappointingly, the third Test followed much the same pattern as the second. The main difference was that the wicket played well for all five days.

Trott again won the toss and Australia batted with much the same consistency as at Melbourne. They were 310 for 2 at the end of the first day, the two left-handers, Darling and Hill, making 178 and 81 respectively. Runs were made by almost everyone, the innings closing for 573. Six catches were dropped, two by Ranji, who had a finger put out in the process.

The English innings never recovered from a disastrous start. Four wickets went down for 42, Maclaren and Ranji both failing, as, inevitably, did Mason. Only some determined batting by Hayward and Hirst prevented a rout. A total of 278 was nevertheless a poor score on a beautiful batting wicket.

Ranji was generous in his tributes to the bowling of Howell, Noble and Jones, as also to the superiority of the Australian fielding.

Following on, England lost Mason for 0, but Maclaren and Ranji took the score to 152. Ranji, hampered by his damaged finger, was never able to play in his usual fashion. Maclaren made 124, but once they were out the rest collapsed against McLeod and Noble. Australia won by an innings and 13 runs.

Ranji, presumably because of his comments on Jones, the local hero, in the match against South Australia, was crudely barracked in his first innings. 'I was at the wicket for about a quarter of an hour, and during the whole of that time uncomplimentary and insulting remarks were hurled at me from all parts of the field.'

For the fourth Test the teams returned to Melbourne. Matches started then on Saturdays in Australia, unlike in England where they began on either Mondays or Thursdays. Trott won the toss for the third time running but this time, on a slow damp pitch, the Australians fared badly against Hearne. Six wickets were down for 58. At this point Trumble joined Clem Hill. Hill, hitting magnificently wide of mid-on and being particularly severe on Richardson, was finally out for 188 early the next morning. The last four Australian wickets had put on 265.

England began with Maclaren and Wainwright, Mason being dropped down to seven. Trott, unusually, shared the opening attack with Howell, bowling leg-breaks. Wainwright was quickly caught off him and Maclaren bowled by Howell. There followed the now customary procession, nobody making more than 30.

Batting a second time England did only marginally better. Ranji made 55, being bowled after hitting the ball onto his boot, and Maclaren 45. They were all out 263, ultimately losing by 8 wickets.

If any match was won by one man, this was it. Hill's batting eclipsed everything else, as Ranji admitted. England's batting, by contrast, was 'the tamest batting I have ever seen'. There were contributory reasons – a bad injury to Storer, Hirst's absence, Maclaren being bowled while having an insect in his eye – but in the end it came down to the superior all-round skills of the Australians.

Ranji once again was the object of much criticism for expressing views on the nature of the play. Rather ruefully he wrote: 'There is a great tendency here to introduce in all matters of cricket, where opinion differs, both the personal element and bitter partisan feeling.'

After the fourth Test and the loss of the Ashes, the team returned to Sydney with the usual feeling of anti-climax. They practised in the mornings, spent the afternoons round the harbour or in the country, and went to the races.

The return encounter with New South Wales turned out to be an extraordinary affair, lasting into the sixth day. At the end of an extremely high-scoring match New South Wales, with totals of 415 and 574 against a weakened attack, won by 239 runs. Druce made a century for the English, Tom Hayward 63 and 62 not out, Maclaren 61 and 140, and Ranji 37 and 44.

This match, too, was not without incident. At the end of the fifth day the English, set to make 600 to win, were 258 for 1, with Maclaren and Ranji in. The next morning the State bowling was begun by Donnan, an opening batsman who scarcely ever bowled. When he did, though, he bowled round the wicket, often cutting up the pitch. On this occasion he ran across a pitch already beginning to wear after five days' play.

Both Maclaren and Ranji appealed to the umpire and then the bowler about the fairness of such a tactic. They got no response. Very soon both batsmen were out to deliveries that pitched in Donnan's footmarks. The remaining nine wickets fell for only 105.

Before the final Test, due to be played at Sydney, the team met a combined universities eleven and then travelled north, along the Darling Downs, to Brisbane. Here they were due to meet an eleven of Victoria and Queensland, but it rained ceaselessly, and only a few hours play were possible.

Test matches played after the series has been decided tend to have a dreamy, unrealistic flavour. England, though, had a point to make and it looked for a while as if they might make it. Batting first, for once, they reached 335 and then, largely through a wonderful performance by Richardson, who took 8 for 94, bowled Australia out for 239. Jones, who took 6 English wickets for 82, 'hurled the ball at a great pace' according to Ranji.

Unfortunately England failed to make the most of their lead. Maclaren was out first ball, Ranji was given out l.b.w. in dubious circumstances for 12, and they were all out for 178. The Australians knocked off the runs for the loss of only four wickets, Darling making 160.

It was not as easy a victory as the scores suggest. McLeod and Hill were quickly bowled and a concerted appeal against Darling was turned down. From that point on the crowd, Ranji remarked, 'behaved disgracefully . . . they behaved in a discourteous and disagreeable manner to the visiting team, and the noise and the jeering commenced, and was kept up right up to the adjournment for lunch.'

There had been thirty-six thousand present on the first day of the match, and it was sad that a series that had begun with such high hopes for the English should have ended in scenes of boorish abuse, especially when there was no longer anything at stake.

A day on the Hawkesbury river and some shark-fishing in Sydney harbour were more to Ranji's taste.

There were still two return State matches to be played before they could leave. Victoria were comprehensively beaten by 7 wickets, Ranji making 61 and 61 not out, and a drawn game was played against South Australia at Adelaide in their last match. Ranji, a model of consistency, made 40 and 36.

The farewell banquets were the occasion for some plain speaking by Stoddart about crowd behaviour – not all the crowd, he was at pains to emphasise, but some of the crowd, everywhere. At Melbourne Archie Maclaren had got married to a local girl and taken leave of the party to go on his honeymoon. The rest of them embarked on the *Ormuz* at Largs Bay for the long voyage home.

With Stoddart in Australia concludes with a summing up of what, despite his great personal success, must have been an increasingly disillusioning tour for Ranji. He analyses the difference in playing conditions between England and Australia – the far greater pace and lack of variety of the Australian pitches, and the light, troublesome to so many English fielders. Strangely, Ranji himself suffered as much as anyone, dropping many catches he would normally have taken with ease. He writes thoughtfully of the adjustments of timing and technique that English batsmen have to make and of the limitations in method and lack of subtlety exposed in English bowlers by the pitches. 'I must acknowledge,' Ranji writes, 'that I should have liked to see, for the sake of variety and for the sake of seeing games played out under all conditions, two games of the Test series played from first to last on wickets affected by rain. There is always more excitement and fun, and more skill displayed on ruck wickets than on perfect wickets . . . The genius and resource and the variety of strokes, the judgment in placing, are all so enchanting to the real cricket enthusiast. The perfect wickets, which are so common nowadays, to my mind level batsmen to a certain degree, at the same time giving them an undue advantage over the bowler . . . The patient batsman with a few strokes is practically as effective as a batsman with a great variety of strokes, which, by the way, he is in most cases unable to utilise on account of the exceptional pace of the turf, and occasionally forgetting himself, he risks it, and meets with failure.'

What Ranji says here remains generally true to this day. There is no doubt, though, that the 1897/98 Australian team was the strongest they had yet produced. The English, after the first Test, never really matched them. Richardson's rheumatism was the main contributory factor, but the batsmen were in and out of form, the bowling lacked variety, and almost always a key player was missing or handicapped by illness or injury. Only towards the very end did some of those new to Australia, such as Hayward, Druce and Wainwright, do themselves any sort of justice. Both Mason and Wainwright were failures as batsmen, averaging only 12 and 15 respectively in the Tests.

NINE

A Season in India

It was always Ranji's intention to miss the 1898 season and spend it in India. On the voyage home he had much to reflect upon: several memorable performances, some barracking, a notoriety that resulted in bats, matchboxes, hair-restorers and chairs being named after him. He was courted by Australian society but also made the butt of Australian cartoonists, especially in the affair of the Sydney jockey. One day at Randwick races Ranji backed an outsider at long odds. He sent a message to the weighing room that if the rider called at his hotel he would be rewarded. In due course an impostor turned up, claiming to have been sent by the jockey.

In the cartoon that appeared in the *Bulletin*, however, Ranji is portrayed as parting with his money to an immensely tall fellow, under the illusion that he was the actual jockey. Maclaren, who had been at the races with Ranji, was responsible for this, spreading tales about Ranji's credulousness as a joke.

Ranji knew, when he left the *Ormuz* at Colombo, that one place he would not be going to was Jamnagar. It would be some years yet before Jaswantsinhji was of an age to be confirmed as the Jam Saheb – if that were to take place at all – but in the meantime Ranji was made well aware that he was not welcome in palace circles.

He had long determined, though, to try and get to know something of the India beyond Kathiawar. He had, after all, left as a schoolboy, with no experience of the world, and little enough of his own province.

He was returning now as an adult and a celebrity. Ranji had recently made friends with Arthur Priestley, MP for Grantham, who had been wintering in Australia and watching some cricket.

They decided to travel together, and for the next eleven months –
the whole of Ranji's time in India – they were inseparable.

If travel, sport (of the princely kind) and social life among
fellow-countrymen were the things Ranji mainly had in mind
during his visit, he had also begun to take a livelier interest in his
future. For ten years cricket had been his guiding light. Perhaps
he might play for another ten, but what then?

A course of action had already been undertaken in England
which was to result in a memorandum being presented on Ranji's
behalf to the Secretary of State for India, Lord George Hamilton.
The latter declined to take any initiative and it became evident to
Ranji that he might do better by working through his fellow
princes.

It could be said, therefore, that the next few months represented
an exploratory journey into the confidence of the rulers of the
Indian states. Ranji was not only unknown to almost all of them,
but he came from one of the smallest princely houses. His lineage
was impeccable, but his assets virtually nil.

The first two weeks were spent in Ceylon, Ranji getting his
land-legs amongst the tea plantations and rubber forests of the
interior. The lush beauty of Ceylon had delighted him on the way
out and he was happy once more, after weeks at sea, to walk among
the tropical trees and flowering shrubs of the island.

From Ceylon Priestley and Ranji travelled up to Rutlam, half-
way between Bombay and Delhi, and the site of a famous battle
between thirty thousand Rajputs, led by Jaswant Rao Rathor, and
the combined forces of Aurangzeb and Murad. Here they were
entertained in the usual manner by the Maharajah, shooting, pig-
sticking, polo.

It was only a short journey from here to Mount Abu on the
southern border of Rajasthan, home of Ranji's uncle, the fiercely
military-looking Sir Pratab Singh.

An invitation awaited him there to call on the Maharajah of
Patiala, now an old man, and at present in Simla. With the weather
already stoking up on the plains it was no hardship for Ranji to go
up into the Himalayas and travel down with the Maharajah the
short distance to Patiala.

The Maharajah's palaces in the Baradari Gardens and at Moti Bagh were Ranji's first real taste of the grand life. The centre of Sikh society, Patiala had been one of the areas most loyal to the British during the Mutiny and had benefited accordingly.

The various visits Ranji made to Patiala – and he returned again and again – provided him with the happiest memories of his stay. The Maharajah was so keen a cricketer that he had not only created a beautiful cricket ground but had engaged Jack Hearne, among other professionals, to come out and coach.

At Patiala, after the monsoon had given way to cold weather, Ranji played his first club cricket in India. He made a century against the Simla Volunteers and a double century against Umballa, being presented by the Maharajah with a pair of Purdey guns on the first occasion and some jewelled studs on the second. There was polo to be had, as well as big-game shooting and tennis. Ranji was enrolled in the Patiala Lancers, the Maharajah's personal bodyguard and, as an honorary ADC, attended on Lord Elgin, the Viceroy, during his visit. He also met Baden-Powell, then a colonel, and known largely for his standard work on pig-sticking.

Ranji did not neglect his family. He spent serene and quiet weeks at Sarodar with his mother, the Masaheb, who in times of distress Ranji always called on in his prayers. In strict purdah the Masaheb was described as being more Italian in features than Indian, and with the face of a Madonna. Ranji's idealisation of her was probably responsible for his general attitude towards women, a combination of extreme courtesy, respect and detachment. During his most severe illnesses it was the sense of her presence, he always vowed, that pulled him through.

There were longer journeys, to Jodhpur and Calcutta, to Mysore and Chial. Everywhere he went he was received with enthusiasm.

It was naturally at Sarodar that he spent most of his time. Here, Charles Kincaid, then only a judicial officer, met Ranji. 'I invited Ranjitsinhji to my house . . . I expected to find a young man embittered by the decision of the Government of India and his head turned by his cricket successes. I found, on the contrary, a charming youth, who treated the Viceroy's decision as a blow of fate to be endured rather than railed against, and who spoke of his prodigious cricket scores with the most becoming modesty. I took him as a guest to the officers' mess at Rajkot, and everyone was delighted with him.'

If, in terms of future influence, the Patialas were the most important of the friends Ranji made on this visit, it was his uncle Sir Pratab Singh, the Maharajah of Idar and Regent of Jodhpur, who became closest to him. Sir Pratab, incorrigibly martial even into his eighties, later served with the British in Flanders and then again with Allenby in Egypt. He gave Ranji the best advice, counselled patience, meanwhile doing all he could behind the scenes to promote Ranji's interests.

Shortly before leaving for England Ranji consulted the celebrated astrologer, Pandit Hareshwar. Roland Wild describes the meeting as follows:

> Hareshwar was called to a bungalow outside Bombay, where he found four men. Behind the chair of one of them stood a servant, waving a fan.
>
> 'Tell us,' said one of the men, 'which of us will be a ruler among men?'
>
> Hareshwar asked the date of their births and inspected their palms.
>
> 'None of you,' he said, 'but I should like to inspect the hand of this servant.'
>
> He was allowed to do so.
>
> 'This man will be a ruler,' he declared. 'But I see also that he is a ruler in another field – in sport, I think.'

Apparently encouraged by this, on the face of it, inspired prediction, Ranji set sail for England.

TEN

1899

Sussex, during Ranji's absence in India, had suffered a lean season, until early August being bottom in the championship. The only good to come out of the summer of 1898 was in the form of C. B. Fry, who made such an enormous advance that his achievements rivalled those of Ranji himself in his great year of 1896. That season Ranji had scored 1,698 runs in championship matches at an average of 58. In 1898 Fry made 1,604 with an average of 59, scoring six hundreds, including, like Ranji before him, two hundreds in the same match. Fry's bowling action had been successfully vetoed by one umpire after another – a course that, *Wisden* observed curtly, should have been adopted long ago – and he bowled no more.

Sussex's first match of the 1899 season at Hove, starting on 15 May, was against Worcestershire, and they won it well by five wickets. Both Fry and Ranji made runs, but it was the bowling of Tate and Bland on an awkward pitch that won them the match.

From Hove, Sussex travelled to Leyton where the previous week Essex had trounced the Australians. Rain, which had affected nearly all matches so far played, resulted in a low-scoring match which Essex won with their last pair in.

At Hove, on Whit Monday, Gloucestershire were the visitors. Grace asked Sussex to bat on a sticky wicket and they were shot out for 97, Ranji contributing 30. Although Ranji made 51 in the second innings, Sussex went down, largely through dropped catches, by four wickets.

These defeats were a disappointment for Ranji, who had himself made a good start to the season by taking 63 off the Australian bowlers in their opening fixture at the Crystal Palace.

These wet Mays were even less to Ranji's liking than to most
people's, the only consolation being that he had persuaded Murdoch he was a bowler ideally suited to the conditions. He bowled
twenty-seven overs of his off-spinners against Somerset, taking
one for 63 in a match won by Sussex by an innings. At Tonbridge,
where Kent were well beaten, he bowled another nineteen overs,
this time without taking a wicket. Back at Hove, and coming on
fourth change against Nottinghamshire, he enjoyed the heady
figures of 5 for 45 in twenty overs. He also followed two scores in
the forties against Kent with 78, but it was the bowling he relished.

On 1 June the first Test was played at Nottingham. Ranji, not
satisfied with his form, had expressed a wish not to be considered.
The selectors, already in trouble with the fast bowling – Lockwood
and Kortright injured, Richardson unimpressive – decided otherwise, luckily as it turned out.

It was an historic match, in more ways than one. Grace,
captaining England, made his last appearance in a Test match. For
some time, grown very stout and slow in the field, he had thought
of retiring, but when the moment came he could not quite bring
himself to do so. He was barracked in the field, made only 28 and 1,
and in the train going home suddenly turned to F. S. Jackson
(who had made 8 and 0) and said sadly, 'It's all over, Jacker; I
shan't play again.' He was never chosen again and that season,
largely because of his acceptance of the management of the
London County team, his long association with Gloucestershire
ended too.

But if it was the finish for Grace it was the beginning for J. T.
Tyldesley and Wilfred Rhodes, and on the Australian side the
entry into Test cricket of the Victor Trumper who had so impressed Ranji in Australia eighteen months earlier. Jessop, too,
was waiting in the wings and it was he, another Gloucestershire
player, who took Grace's place.

The match itself, the first on the newly rebuilt Trent Bridge
ground, was an affair of swiftly changing fortunes. Just before
lunch on the second day Australia, having won the toss, had been
bowled out for 252, Rhodes and Hearne sharing eight of the

wickets, and England, with Grace and Fry together, were 70 without loss.

Grace now got out. Jones, bowling at terrific pace, hit the stumps of Fry, Gunn, Storer and Ranji in succession, and England were dismissed for 193. Fry got 50, Ranji 42.

Australia had been criticised for their exceptionally slow and cautious batting on the opening day. Clem Hill, who had been top scorer with 52 in the first innings, again led the way and Noble contributed his second 40 of the match. Trumper made 0 and 11.

The Australians declared at lunch on the third and final day, leaving England to get 290 to win. Rather more realistically, they had to survive for four hours.

The start was disastrous, Howell bowling Grace and Jackson with break-backs in the same over, with the score 1. At 10 Jones bowled Gunn and at 19 Fry was caught off Trumble.
Hayward and Ranji took the score to 82, Hayward, badly dropped when he was 12, lasting for 85 minutes.

Tyldesley hung on by his eyelashes for a while and then Ranji, farming the bowling, saw England through to the end. His manner of doing so, though, was scarcely the usual one, for he unleashed an array of dazzling strokes, as if winning the match, not saving it, was in question. In the end England were 155 for 7, Ranji 93 not out.

Wisden remarked: 'Never probably did a batsman, in the endeavour to save a match against time, play such a free and attractive game as he did during the last forty minutes he was at the wicket.'

Probably Ranji, after a careful and responsible start, decided that his natural game was the safest way for him to play. *Wisden* was critical of his running between the wickets: 'what should have possessed him to attempt short runs when there was nothing to gain and everything to lose one cannot pretend to explain.'

'Ranji Saves England', the placards announced all over London, and so he had done. It had been an exciting match, played in lovely weather. There was no doubt, though, as to who had had the better of it.

The summer of 1899 was one in which people needed distractions

from the first ugly phases of the Boer War. There were those, like
Kipling and the British Government, who conceived of the whole
enterprise as more of a brief colonial adventure than a war to be
taken seriously. Others, the Liberals particularly, were suspicious
of the motives behind the campaign against Kruger. People were
so divided that, as Priestley remarked in *The Edwardians,* 'old
friends shouted one another down and political meetings often
ended in uproar and brawls'. Sir Pratab Singh, offering his services
loyally to the King Emperor, may have had no doubts about the
issues, but many people did. South African gold and diamonds
were at least as much at stake as Imperial honour.

The summer and autumn of 1899 saw unexpected British
reverses on the field. A year later Roberts and Kitchener would
combine to scatter the Boers, but in the meantime it was an uneasy
and nervy country that welcomed the diversions of Test matches.

Sussex had a rest from championship cricket in June. Cambridge
came to Eastbourne and were bowled out for 78 and 159 on an
over-watered and then rained-on pitch. Ranji took 2 for 19 in the
second innings, after having made a masterly 107, in the most
difficult conditions, batting only 90 minutes. Against Oxford at
Hove, in a drawn match, he scored 85 and 58 not out.

The next county match at the Oval, a ground on which Ranji
had never shone, was the strangest of games. Richardson, bowling
better than he had done all summer, shot Sussex out for 128, of
which Ranji made 40. Surrey, for whom no one made less than 20
and no one more than 88, scored 457 in reply.

Fry was cheaply out when Sussex batted again, but George
Brann and Ranji put on 325 in 250 minutes for the second wicket.
Sussex eventually reached 561 and the match was drawn. Ranji's
share was 197.

This great run of scores by Ranji had been interrupted by the
second Test at Lord's. He was caught and bowled by Jones for 8
in the first innings and caught off Howell for a duck in the second.
For Australia Trumper made his maiden Test century; Hill, in
tremendous form, 135. Australia won by ten wickets, the only
match of the series that was not drawn.

In the eyes of many good judges this was the best Australian side ever to tour England, certainly superior to any since Murdoch's celebrated side of 1882. Murdoch, in a wet summer, had an attack that contained Spofforth, Giffen, Garratt, Palmer and Boyle, while Darling, in the hot dry months of 1899, had at his disposal Jones, Trumble, Howell, Noble and McLeod. There cannot have been much in it. Both teams were immensely strong in batting, the 1882 side richer in hitting power, the 1899 one notable for its dour determination.

After making his 197 at the Oval Ranji had to travel up to Headingley for the third Test. Maclaren was now installed as captain, and Jessop and Rhodes dropped with three others from the eleven that had lost at Lord's. The match was washed out by rain, England needing only 158 to win with all their wickets in hand. It was in this match that Hearne did the hat-trick, his victims being Noble, Gregory and Hill. More sadly, Johnny Briggs, the great Lancashire all-rounder, who had toured Australia with Ranji, was taken ill on the first evening and removed to Cheadle Asylum. Briggs had suffered all his life from epilepsy and he never properly recovered from this attack, dying three years later. Ranji made 11 in his only innings but took three good catches.

The Gentlemen v. Players match at Lord's, Ranji's next important engagement, was notable mainly for a hundred by Fry. No sooner was this over than he had to travel north again, to Old Trafford, for the fourth Test.

Jones got Ranji's wicket again, on the first morning, for 21, England losing the wickets of Quaife, Fry, Ranji and Maclaren for 47. Tom Hayward hit a magnificent 130 and England eventually reached 372. The Australians, all out 196, followed on, but recovered to make 346 for 7 declared. Ranji was 49 not out when the game ended, England at 94 for 3 being 76 runs short of victory.

Surrey were due at Hove the next day. Ranji, not arriving at his Norfolk Hotel rooms until the early hours, put himself down to bat at number five. He had a few weeks earlier taken over the captaincy from Murdoch, who, after a string of failures, had dropped out. It was not until well into the afternoon that Ranji had to go to the wicket. When he was out on the next morning he had made 174. Surrey, too, scored heavily, and Ranji, going in a second time on the last afternoon with no chance of a result, amused himself with 83 not out.

Middlesex were beaten at Hastings in two days by 8 wickets, Tate and Bland exploiting a drying pitch. With runs at a premium only P. F. Warner with 69 for Middlesex, and Fry, 94, and Ranji, 36, stayed long.

The Australians were due next at Hove. Ranji, who for all his heavy scoring in county matches did himself rather less than justice against the Australians, failed in both innings. Fry, however, made 181 and Victor Trumper, in an Australian total of 624, 300 not out, beating the previous record of 286 by Murdoch on the same ground in 1882.

The first week in August saw Sussex at Worcester, the riverside beauty of that ground, with its soaring cathedral and sailing swans, bringing out the best in Ranji. Sussex narrowly escaped defeat but Ranji played two elegant innings of 80 and 78.

After this Sussex travelled to Bristol for a week in the west country. In another drawn match Ranji made 154, at a run a minute. At Taunton, on a perfect wicket, Ranji's scores were 86 not out and 42. In Somerset's innings of 554 on the first day, Ranji bowled twenty-two overs, taking 2 for 67.

While Sussex made their way back to Brighton, Ranji took the train to London where next day the fifth Test was to start at the Oval.

This was a match England needed to win, but although, after batting first and running up a total of 576, they made Australia follow-on, they could only take five of their second innings wickets. On the first day England, under instructions from Maclaren to score as fast as possible, reached 435 for 4. Jackson and Hayward, opening the innings, each made centuries, Ranji 54, Fry 60, and Maclaren 49.

Sussex, for the last fortnight of August, were at Brighton. They looked like being beaten by Essex, having to follow-on, but Ranji, having made 48 in the first innings, batted three hours on the last afternoon to save the match.

Lancashire came next and were thoroughly defeated, Ranji

making 102 in his only innings. Yorkshire had the better of a draw, but Ranji's golden run continued with scores of 57 and 70. At Portsmouth, where Hampshire were defeated by an innings, Ranji made 72 not out, before declaring.

This had been a much better season for Sussex. They rose to fifth in the championship, winning seven of their matches. They were an immensely attractive batting side but with no reserve strength in their bowling. Nearly all their wickets were taken by Bland and Tate, both of whom took more than a hundred. It says little for the others that Ranji, capturing 31 wickets at 28 each with gentle off-spinners, was the next most successful of the regular bowlers.

Several Sussex batsmen had good seasons, especially Fry, who scored 1,500 runs at an average of 42, and Brann who made 1,200 at an average of 32. Ranji, though, towered over them all. In championship matches he made 2,285, averaging 76.16 and hitting seven hundreds. In all first-class matches he scored 3,159, beating his own record of 2,780 in 1896. Abel came next with 2,685, then Hayward with 2,647.

This was Ranji's first experience of captaincy. He was criticised in *Wisden*, perhaps unfairly, for changing his bowling too frequently 'so as to quite upset his team'. Ranji always carried a small aneroid barometer on him in the field and claimed that it was of much tactical value to him.

Personally successful as the season was for Ranji, it had also been an extremely tiring one. Going through his innings one by one gives some idea of his consistency and the amount of travelling involved between matches. He had few days off, and, gregarious to a fault, rarely spent an evening quietly. Insomnia and asthma were so much part of his expectation that, even when suffering most, he was generally able to perform the next day with the lightest of touches.

The season had not been over a fortnight before Ranji was in action again. Agreeing to a request by the Associated Clubs of Philadelphia to take out a strong amateur side for a short tour he sailed on the Cunard liner, *SS Etruria*, with a party of twelve that was little below Test quality. Maclaren, Stoddart and

Jessop were among them, as were Woods, Brann and Bosanquet.

Ranji as usual was seasick most of the trip, which was extremely rough, and was not alone in preferring his cabin to the deck.

The first match, played in Philadelphia in the last week of September against a team of twenty-two Colts, was ruined by rain. In the second match, at Haverford, the Gentlemen of Philadelphia were beaten by an innings and 173, Jessop and Woods bowling them out, and Maclaren, Ranji, Stoddart and Jessop all making runs.

A team of '14 of New York' were similarly outplayed on Staten Island, and the Gentlemen of Philadelphia equally easily defeated in a return fixture. In a final match against Canada in Toronto, the Canadians were beaten by an innings. Ranji, at no time in the best of health, batted only three times, scoring 42, 57 and 68.

They were away five weeks altogether, as much as Ranji could happily accommodate from the shooting and fishing that meant so much to him. The Americans had found his princely rank and bachelor status a source of much speculation, as were his clothes and appearance. He was plumper than the correspondent from the Philadelphia *Inquirer* had expected, and his walk was described in the same paper as 'rolling about like a barrel on pins'.

After a visit to the Niagara Falls, Ranji's party sailed for home on the *Oceanic*, docking at Liverpool. Ranji made straight for his old rooms at Cambridge, basing himself there for the rest of the winter.

ELEVEN

1900

1899 is generally accepted as being one of the great landmarks in cricket, particularly Anglo-Australian cricket. Not only was it the end of the Grace age, but it saw the flowering of such superb players as Trumper, Gregory, Darling, Hill and Armstrong for Australia, and Rhodes, Barnes, Tyldesley, Braund, Hirst and Jackson for England.

Ranji, after a quiet winter at home, was able to give all his attention to Sussex. There was no touring side to interrupt his captaincy. Unfortunately Sussex, for whom once again Ranji and Fry did marvellous things, proved quite unable to bowl their opponents out. They made huge scores themselves but then often had to field out a drawn match. Out of twenty-four matches, eighteen remained unfinished. Although Sussex lost only two, they could win only four.

Their fielding improved, largely due to Ranji's constant encouragement, and Joe Vine emerged as one of the best outfielders in the country. But the bowling was weaker than the year before and only Fred Tate had reasonable figures.

There is no need to go into detail again over Ranji's Sussex season. In 1899 he batted 35 times in championship matches, scoring 2,285 at 76.16; in 1900 he played 34 innings, scoring 2,563 at 85.43. He hit nine hundreds, as did Fry, and five double hundreds. Sometimes they scored runs together, equally often when one failed the other thrived. Fry, who watched many of Ranji's innings from the other end, wrote:

He had no technical faults whatever; the substratum of his play was absolutely sound. What gave him his distinctiveness was the combination of the perfect poise and suppleness and the quickness peculiar to the athletic Hindu. It is characteristic of all great batsmen that they play their strokes at the last instant; but I have never seen a batsman able to reserve his stroke so late as Ranji nor apply his bat to the ball with such electric quickness. He scored his runs on dry wickets very fast. I have often been in with him while he scored eighty to my twenty. It was impossible to bowl him a ball outside the off stump which he could not cut, and he could vary the direction of the stroke from square to fine. It was almost impossible for the best of bowlers on a fast pitch to bowl him a ball on the wicket which he could not force for runs somewhere between square leg and fine leg. These strokes were outside the repertoire of any other batsman I have ever seen. It was not only that he made strokes which looked like conjuring tricks; he made them with an appearance of complete facility. So distinctive was Ranjitsinhji's cutting and wrist play on the leg side that one almost forgot to notice his strokes in front of the wicket; but not only was he a beautiful driver on both sides of the wicket in the classical sense, he could drive if he liked hard and high just like a professed hitter. Old Bob Thomas, the first-class umpire who probably saw most cricket from 1870 to 1900, and who was reckoned a fine judge of the game, told me that 'the Prince was a greater batsman than the Doctor because he had more strokes'.

In discussing the fast bowlers of the key year of 1899, Fry interestingly puts Lockwood above Richardson and Mold, though Richardson and Kortright were certainly faster. 'Ranji once said to me,' Fry writes, 'and I concur, that one could be 120 not out on a plumb wicket and then be clean bowled by Lockwood and walk away to the pavilion not knowing what one would have done if one had another chance at the ball.'

One cannot quite leave Ranji's 1900 summer there. He was in some discomfort during a cold and wet May, often limping, and after an opening 158 against Cambridge at Fenner's did nothing spectacular. But with the arrival of June and warmer weather he blossomed: 97 and 127 against Gloucestershire at Hove, 222 in the next match against Somerset, 215 not out against Cambridge.

He failed twice in a very low scoring match against Nottinghamshire, rain making batting hazardous, but then took 192 not out off the Kent bowlers at Tonbridge. Two low scores against Essex at Eastbourne were followed by 158 at Trent Bridge. At Old Trafford he did nothing in either innings against Lancashire but bounced back with 72 and 87 off Hirst, Rhodes and Haigh at Sheffield. 'Ranjitsinhji had never before been seen at Bramall Lane,' *Wisden* records, 'and his presence proved an enormous attraction, the crowd on each of the first two days being estimated at fully 15,000. He played splendidly in both innings.'

On the way south, in a bizarre match against Leicestershire in which both sides amassed over 600, Ranji batted five hours for 275.

Ten days at home in Brighton produced 41 and 88 not out against Hampshire, 8 and 103 against Surrey, 202 against Middlesex. In the Middlesex match Fry reached his third successive hundred. After a thunderstorm Ranji, in only three hours on a bowler's wicket, made 180 on the last day, the remaining batsmen managing only 34 between them.

At Bristol, in his next innings, Ranji scored 109, following this with 89 at Taunton. Back in the south-east for the last half of August he finished off the season with a sequence of 66, 18, 73, 87, 58, 6 not out, and 220. This last, against Kent, was his eleventh three-figure innings of the season. Earlier in the season G. J. V. Weigall, the Kent amateur and one of the most opinionated men in cricket, remarked to Ranji that he never seemed able to make big scores against Kent. His reply was 192 not out and 220.

TWELVE

1901

In January 1901 Queen Victoria died. Ranji, interrupting his round of shooting and fishing expeditions, brought the two daughters of his old guardian up to view the procession. The Miss Borissows and Ranji, unable to find proper accommodation, had to spend the night in a third-class hotel, Ranji stretching out in the corridor outside their door.

The succession of Edward VII as King, once the period of mourning was over, led to a brighter, livelier atmosphere in London. The King wanted to enjoy himself, and he wanted the country to enjoy itself, too. The hedonistic feeling of release among the upper classes, with no shortage of money or servants, led to an endless round of country house weekends, visits to the theatre and night clubs, bridge parties, expeditions to Henley and Cowes, to the grouse moors and Scotland. It was a style of life totally congenial to Ranji. He may not have had the resources to sustain it but that rarely deterred him. He entertained continually in his Cambridge rooms and was himself in great demand. It was undeniably a self-indulgent and shallow decade that ushered in the new century, but to an Indian prince the problems of unemployment and slum housing in London could scarcely be of great concern. The sweat shops of the East End and conditions in factories and collieries must have been as remote to Ranji in 1901 as life in the bazaars of Jamnagar. Of more interest to him were the gleaming new cars of the period, the Sunbeam Mableys and Wolseleys, the Rolls-Royces and Lanchesters, with their folding hoods and shining brass lamps. He enjoyed, too, the music-hall, Marie Lloyd and Little Tich, Cinquevalli and Harry Tate, at least when he could be prised away from the bridge table or from playing billiards at Thurstons.

After a shooting weekend in early spring Ranji was laid low with influenza. It took him some weeks to recover and it was 27 May before he was able to play his first innings. It was hardly to be expected that he would find his touch immediately, but though noticeably frail and short of practice he appeared to continue much as he had left off.

His first two matches were at Hove. In the first, against Gloucestershire, he made 64 in the first innings and then was bowled by Jessop for 0 in the second. 'Bowling as fast as he had ever done in his life,' *Wisden* observed, 'Jessop quite unnerved the Sussex batsmen.' Somerset were Sussex's next opponents and Ranji took 133 off them, Sussex winning by an innings.

The South Africans played MCC at Lord's early in June. They were not, at that time, quite up to county standard, and most counties played less than full strength sides against them. MCC, however, did them proud, their side including Grace, Ranji, Murdoch, Storer, and Trott among others. MCC won only narrowly, nobody making fifty for them in either innings.

Ranji went straight off to Trent Bridge on the last evening and next morning scored 85. Sussex beat Nottinghamshire for the first time at Trent Bridge for over forty years, Vine taking fifteen wickets with quickish leg-breaks and Fry carrying his bat for 170 in the second innings.

Although Ranji scored no hundreds in June he was consistent enough – 35 against Kent, 37 against Leicestershire, 70 not out against Cambridge, 34 and 84 at Eastbourne against Oxford.

July and August, however, were golden months. On Sussex's northern tour Yorkshire bowled them out at Bradford for 52 and 155, Hirst and Rhodes being almost unplayable on a damp pitch. Ranji still managed 57 in his second innings, by some way the top score of the match.

Moving across the Pennines he took 69 and 170 not out off the Lancashire bowlers, Sussex winning by 94 runs. Back at Lord's, for the losing Gentlemen against the Players, Ranji made 36 and 15. Fry scored 126 in his first innings, almost all his runs coming on the leg side. Few Gentlemen elevens can have looked so strong on paper: Fry, Warner, Ranjitsinhji, R. E. Foster, Mason,

A. O. Jones, Jessop, Jephson, Wells, McGregor and Bradley.

Ranji's next three innings, on Sussex grounds, were 55, 219, and 15. At Lord's against Middlesex, Trott bowled him twice, for 21 and 26, but back at Hove he hit the Surrey bowlers all over the ground for 100 not out.

Ranji always enjoyed Sussex's excursion into the west country at the beginning of August and this year was no exception. At Worcester, after being run out for o in his first innings, he made 139 in his second. Gloucestershire were beaten by an innings at Bristol, Ranji making only 1. At Taunton, however, when Sussex were in some danger of defeat, he followed 45 in his first innings by batting out the match for 285. There had been some criticism recently of Ranji's social habits – dinner parties going on late, bridge and billiards into the small hours, night fishing. To refute any suggestion that his play was being affected he spent the whole of the previous night on the river, having put his boots outside his bedroom door to give the impression he had gone to bed early.

Fry relates the incident more specifically in relation to Ranji's passion for bait-fishing. 'Once when Sussex were playing Somerset at Taunton, he heard that perch could be caught in a mill-pool close by. He asked Tyler, the Somerset left-hand bowler, about this. Tyler and some pals, egged on by Sammy Woods, the Somerset captain, persuaded Ranji that it was no good except at night, so Ranji agreed to fish all night. Billy Murdoch, our captain, heard of this and absolutely forbade it. Ranji assumed obedience, went to bed early, and displayed his shoes outside the bedroom door.' In fact, Murdoch had retired from the captaincy a year earlier and neither Tyler nor Woods were then playing for Somerset.

This innings seemed to increase, if anything, Ranji's appetite for batting. He returned to Hove and immediately – Maclaren putting Sussex in on a rain-affected pitch – took 204 off the Lancashire attack. Yet for all the huge scores he made, Ranji never batted for the mere sake of it; nearly always he scored at about a run a minute, and while he was in he always put on some kind of display, each innings an expression of personality, an exercise in technical skills, a series of experiments. He set out to demonstrate the most that could be achieved in certain conditions, consciously wanting to enchant as much as to dominate.

The two successive double centuries were Ranji's last long innings of the summer. He made 33 and 55 at Portsmouth, 86 not out against Yorkshire in Fred Tate's benefit match, 74 against Middlesex at Hove, 30 against Kent, and then, early in September, 115 for an England eleven against Yorkshire during the Hastings Festival. Fry had begun a magical run of six centuries in a row and Ranji could afford to watch and admire.

Sussex, though still weak in bowling and putting down almost as many catches as ever, rose to fourth place in the championship, their best position since Ranji joined them. 'The Sussex captain,' *Wisden* noted, 'became more and more a driving player. Opposing teams endeavoured to cramp his game by putting on additional short legs but, without abandoning his delightful strokes on that side of the wicket, or his beautifully timed cuts, he probably got the majority of his runs by drives – a notable change, indeed, from his early years as a great cricketer.' About Fry *Wisden* remarked: 'He rarely cuts, he scores scarcely at all in the slips, and he often puts together a big innings without making any appreciable number of off-drives.' *Wisden*, acknowledging Fry's on-side skills, suggests that his eminence was largely due to 'intelligence and application', but if he was really so one-sided a player as this implies it is surprising good bowlers did not contain him more successfully.

In the autumn Ranji returned to Sarodar. His saddest duty during his stay was to attend the mourning ceremonies after the death of his friend and benefactor, the much loved Maharajah of Patiala, always 'uncle' to Ranji since their first meeting on his return from Australia.

It was a relief to have a break from the continual grind of county cricket, much though he loved it. 'In those days,' Fry wrote in *Life Worth Living*, 'one never saw one's garden or home from the beginning of May till the end of August.' Ranji as yet had no home of his own, only his rooms in Cambridge and his suite at the Norfolk in Brighton.

This time Ranji spent most of the winter in Kathiawar. He

played cricket at Patiala and in Poona, made a round of visits to
relations, but for the most part was content to ride across the
stony plains searching for panther, each evening watching the
sunset drop like a flare over the Barda Hills. This brown, flat
country, with its hostile rocky outcrops and low scrub, its tent-like
inclines and dried-up river beds, was always dear to Ranji and
long after he had become Jam Saheb it was where he came for rest
and solitude. He could well gaze west towards the blue waters of
the Gulf of Cutch and wonder at what was happening in Jamnagar,
the domes and towers of which were to him as yet only imaginary.
What he heard was not encouraging; tales of corruption and disease, of exploitation and poverty.

Each time Ranji returned to India interest in the affairs of his
State revived. In England cricket occupied his days and his
thoughts, and when it was not cricket it was those other pursuits
of the countryside to which Ranji devoted himself more assiduously than most Englishmen.

In Sarodar, almost within earshot of the Jadeja capital, it was
another matter. The bullock-carts creaking under the fever trees,
the rice-green parrots throwing themselves like darts from the
eaves of the courtyards, the constant parade of villagers to and
from their cultivations in the valley, were all reminders of a childhood spent in preparation for rule, whatever had since occurred.
Sweat on his horse's flanks after a gallop, the gargling of Sarodar
doves, the echo of rifle shots ricochetting over the thorn bushes,
these were memories he could take back to England. All the same,
he was not yet reconciled to the life of a small landowner; it was
not what he had been promised. The sophistications of Cambridge
and London, travel round the world as one of the greatest cricketers ever, had opened up larger horizons than this one.

THIRTEEN

1902

Ranji was back in Sussex for the start of the new season, one notable for its quantity of rain as well as for the visit of the Australians, again under the captaincy of Joe Darling. W. G. Grace, at the age of 54, played his two-hundredth three-figure innings, 124 of which had been in first-class cricket. He made two more, for London County, on the Crystal Palace ground.

Despite the appalling weather and the number of drawn games, Sussex made further progress in the championship, finishing second to Yorkshire. As a team they were more balanced than usual, less reliant on Ranji and Fry, both of whom played many fewer matches for the county. The fielding was still atrocious, but Fred Tate had a marvellous season with his off-spinners, taking 153 wickets. Vine, Relf and Killick all batted well and even with Ranji and Fry away Sussex were a difficult side to bowl out.

It was a strange summer for Ranji, half a dozen superb innings alternating with an unusual number of low scores. He was picked for the first four Tests, but was unable to play at Sheffield in the third, and was dropped for the fifth. He never played in a Test match again. Indeed, his Test scores, no less than Fry's, make sad reading; 13 at Birmingham, where Australia were bowled out for 36 by Rhodes and Hirst, and then saved by the rain; o at Lord's, where less than two hours play was possible in the whole match; 2 and o at Old Trafford, where Australia won a thriller by 3 runs. At the Oval, where Ranji was left out for the first time since he had begun to play for England, Jessop hit his famous hundred in 75 minutes and England won by one wicket. Fry, with scores of o, o, 1 and 4, was dropped after the third Test.

These scores by two of the greatest batsmen in the world are

hard to account for. In the first Test Ranji, visibly upset by a misunderstanding that resulted in Maclaren being run out, was
bowled in the next over. The second Test was an unreal affair, half
the Australians being down with 'flu and the skies laden with rain.
At Old Trafford Ranji again had to bat in the gloom and was
twice l.b.w. to Trumble, the second time questionably. It was a
melancholy way for such a great Test career to end. The day after
the Oval Test ended Ranji, playing for MCC at Lord's against the
Australians, scored 60 on a nasty wicket. It was, though, scarcely
the same thing. Trumble, moving the ball either way with his
high action and great height, got him cheaply in the second
innings.

But if 1902 saw the end of Ranji as a Test cricketer he was far
from finished so far as Sussex were concerned. It is true that 600
of his 1,100 runs for the county came in three innings – 135 against
Surrey at the Oval, 230 against Essex at Leyton, 234 not out in the
return Surrey match at Hastings – but he often batted well on the
sticky wickets that prevailed throughout the season. He averaged
66 for Sussex and though his average for all first-class matches
dropped to 46, he was still second in the whole country, only the
46-year-old Arthur Shrewsbury, helped by seven not outs, being
above him.

Ranji had, for him, a poor May, being often off colour in the
cold and wet, and then straining a muscle in his leg. Apart from
67 for MCC against the Australians at Lord's he batted only four
times, in the last two matches of the month, managing never more
than 23.

After leaving the England side at Birmingham he failed to score
at Trent Bridge against Nottinghamshire, Tate bowling the home
side out for 46 and 150. At Leicester, in appalling weather, he
made only 4, Tate taking nine Leicestershire wickets for 73 and
then four for 44, only rain preventing another easy Sussex victory.

Ranji had begun now to drop himself down the order. At the
Oval in the next match he batted at number seven, Lockwood and
Richardson having torn open the Sussex batting. In his first ninety
minutes at the wicket, with Sussex reduced to 105 for 7, Ranji
made only 44. After lunch, however, he flayed all the Surrey

bowlers, 'rising to the occasion,' *Wisden* observed, 'like the great master he is.' Out of 115 for the ninth wicket he made all but 24.

Ranji batted agreeably for 28 at Lord's against Middlesex, Tate then bowling out Middlesex twice in a day. But it was at Leyton that he came into his own, savaging the Essex bowling for 230. No one else made a double century in county matches during the rains of 1902, but Ranji soon after made a second one at Hastings, at one stage putting on 160 in 70 minutes with Tate off the bowling of Lockwood and Richardson.

The Australians came to Hove over the first weekend in August, Noble and Armstrong putting on 428 together after the Australians had lost 5 for 152.

Ranji, in his last innings of the season for Sussex, made 19. His subsequent non-appearance for the county caused considerable speculation. *Wisden* observed: 'For some reason which was not allowed to become public Ranjitsinhji dropped out of the team altogether during the last few weeks of the county season, finishing up with the Australian match at the beginning of August. Rumours were freely circulated as to his having had differences with one or more of the professionals, but on this point, in the absence of definite information, one can say nothing. The fact remains, however, that, for the time at least, the great cricketer withdrew himself from the team with which his fame has been so closely associated. Ranjitsinhji was not last season half such a dependable batsman as in previous years, but his absence of course made a great difference, and it says much for the general excellence of the Sussex eleven that even with their captain away, they went through their August matches with only one defeat.'

In fact, during August, Sussex beat Essex and Hampshire in very low-scoring games, went down to Lancashire at Hove, and drew with Somerset and Kent.

It is inconceivable that Ranji, to whose heart Sussex's fortunes were so close, would have neglected them without good reason. It was far from uncommon in those days for amateurs to take weeks off for business purposes, or for shooting or fishing expeditions, or simply because they preferred to do something else. Ranji, however, had never done this.

Yet from the end of July to the end of the season he was not
with the Sussex side at all. He had on his hands, it is true, various
relatives and friends, Sir Pratab Singh and the Cooch Behars
among them, whom he felt obliged to entertain. King Edward's
coronation, for which they had travelled especially, had been
postponed because of the King's illness. As a result there were in
England, long after in normal circumstances they would have
been due home, numerous people to whom Ranji, for one reason
or another, felt obligations.

Ranji could, no doubt, have entertained his friends in Brighton
and continued to play when he could for Sussex, at least once the
West country tour was over. He chose instead to appear only in
the MCC v. Australians fixture at Lord's, thereafter taking a party
up to Gilling where Borissow was now Rector. Here he rented a
shoot, played village cricket, and fished.

It was in Yorkshire, therefore, that Ranji's Indian summer was
played out. When his friends departed Ranji stayed on. The winter
of 1902/3 was for him to be a complete rest from cricket, though
he helped prepare a new edition of the *Jubilee Book* with additional
chapters on Australia, India and South Africa. He interrupted his
country pursuits only once, and that was when, on 24 February,
he wrote a letter to *The Times* on the then crucial question of wider
wickets.

It had been proposed, at a meeting of county captains, that the
width of the wicket should be increased from eight to nine inches.
The motive was to reduce the number of drawn games and the
excessive scoring on hard wickets. For some reason the committee
of MCC, not known for their haste in bringing in new legislation,
expressed the wish to try out the proposals – without preliminary
test – during the forthcoming season.

On 7 May the proposal, supported by both the MCC sub-com-
mittee concerned with the matter and the full committee of the
club, was voted on. A. G. Steel, the retiring President, supported
by Lord Harris, appealed to the members to support the proposal.
In the event, the two-thirds majority required was not obtained,
the voting being 215 for, 199 against.

The subject died a natural death. The Editor of *Wisden* was strongly against it. 'Personally, though I think it would very likely have helped the bowlers on bad wickets, when they need no assistance, I do not think it would have made any difference to them in fine weather. When batsmen of the class of Ranjitsinhji, C. B. Fry, Maclaren and Victor Trumper – I mention only the most famous names among contemporary players – are making long scores the ball, unless intentionally let alone, so seldom passes the bat that I cannot believe the widening of the wicket by an inch would have any effect.'

Maclaren, it turned out, was against the idea, too. Ranji's main contentions were, firstly, that dropped catches or bad weather were the principal reasons for drawn games, and, secondly, that earlier finishes – on the second evening or early on the third day – would bring financial ruin to the counties. 'All but one of the drawn first-class games in which I took part last season were unfinished thanks to bad fielding on the part of one and often both sides in most games, and in the remaining ones owing to the weather. I may add, by way of parenthesis, that for the last three years the average of easy catches dropped by one county team [Sussex presumably], holding a high position in the championship, during Whitsun week alone, at the lowest computation, cannot be less than 15.'

Ranji had spent lavishly on the entertainment of his friends: hotel suites, private cars with chauffeurs, boxes at Lord's, theatre and supper parties. Not that his life at the Norfolk in Brighton was lived under noticeably different conditions. He handed out presents and gave dinner parties at the faintest opportunity.

It was predictable, therefore, that the financial problems of the Cambridge years should recur. In fact, many of his debts from that period were still outstanding. They were lately increased to an extent that creditors' meetings had to be held and it needed all Ranji's charm and assurances, as well as personal guarantees from family and friends, to satisfy them. He seemed constitutionally incapable of changing his way of life.

At Gilling temptations were reduced. Some money came in from journalism, largely for the popular papers, and Bottomley,

the *Sun*'s proprietor, as one of his scoops, persuaded Ranji to edit
the paper for a day. Bottomley, however, was no reliable source
of revenue and he was soon in more trouble than Ranji.

The quiet of Gilling was briefly disturbed for Ranji in the spring
by reports of the installation of Jawantsinhji, now called Jassaji
as Jam Saheb. Imagining the ceremonies taking place at Jamnagar,
the congregation of relatives, the arrival of princes and government functionaries from all over India, he inevitably felt left out.

Jassaji was a young man, unattractive and graceless though he
might be. He was provided with five wives. There appeared no
sense in Ranji holding on any longer to dreams of succession. He
returned to Brighton in April, more single-minded than he had
been for some time.

FOURTEEN

1903

1903 was, in terms of wetness, worse even than 1902, but with fewer distractions from family, no touring side and India as far out of mind as he could put it, Ranji was able to concentrate once again on Sussex. He played in twenty-one matches as against eleven the year before and with great enthusiasm.

With Fry now as vice-captain, in preparation, as it turned out, for taking over from Ranji the following season, Sussex held their second position, this time to Middlesex, with Yorkshire third. This was, above all, Fry's summer. The Test failures of 1902 behind him, Fry batted in all sorts of conditions with extraordinary consistency. He scored 174 in the opening match at Hove against Worcestershire, made six further centuries and finished with an aggregate of 2,413 at an average of 80.43. Only Tom Hayward also passed 2,000, and he averaged only 35.68.

Second to Fry, and averaging nearly ten above the third, George Hirst, came Ranji, with 1,394 runs at an average of 58. Even Ranji, well though he batted on occasions, could not compete with Fry. Whereas in his early days Fry was almost entirely an on-side player, he now blossomed out as a handsome driver through the covers and past mid-off. Ranji expressed the opinion that he was now at his peak, having learned 'the limits of his own resources'.

Ranji eased himself gradually into form. He went in at number seven in the opening game, scoring 11 and 27, but in the next match, against Nottinghamshire, abandoned on the last day because of Arthur Shrewsbury's suicide, he managed only 8. At Leicester, on the way north, he made 27 and 28, but at Old Trafford, on a fiery pitch against Barnes and Brearley, came right back to his best with 105. 'Ranji played absolutely faultless cricket,' commented *Wisden*, 'the great feature of a splendid innings being his cutting and driving.'

Sussex returned to Brighton and in a high-scoring match against Gloucestershire Ranji, after being bowled for 0 in the first innings, scored 162 not out in the second. Jessop on the first day hit 286 out of 355 in less than three hours, an astonishing performance.

Against Somerset at Hastings, where Sussex won by 8 wickets, Ranji got 57. They moved on now to Bradford, Fry making 234, Ranji 93 and Sussex beating the reigning champions by an innings and 180. The Essex match at Leyton was rained off and the meeting with Kent at Tonbridge abandoned without a ball being bowled.

Back at Hove Sussex were due to play Middlesex, both teams being unbeaten at that point. Unfortunately, after Sussex had made 287 on a slow pitch – Fry 89, Ranji 99 – the last two days were washed out.

Ranji stood down for Sussex's next two matches, against Oxford and Cambridge, but played for MCC against his old university at Lord's in the last of their trial matches, going in first with Weigall and making 88.

He pulled a muscle in this match and was not properly fit until the beginning of August. Nevertheless, though badly lame, he appeared for the Gentlemen at Lord's, scoring 9 and 60. Fry in the second innings made 232 not out and Maclaren 168 not out.

Ranji, nursing his leg, now missed two or three matches and did little in those he played in. Rain fell almost every day. At Hove, in another match ruined by the weather, he once more hit Barnes and Brearley all over the ground, making 144 not out. He followed this up with 95 at Portsmouth, easily the top score on a damp pitch for either side, and 55 not out against Middlesex at Lord's, play only being possible on one day.

The rain wrecked match after match. In between whiles Sussex beat Yorkshire at Hove, their second victory of the summer over them. Fry continued to make hundreds whenever he could – two against Kent in the last match of the season – and Ranji ended up with 28 and 72 not out in the same match.

Despite the appalling weather it was consolation to Ranji that Sussex were again second and he could hand over to Fry with some pride. He himself played one other satisfying innings, making 132 out of 204 for Grace's London County side against MCC at the Crystal Palace. Nine wickets fell for 68 but Ranji, farming the bowling, saw 136 added in 70 minutes. Grace thought it one of Ranji's very best innings.

Ranji returned in the autumn to India. There was nothing for him at Jamnagar but from Sarodar he made repeated hunting trips to the Gir Forest in the south-east of Kathiawar looking for lion. He shot his first lion staying with the Nawab of Junagadh and was nearly killed by a panther. He rode vast distances, shot snipe from horseback, and fished. It was the princely life without either the responsibilities or the perquisites of a ruler.

FIFTEEN
1904–6

Ranji was content, now in his ninth season with Sussex, to play under Fry. He batted rather less than in the previous summer – in sixteen matches as against twenty-one – but his form was better. The weather was generally fine and on the correspondingly harder pitches Ranji hit eight hundreds, including a double century against Lancashire at Hove. Three of his centuries were made at Lord's, two of these for MCC against Oxford and Cambridge, and the other for the Gentlemen. When the season finished he was top of the first-class averages, scoring 2,077 runs at an average of 74. Fry came next with 2,824 runs at 70.60 and J. T. Tyldesley third with 2,439 at 62. For Sussex Fry averaged 79 and Ranji 73.

Once again, during the hot midsummer days of 1904, the crowds flocked all over England to watch Ranji and Fry. About Ranji's 207 not out against Lancashire, *Wisden* reported: 'From the first ball to the last in that superb display he was at his highest pitch of excellence, and beyond that the art of batting cannot go.'

Although Sussex were as powerful and attractive a batting side as any in the country, their bowling was even tamer than usual. They had no bowler of pace. Tate, now 37, could not always command a place, and Cox and Relf not only opened the bowling but had to bowl most of the time. Both were in their thirties.

Fry, stricter on and off the field than Ranji, was no more successful than Ranji had been in getting catches to stick. Sussex as a result dropped to sixth, following days running up large scores with long days in the field.

It is possible to detect in Ranji's play in 1904 a less serious commitment to routine. He had always been a player of airs and graces, of such apparently spontaneous invention that he had made batting seem the most casual of arts. But throughout all his seasons with Sussex he had stuck dutifully to the county grind, travelling up north to Old Trafford and Headingley, to the unfashionable grounds at Derby and Leicester and Northampton. He usually went on Sussex's west country tour to Bristol and Taunton, the happiest of hunting grounds for fish as well as for runs. But now he began to pick and choose, and when he batted, to experiment even more.

He liked to play at Lord's almost as much as at Hove, and it was at Lord's, on 19 May, that he opened his season with 36 against Middlesex. He played his first innings at Hove on 23 May, scoring 82 against Gloucestershire. He followed this up with 48 against Somerset, also at Hove, and 27 at Leicester. In different innings he set himself the task of concentrating on and embellishing certain strokes at the expense of others. He would test out the various ways in which the same kind of ball could be played. An innings marked by cutting would be succeeded by one in which his runs came from pulls and on-drives. The glance and late cut, perfected so long ago, were seen less frequently. He had nothing to learn about them.

What his nephew Duleepsinhji wrote about him remained generally true: 'It was Ranji who made the back stroke an attacking stroke. The idea of batting up to then was that the ball must travel back more or less in the same direction from which it came to the bat. He changed this by helping the ball in the same direction, more or less, by slightly deflecting it. This was the great difference between him and others before him. He used the forward stroke for attack and the back stroke for both attack and defence.'

The essence of Ranji's technique is in that observation. But as he grew older he liked to put on a show, even when the context scarcely warranted it. No one who came to watch Ranji was disappointed if Ranji could help it. There was a mischievous element in his make-up and he enjoyed exploiting it. He wanted to surprise as well as seduce. Thus, those uncharacteristic innings in which all the renowned strokes were exchanged for unfamiliar ones. His eye was so good and his footwork so neat that he could get away with almost anything.

In his two matches at Lord's for MCC he took 59 and 166 not out off Cambridge and 142 off Oxford in the same week. He put on the grandest of exhibitions and then departed. Ranji was never one to hang about when he had made his point and his presence was no longer necessary. Yet time after time he saved matches for Sussex by playing long innings on the last day, usually scoring, it is true, as fast as if he were trying to win them.

It was typical of Ranji, for instance, that he should make 178 not out against the touring South Africans, and what is more, make them in three hours. They would have tales to tell back on the veldt. Typical, too, that in a thrilling win for the Gentlemen over the Players at Lord's he should have produced one of his greatest innings. The Gentlemen, on the last day, were set to make 412 to win off the bowling of Hearne, Braund, Rhodes and the very fast Arnold among others. Ranji and Jackson, joining forces at 108 for 3, added 194 in two hours and a half. 'Ranjitsinhji's batting was beyond criticism,' *Wisden* records. 'Even he has rarely played a greater innings.' Ranji was eventually out for 121.

Against Yorkshire at Sheffield Fry and Ranji put on 255 together. At Hove against Surrey a month later they batted in partnership while Fry made 181 and Ranji 152. In August at Hove there were the two thrilling innings of 99 and 207 not out against the Lancashire bowlers. In their penultimate match Sussex were beaten by Middlesex, Bosanquet taking fourteen wickets in the match with his googlies and leg-breaks, but Ranji batting in masterly fashion against him on a late summer afternoon for 52.

No one knew it at the time, probably not even Ranji himself, but that last innings, Ranji darting down the pitch to scotch Bosanquet's skilfully flighted spinners, was the last he would play as a regular member of the Sussex side. If it was the end for K. S. Ranjitsinhji, it was not however quite the end for that great enchanter about whom Neville Cardus mused: 'Did he really happen? Or was he perhaps a dream, all dreamed on some midsummer's night long ago.' It was as the Jam Saheb of Nawanagar that he returned three times to play for Sussex; four years later, in 1908, again in 1912, and finally, rather sadly, in 1920. In 1908 he hit three hundreds, in 1912 four. But successful though he was in 1908 and 1912, he was not the magical player of his youth. He was, instead, an Indian ruler amusing himself on leave. Henceforth Ranji would impress with the correctness of his technique, the solidity of his defence. But the eye that once allowed such magnificent, last-minute improvisations now saw just that much slower. He was reduced by both eyesight and figure to playing within limits, in the manner of a mere mortal.

Cardus, in his essay 'Ranji, Fry and Sussex', quotes Ted Wainwright of Yorkshire: 'Ranji and Fry at Brighton on a plumb wicket. It were t'same tale every year . . . Sussex 43 for 2 at one o'clock, but, bless your soul, we knowed there were nowt in it.' Ranji would join Fry, 'swishing his bat like a cane' and at the end of the day Sussex would be 390 for 2.

Cardus may not often have seen Ranji bat – he was, after all, only fifteen when the season of 1904 came to an end and he did not join the *Manchester Guardian* until 1917 – but he gives a vivid impression of the contrasting styles of Ranji and Fry in a long partnership:

> Fry played by the book of arithmetic; his was the batsmanship of the rational mind. If it sent out a light at all it was the dry light of science . . . He was the acutest thinker ever known to the game; his every stroke was an idea, a principle, and his every innings a synthesis. Even when he drove straight – and few cricketers have commanded a stronger drive than Fry's – his energy was disciplined.
>
> When you looked upon Fry at the wicket you looked upon the schoolman glorifying a system, even though it bound him, body and soul. It was all superb but of the comprehensible earth. When you looked upon Ranji at the other end, you turned from the known world of law and order to the occult; you turned from the West to the East. Ranji was the most remarkable instance in all cricket's history of a man expressing through the game not only his individual genius but the genius of his race. No Englishman could have batted like Ranji. 'Ranji,' said Ted Wainwright once, ' 'e never made a Christian stroke in his life'

... The bowler, knowing he had aimed on the middle stump, saw, as in a vision, the form of Ranji, all fluttering curves. The bat made its beautiful pass, a wizard's wand. From the very middle stump the ball was spirited away to the leg-side boundary ... When Ranji passed out of cricket a wonder and a glory departed from the game for ever. It is not in nature that there should be another Ranji. We who have had the good luck to see Ranji, let us be grateful.

In another piece on Ranji Cardus wrote:

Happy the man who today can close his eyes and see again the vision of Ranji, his rippling shirt of silk, his bat like a yielding cane making swift movements which circled round those incomparable wrists. He caused a revolution in the game: he demonstrated the folly of the old lunge forward to a ball seductive in length. Ranji's principle was to play back or to drive, and his many imitators contrived in the course of years to evolve the hateful two-eyed stance from Ranji's art, which, of course, was not for ordinary mortals to imitate.

Curiously, the lesson was not fully learned, for which of us, as schoolboys in the twenties, thirties, forties and fifties – perhaps even now – was not brought up on the 'forward defensive', that constricting lunge at the blind spot?

When Andrew Lang's 'old happy days of burned-out Junes revive' there were few, if any, who figured quite so much in cricket talk as Ranji. When he was back in India and it was only Fry whom bowlers opposing Sussex had to get out, it was never quite the same.

In November 1904 Ranji sailed for India. What he had in mind is not clear. There is no reason to suppose he was not intending to be back in Brighton for early season practice in April. He had invited Lord Hawke to accompany him on this trip. The plan was for them to be based at Sarodar but to look for lion in the Gir Forest. These days the Gir lions are few and far between, and the remaining half-tame and shabby beasts more accustomed to going through their paces for the camera than evading big-game hunters.

They are, though, the sole surviving lions in south-east Asia. In Ranji's day they were hardier and more resourceful creatures, residents, with a community of African negroes, of a thickly forested belt inland from the south-east coast of Gujerat.

Lord Hawke was a shot of some distinction, and it was not unknown for him to make grouse shooting a more urgent priority than cricket at whatever level.

When they had exhausted the possibilities of the Gir they camped, under the Datar Hills, near Junagadh. From here they travelled to Palitana, a horse-breeding centre and a transit stop for pilgrims on their way to the nine hundred Jain temples on Satrunjaya Hill, the 'Holy Mountain'. From the top of the hill you can look eastwards across to the Gulf of Cambay, north to the granite peaks of Sihor, and south-west, across the plain scrawled over by the Satrunjaya river, to the Talaja Hills. The Jain temples, with their inner gates and courtyards, some of them dating from the eleventh century, marked the eastern end of Ranji's hunting territory. There was nothing of this dramatic quality in Kathiawar but from the Barda Hills and Kileshwar, where Ranji later built his own hunting lodge, they were within reach.

Since he had been a boy at the Rajkumar College Ranji had enjoyed little family life. He planned to make up for it now. Although he kept well away from Jamnagar itself he became a familiar figure in Rajkot and other parts of the state. He made friends with his fellow princes, embarking on happy visits usually related to sport of one kind or another. He attached as much importance to seeing British officials, to whom his cricketing exploits had already made him a legendary figure. On the face of it he had no statutory future in the State, but Ranji rarely underestimated the indirect value of sociability and charm.

Ranji was not without his superstitions. A year earlier he had consulted his *joshi*, Pandit Hareshwar, a second time. His palm was read, the other necessary calculations made. A week later Ranji received the verdict: 'If you do not sit on the *gadi* of Nawanagar on 11 March 1907, I will give Rs 2,000 to charity and will give up my work.'

How much this unlikely prophecy sustained Ranji during the
monsoon and hot weather of 1905, it is impossible to estimate.
Ranji protested a light-hearted attitude to fate or 'luck', but at a
deeper level was affected by propitiatory or hostile signs. Hardly
a single one of the Jams had come to power by normal routes to
succession. Poisoning, murder, illness, death in battle, court
intrigues; all, in one reign or another, were agents of inheritance.

Jam Jassaji's entourage, even with British advisers, showed few
gifts of administration. The affairs of Jamnagar, a city 'fit for the
body of a gallant but dirty animal', according to a contemporary
political officer, slid further into chaos. One epidemic succeeded
another in the narrow, congested streets and bazaars. The main
sources of satisfaction in court circles, still implacably hostile to
Ranji, were his financial difficulties, caused, as rumour had it, by
a life of dissolution. By extravagance of style and open-handed
entertaining, possibly, but by dissolute habits not at all.

Lord Hawke had returned in the spring to lead Yorkshire to
yet another county championship, one based almost entirely on
their great quintet of bowlers, Haigh, Rhodes, Hirst, Myers and
Ringrose. Hawke used to bat modestly at number nine or so, but
he was the kind of paternalistic, responsible and resourceful
captain under whom Yorkshire have always best flourished.

After the season was over Hawke returned to India to stay with
Ranji. There was much cricket to talk over on *shikar*, or in the
warm evenings over whisky and cigars at Sarodar. The Australians had been in England, with Joe Darling again captain and
such old adversaries of Ranji's as Noble, Gregory, Armstrong,
Hill and Trumper under him. F. S. Jackson, now captaining
England, had won the toss in all five Tests and, partly as a consequence, the series by two Test matches to nil. Jackson headed
both the batting and the bowling, the Test successes of the summer being the batting of Fry, Tyldesley and Maclaren, and the
bowling of Brearley and Bosanquet. The Australians, for all the
potential brilliance of their batting, proved as vulnerable in the
Tests as they were mostly unbeatable outside them. Trumper, so
admired in his infancy by Ranji, managed a top score of only 31
in eight innings, Clem Hill averaged only 20, Noble 19.

Sussex, too, had one of their better seasons, winning thirteen matches, losing only four, and finishing third to Yorkshire and Lancashire. Fry, again captain, hit seven hundreds and the bowling of Cox, Killick and Relf came on to such an extent that Cox took 154 wickets, Killick 101 and Relf 98. Ranji was always anxious for news of the goings-on at Hove and at Lord's, and the company of the seventh Lord Hawke, twelve years Ranji's senior, must have been consolation to him.

They went once more to the Gir, and together were fellow guests of the Agent to the Governor of Rajkot, Colonel Kennedy. Jassaji, the Jam Saheb, had also been invited. Kennedy's gesture was certainly intended as an act of conciliation but Jassaji, learning of Ranji's arrival, refused to stay on. He packed his bags and departed in a cloud of dust.

Colonel Kennedy and Ranji had long been friends, Kennedy's official obligations to Jassaji and his loyal support of Viceregal policy notwithstanding. Formalities were strictly preserved between the two in the discussion of all State business.

Lord Hawke set sail for home in the early spring. Soon after his departure news came through from Jamnagar that the Jam Saheb was seriously ill with typhoid. He struggled on for several weeks and then died. He was twenty-four.

Few successions to the throne of Nawanagar had been formalities. Although, in this instance, there were no genuine rivals to Ranji, the Government of India were in no hurry to come to a decision. There was the matter of Jassaji's five widows, a rumour of the time suggesting that one of them might be authorised to adopt an heir.

Neither of Ranji's brothers, Devisinhji and Jawansinhji, the only other survivors of the House of Jam Rawal, showed personal interest in the matter. What, in the circumstances, could have been a simple and logical decision was, however, turned into a long-drawn-out affair by the Agent to the Governor of Bombay, the white-bearded Mr Percy Seymour Fitzgerald.

It was in Fitzgerald's nature to spin out drama. He received deputations, studied documents, filed letters of support. Fitzgerald had long been on close terms with Ranji's family, his father especially. He called in Sir Pertab Singh, another old friend.

Since there was no realistic alternative the succession could quickly have been disposed of. Ranji had already sent in a persuasively-worded petition to the Secretary of State for India. But that was not Fitzgerald's way. While Ranji stayed with his mother at Sarodar he sat on at Rajkot sifting and considering.

During the weeks of waiting Ranji expressed confidence in the outcome in his letters to friends. To Edith Borissow, daughter of his old guardian, he wrote: 'I think I can be certain of sitting on the *gadi*, but I am not altogether certain that I want to . . .'

In due course Fitzgerald announced the result of his deliberations on behalf of his Government. The events that had been set in motion by Jam Vibhaji all those years ago came, after all, to fulfilment. The *joshi* would not have to shut up shop or part with his money.

PART TWO

The Jam Saheb

SIXTEEN

Coming
into his Own

Nobody is forgotten sooner than a famous cricketer, Ranji once observed drily to Charles Fry. It happens not to be true in his case, but from the moment of his succession as Jam Saheb of Nawanagar Ranji did his utmost to bury his fame as a cricketer. It stood, he felt, in the way of his being taken seriously. While other leading men of affairs, when they met him, always wanted to talk cricket, Ranji insisted on talking tariffs.

He was installed at Jamnagar on 10 March 1907, an event the timing of which had been set by the astrologers, Pandit Hareshwar chief among them.

Ranji arrived in a special train from Porbander, accompanied by Fitzgerald. The Rana of Porbander had given a farewell party for him the night before and the Nawab of Junagadh had provided a luxurious saloon. The train steamed in to Jamnagar at exactly half-past six, but it was seven o'clock before the committee of *joshis* decided that it was an auspicious moment for Ranji to emerge. Before he did so, however, high-born Hindu maidens, according to custom, entered the carriage to perform the ceremony of happy augury and welcome.

When Ranji, in silk Durbar dress, jewelled sword belt and thick rope of pearls, finally stepped out, it was to receive the Dewan, Mirwanji, and a line of waiting dignitaries. His elder brother, Devisinhji, was present to witness his frequent garlanding and opposite the station entrance the Jamnagar troops, forming three sides of a square, presented arms. Along the fourth side the elephants flicked their tails under the brilliant carapaces of their howdahs.

The band struck up, and Ranji, advancing to his carriage over a carpet of strewn marigolds and hibiscus, posed for the first of his many photographs as ruler.

The route to the summer palace, chosen after much pondering by the *joshis*, was lined with cheering crowds. Banners and flags fluttered from buildings festooned with shields and arches. Flowers were showered from balconies.

Such was the poverty of the State that almost everything for the celebrations had to be borrowed – carriages, tables, beds, tents, cutlery. Because of the urgency of the preparations – the astrologers had warned, according to the Hindu *sashtras*, against the days between 11 March and 11 May – invitations had to be sent out in a hurry.

Nevertheless, soon after Ranji, having halted to offer prayers at the various temples, had reached his palace, the special trains began to steam in. Among the first batch of arrivals were his old ally Colonel His Highness Maharajah Sir Pratab Singh of Idar, the Maharajahs of Alwar, Jodhpur, Porbander, and Junagadh and the Kumar Manchir Kachhar of Jasdan.

The Nawab of Junagadh provided Ranji with a large staff of Arab guards for his personal safety and his own servants supervised the food. Among the presents pouring in from distant rulers was a horse and sword presented by the Maharao Saheb of Cutch, most senior of all the Rajput Jadeja chiefs.

The Masaheb, Ranji's mother, had already arrived with other members of the family. During the night, with dozens of illuminated and decorated camps laid out on the *maidan*, mantras were chanted by the brahmins and prayers offered in the temples. Princes and their retinues from all over western India continued to arrive, the Thakore Sahib of Bhavnagar, the Maharajahs of Kotah, Rutlam and Sirohi among them. From Ahmedabad came the Gowswamji Maharaj, spiritual leader of the Vaishnavites and of the ruling house of Jamnagar. Telegrams poured in from all his old friends in England. Far into the night Ranji greeted visiting officials, both British and Indian.

Before the formal acts of installation the Pattabhishek ceremonies had to be carried out by the priests in the temple of the Old Palace. Ranji, dressed in the saffron robe of holiness, took his seat on the throne, holy water was sprinkled on his head and the sacred torch waved before him. A holy caste mark was smeared on his forehead and the crown placed on his head.

The installation was due to take place at three-thirty on the next afternoon in a grand *shamiana*, decorated with richly embroidered shawls and carpets, that had been erected outside the palace. For various reasons – the late arrival of trains particularly – it was five o'clock before the guns boomed out the departure of the Agent from the Guest House for the Durbar. At the entrance to the *shamiana* Fitzgerald was greeted by Ranji, who had arrived on an elephant, and the political officers, a salute of thirteen guns were fired and the guard-of-honour, consisting of State troops and Imperial Service Lancers, presented arms. Lavishly caparisoned elephants, bearing gold howdahs, lined the square opposite.

Inside the *shamiana* the jewellery of the assembled princes flashed and glittered. Ranji, never reluctant to dress up, wore a magnificently jewelled sword belt across his shoulder and carried a sword sparkling with precious stones.

The ceremony was simple and to the point, consisting of no more than a speech from Fitzgerald on behalf of the Government of India, the handing over to the new Jam Saheb of the Seal of State and keys to the Treasury, and a reply by Ranji.

Fitzgerald began his speech by referring to Ranji's ancestor, Jam Raysinhji, 'who ruled this state more than 250 years ago and after a brief but brilliant reign met a soldier's death in a battle with Kutubudin at Sheakhput in 1664.' After mentioning other valiant Jadeja forebears, Fitzgerald struck a more personal note:

Times have changed and you have won fame on a more peaceful field. Your reputation as a cricketer and as an athlete is world-wide, but in the making of it you have shown that you possess all the gifts of the fine old Rajput race from which you are descended. I knew your grandfather Jhalamsinhji, whose gallantry at the time of the Wagher rebellion won for him the confidence and favour of Jam Vibhaji and the high considera-tion of the officers of the British Government. I knew your father Jiwantsinhji and esteemed him as the beau ideal of a

Rajput gentleman and I have known you since you were a little boy, ever since you were designated as his heir by Jam Vibhaji. I have seen you tried by sore adversity and have admired the pluck, the patience and the restraint with which you have met it and I have no fear for the future . . . To the instincts of a great ruling race you have added the experience of a man of the world, an experience gained over a wide field in the West and in the East, but your long residence in England and your Western training have never diminished your love for your people and I feel that no Jam ever sat to rule this State better equipped for his task than you are.

Having welcomed Ranji, Fitzgerald went on to offer words of advice. 'I feel there is no need to warn you against the flatterers, intriguers and sycophants.' He referred to the 'ten sad years of plague, pestilence and famine' but also to the fertile lands, the pearl fishery and the harbours. 'It will behove you in the present financial circumstances of the State to proceed with caution at first, but as your means permit you should extend your railway towards Dwarka; irrigation, forestry and the development of the magnificent harbour which you have at Salaya should claim your attention; and you should be strong to maintain and lose no opportunity of extending the reforms which were inaugurated during the period that the State was under the direct administration of the British Government.'

This last was the only reference to the period between Jam Vibhaji's death and Ranji's accession. Fitzgerald concluded: 'Here your subjects acclaim you, throughout the Native States of India the tidings will be received with great joy and nothing but the shortness of the notice has prevented an assembly of chiefs in this Durbar such as has never been seen in Kathiawar before. While in England where you lived so long there will be thousands who will rejoice that 'Ranji' has come into his own.'

Ranji was conducted to the Chair of State, and when he was seated a salute of eleven guns was fired. Ranji, in the course of his graceful speech of reply, turned directly to the Agent: 'To you, Mr Fitzgerald, I can hardly express how deeply thankful I feel, you being my life-long friend from my childhood and it is a strange coincidence, showing the divine hand therein, that it was you who was the Prant Officer at the time of my adoption by His Highness the Jam Shree Vibhaji, by which act my position and status was changed from that of a son of a Bhayad to that of heir to the *gadi*, and that it is you who now, as the head of the province, are carrying out, as it were, the final step that ought to come out of that act.'

Ranji ended: 'I hope to abide by the traditions of this State, in its deep, unswerving loyalty to the British throne, in which I could not have a better example to look up to than my friend, the famous Sir Pratab Singh, the Maharajah Saheb of Idar.'

By the next morning the *shamiana* had been dismantled, the tents folded. The same special trains that had borne so many rulers and guests to Jamnagar two days before departed, carrying them and their entourages back to their territories.

When all the flags and tributes of welcome had been put away Ranji was left, for the first time, to contemplate his capital, a disease-ridden, squalid and dusty city.

SEVENTEEN

A Thirsty Land

Ranji's territories extended to 3,791 square miles, roughly the equivalent of three English counties. The population was in the region of 350,000, distributed over four hundred villages, and the gross revenue twenty-one lakhs, the equivalent of £140,000. Some years later J. A. Spender, visiting India as the special correspondent of the *Westminster Gazette*, described Nawanagar in these terms:

> It is not a territory, like a stretch of green and smiling English countryside, where the rain falls plentiful and one crop or another is sure; it is during nine months of the year a great brown waste with a few oases in it, and but for an incessant struggle to conserve its scanty water, might fall back into desert and famine. I can imagine a painter thinking its landscape delightful; the faint blue hills to the east, the rolling plains, the dark green mangrove plantations in the salt marshes, and the line of sea beyond give an exhilarating sense of space, colour and atmosphere. But one can see at a glance that it is a thirsty land.

The thirst of the land was only one of the many immediate problems facing the Jam Saheb. Jam Vibhaji, for all his wisdom and virtues, had been an extravagant ruler and the effects of his open-handedness lingered on. The Government Service was hopelessly corrupt; large grants annually made their way into the pockets of eunuchs and dancing girls, the descendants of favoured concubines; and the maze of narrow streets and bazaars that constituted Jamnagar continued to breed every known disease.

Ranji was never happier than when there were new schemes to

be launched or elaborate entertainments to be devised. There was little money for either in his first years, but he set at once to eradicating wasteful expenditure and to preparing plans for a new and cleaner city.

The eunuchs, who had acquired large tracts of State land and whose main function was to repel evil spirits on State occasions, were expelled. Since they represented both power and wealth this was an act that required courage. The dancing girls' inherited pensions were stopped. The Khawas of Amran, an over-ambitious and unscrupulous landowner in the north who had opposed Ranji's accession and continued to harass him, was bought out.

These, however, were minor affairs. Ranji's long-term plans included the razing of Old Jamnagar, so that light and air could be let in; the suppression of rabies, widely prevalent owing to the hordes of pariah dogs; and the establishment of a proper system of irrigation so that when rain did fall it could be contained. In due course he succeeded in all three aims.

Fitzgerald, in his installation address, had referred to the pearl fisheries, the extending of the railway system, and the development of the port. These projects became increasingly dear to Ranji's heart and as time went on occupied him disproportionately.

Before Ranji could do much more than set plans in motion he himself was struck down by typhoid. Rumours exist today that Jassaji, like so many previous Jams, died of poison, but whether he did so or not, typhoid and cholera were raging in Jamnagar and continued to do so long after his death.

Ranji was ill for several months, and more than once seemed to be losing his battle. He was removed from Jamnagar, first to Bombay, then to Poona, where Colonel Child, of the India Medical Service, took charge of him. The Masaheb rarely left his side. Ranji wrote in a letter to a friend during his convalescence, 'I woke up one night to find her praying beside me and I knew that I had been drawn back into life.'

All that first summer Ranji languished, unable to walk. In the early autumn he was pushed about the slopes and squares of Poona, fretting to return home. When he did so he was frail and weak, and three stone lighter.

The most pressing task on his return to Sarodar was the treatment of sewage. Ranji did all he could to supervise essential health-work but it was soon clear he himself had not properly recovered. Despite his protests his doctors insisted on six months out of India and a rest from all State involvements.

In the middle of October Ranji sailed with his younger brother and other members of his family for England. Arriving in November, after yet another of those long sea voyages he so disliked, he fell ill again. For the whole pre-Christmas season he could do little more than sit in his hotel room or potter about the Bond Street shops to which he was mesmerically drawn. He visited Purdey, from whom he was later to buy all his guns and ammunition, and Cartier, with whose advice he started a collection of jewels that was to rival the best in India.

To Ranji's immense pleasure he was given a formal audience at Buckingham Palace. After Christmas, having lavishly entertained all his old cricketing friends, he left for Sussex where he had rented Lord Winterton's house, Shillinglee Park. In London there had been plays by Granville-Barker, Maugham, Galsworthy, Barrie, Synge; Mrs Patrick Campbell, Ellen Terry, Marie Tempest, and Gladys Cooper were among those he had seen on the stage.

At Shillinglee he gradually came back to health. He rented additional shoots, re-stocked the lake with trout, laid a cricket pitch. Soon all thoughts of returning to Jamnagar in the spring had disappeared. He received reassuring messages from his Dewan Saheb and from the Agent. It was not surprising, therefore, that instead of spending the next few months on the baking plains of Kathiawar, Ranji should have chosen to stay on in the lush Sussex countryside. By the middle of May he felt able to practise in the nets and later that month Grace brought a side to play some high-class but light-hearted country house cricket at Shillinglee.

Ranji was having his portrait painted at the time by Henry Scott Tuke – a picture that hung in the 1909 Academy exhibition – and during the weekend of the match Tuke did a portrait of Grace wearing a scarlet puggaree belonging to Ranji.

The warm weather, the good company and the exercise put Ranji in a frame of mind to try his luck once more for the county.

He was thirty-six and had not played in a first-class match for nearly four years.

It was scarcely to be expected that Ranji would at once slip back into his old form. Initially, he was most concerned to show he was worth his place. 'He played what might be described as an orthodox game,' *Wisden* observed, 'being very sparing with the daring strokes on the leg side which at one time drove even the best bowlers to despair. . . . His defence was as perfect as ever but after the loss of three seasons he could not trust himself to run the old risks with good-length bowling.'

Ranji's first appearance for the county was against Kent on 8 June. He received a tremendous ovation when he went out to bat but he was soon back in the pavilion for 3. He did rather better in the second innings, batting fluently for 29.

From Hove, Sussex went up to Lord's and there, where it had rarely failed, the old magic returned. Sussex batted first and at close of play Ranji, going in at number six, was 141 not out; 'an innings full of beautiful hits.' He scored 78 in the second innings, so it was with few misgivings that he returned to Shillinglee.

Sussex in their next match met Essex at Horsham and Ranji was made captain. There was little play owing to rain, but a week later Ranji made 17 and 15 at Hove against Cambridge. He missed Sussex's next four matches, at Gloucester, Portsmouth, Old Trafford and Huddersfield, but returned on 13 July for the Somerset game at Hove. He batted solidly for 33 before taking a number of the team back to Shillinglee to stay. His old friend Fry, who only played in eight matches that summer, was of the party.

The next match, due to start on the following day at Chichester, got Ranji into some trouble. The rain streamed down all Thursday, but on the Friday morning, though it was still pelting twenty miles away at Shillinglee, play seemed briefly possible. The Hampshire side were all present, but only two Sussex players were on the ground. Before any decision could be taken it began to rain again. Fry and Vine turned up about noon and the rest, including Ranji, between three and four.

The match got under way on the Saturday and Ranji made 51. But a report had to be sent to Lord's and a rebuke was administered.

The weather improved and back at Hove Ranji, after making only 1 in the first innings, batted sleekly to take 44 off a strong Lancashire attack.

This was the start of a golden week, for on the following day Ranji batted gloriously for 87 against Worcestershire and then, at the weekend, batted for five and three-quarter hours at the Oval – once so unlucky a ground for him – to make 200.

Satisfied with his form and his stamina, Ranji returned to Shillinglee. He took a month off in all, fishing, shooting and entertaining. He travelled up to Gilling to see the Borissows and took part in a charity match, in aid of the bell-tower clock, bringing with him a number of famous cricketers. The money was raised and a month later Ranji went north again to start the clock himself. 'Very appropriate,' a lady parishioner remarked drily. 'They've both got gold hands and a black face.' More innocently, a countrywoman was heard to remark: 'Fancy! A Christian clock started by a heathen.' The Gilling Church clock is known today as 'The Christian Clock'.

In the last week of August he was ready for a final fling at Hove. Unfortunately the weather ruined Yorkshire's visit but in his single innings against Gloucestershire Ranji made a relaxed and entertaining 29.

In all he played ten matches for Sussex, averaging 65.09 and making 716 runs. Fry, who with Ranji was a long way ahead of the other Sussex batsmen, scored 589 at an average of 59.80. *Wisden* compared the two to the stars of an opera company, achieving brilliant individual performances but not greatly helping the *ensemble*. It was probably a fair criticism.

Outside the county matches Ranji played twice for the Gentlemen, at Lord's and the Oval in July, batting well enough to make 20 and 6 at Lord's, 19 and 47 at the Oval. There was ill-feeling that neither Ranji nor Fry was asked to captain the Gentlemen at Lord's, P. F. Warner being given the job.

Probably Ranji's most characteristic innings of the season was his last. He went up to Scarborough during the September Festival and scored a marvellous 101 in his best vein for Lord Londesborough's England eleven v. MCC's Australian eleven.

Ranji had not batted at Scarborough since 1894 and he received a tremendous ovation. Blythe, Crawford, Braund and Rhodes were among the MCC bowlers and Ranji, conscious of the huge crowd that had turned up especially to see him, glanced, cut and improvised as of old.

When the first-class averages were published later in the month Ranji appeared in sixth place, averaging 45.5, only Bosanquet, Fry, H. K. Foster, Hayward and Warner being above him.

Ranji determined to spend the autumn at Shillinglee before returning to Jamnagar. Photographs of the time show him contented and in good spirits, fishing from a punt in the lake, behind the wheel of his new car, at the head of large dinner parties.

On 19 October he was the guest of honour at a second Cambridge banquet. Among the hundred and fifty guests were England and Sussex cricketers, including W. G. Grace, dons, scientists, politicians and local dignitaries. Most of the speeches centred on cricket but Ranji, when his turn came, effected a change of mood. Something had upset him during the preceding weeks, causing him to write to a friend: 'I have had a great holiday but not so much freedom as I would have liked. And there are things which simply turn one inside out, and sour our hearts. As an Indian loyal to the Crown, I regret this beyond measure.'

Now, after a genial opening to his speech, he introduced an unexpectedly defensive note: 'When you read from day to day that there are malcontents in England, might I not make an apology for the malcontents in India? But there is one thing I would like to point out, merely as my own suggestion. I think that the British Empire should treat all British subjects alike. The doors to Indian peoples have unfortunately been shut in Australia, and in Canada and South Africa. I cannot but regret it, and I think that the home Government ought to try and make out some scheme by which Indians could give their labour and trade in our colonies. I honestly believe that the present agitation arose, not so much from any dislike of the British Government, because they saw from the Government peace, progress and prosperity, but when people got no employment they were apt, as in this country, to brew mischief.'

Ranji ended up: 'I leave England with a sorrowful heart. But I am starting a new career with this one idea – to do my duty to my country and my people, to uphold the honour of my house and my race, to maintain the unity of our common Empire, and to show unswerving loyalty to the Sovereign.'

No imperialist could have spoken plainer and yet the mystery remains. What particular incident – unless it was the anti-Indian legislation in the Transvaal, the 'Black Act' that resulted in the imprisonment of Gandhi – touched him that autumn on a raw spot?

He was back in Jamnagar for Christmas. He had been away a year and a month.

Restored in health, Ranji set about the work that had been interrupted by his illness. Probably he was well enough to have returned in September, but what are a few weeks in the eternal fight against the Indian climate, Indian poverty and Indian disease?

Once back, he quickly got down to business. Street by street, as tactfully as he could manage, he opened up the old city. He laid out new roads. He waged war on the hordes of dacoits that roamed Kathiawar pillaging and terrorising. He ordered work to be begun on the extension of the railway to Dwarka, so that the annual Hindu pilgrimage to the shrine of Krishna could be made in safety. He put in hand the construction of a pier at Rozi so that Nawanagar could have its own port and a distribution centre for exports.

It was an altogether more austere and spartan Ranji who began to emerge. He made occasional shooting expeditions into the Gir, he played some cricket on the pitch he had laid outside the palace grounds, now and again he went fishing. Mostly, though, he was at his desk dealing with State work and receiving visitors, or travelling the country inspecting and supervising. The most urgent task of all, the digging of wells throughout the State, he made the highest priority.

It was inevitable that Ranji, with his experience of sophisticated modern cities, would not be satisfied with what he had found in Jamnagar. He was a natural town planner and if he lacked the immediate resources to build a beautiful capital he had the ideas. Tree-lined boulevards and crescents were laid out, with vistas of hitherto concealed temples; lakes were constructed and public gardens created. Modern markets on wide streets began to replace the congested, disease-ridden bazaars.

In 1911, the monsoon that in normal years only just touched Kathiawar, failed to materialise at all. In a whole year the rainfall amounted to no more than three inches. Following the drought came famine, one of the worst in the history of the State. Only by halting all schemes for improvement and requesting a huge loan was Ranji able to relieve the distress of his people.

1911 was also the year of the Delhi Durbar. It seems, in the light of such appalling conditions in Jamnagar, frivolity bordering on the callous that Ranji should have thought it necessary to compete with far wealthier fellow-princes in lavishness of hospitality, the exchange of gifts, and magnificence of appearance. But Rajput pride deemed that in the City of Tents the oyster-shell outline of that of Jamnagar should be as dazzling as any other.

'He drove to the Durbar,' Roland Wild wrote, 'in a silver coach, and jewels flashed in his raiment, in his sword belt, on the hilt of the thrusting dagger which had rested at Jam Rawal's side . . . His emblem floated bravely in the wind, and on the shield of State there were the historic symbols of Jamnagar – a fish, token of esteem when given by a friendly neighbour; a galley, denoting a State on the seaboard; a lion, denoting loyalty to the British throne; and antelopes as supporters to the shield.'

The splendour of Ranji's entourage and entertaining rebounded on him. The Government of India, anxious over the extent of the loans received by Ranji on both counts – welfare and pageantry – insisted on the appointment of a financial adviser.

Ranji was hurt. He believed himself the victim of prejudice and envy. 'Injustice,' he wrote, 'is felt as keenly by princes as by peasants.'

He was advised to economise and build out of revenue. But the famine had wiped out most of the revenue. The Gaekwad of Baroda offered him money but the Bombay Government declined to guarantee the loan.

The pearl fisheries in his own State, to whose development he had given much care, came to the rescue. As the greatly increased income from these started to roll in, Ranji was able to resume some of the schemes that had been launched so hopefully three years earlier. Drains were laid, slums pulled down, work on the wells re-started.

With the Indian cold weather over and the prospect of another burning season under the Kathiawar sun ahead of him, Ranji sailed again for England. Isolated in Jamnagar, he had begun to feel the need of old friends, of a more soothing climate. Perhaps he was missing cricket. It had been three years since he had picked up a bat, driven through green lanes, or sat by a trout stream.

Sussex, now under the captaincy of H. P. Chaplin, had not fared well in Ranji's absence. 1911 had been a particularly poor season. In 1912, the year of the Triangular Tournament, both the Australians and the South Africans were in England. The tournament, in which each country played three Tests against each of the others, was won by England, who had only recently returned from winning four consecutive Tests in Australia under the captaincy of J. W. H. T. Douglas.

It was as wet a summer as any Ranji had encountered in his heyday. Nevertheless, he was soon re-installed at the Norfolk in Brighton and practising assiduously at the Hove nets, or at Lord's. Fry, unfortunately, was going to be absent most of the summer captaining England, with Hobbs and Rhodes opening the batting in Test matches, and Barnes and Foster the bowling.

For Ranji it was a challenge batting against bowlers he only knew by repute and a pleasure watching the advance in batsmanship made by such as Spooner, Hobbs and Woolley. Fry, describing Hobbs that summer, wrote: 'He sailed along through sunshine and storm on a perfectly even keel with an alert pair of aristocratic hands on the helm of the game. His quiet gentility disguises a thoroughly resolute and pugnacious subsoil of temperament.'

Despite the damp Ranji was in action on 23 May, captaining Sussex for the occasion against Derbyshire at Hove and making 33 in an eight-wicket Sussex victory.

Ranji, now nearly forty and plump, made no attempt this summer to become a regular member of the side. But, picking his matches carefully, mostly at Hove, he showed better form than he had done four years earlier. At Hove, on 13 June, he hit up 128 in three and a half hours against Kent, before being stumped off Woolley. A fortnight later he made a duck at Hove against Leicestershire, but followed this with 101 against Cambridge at Lord's.

Ranji sprained his wrist in this match and was never free of discomfort for the rest of the season. This did not stop him from taking 176 off the Lancashire bowling and 125 off an Australian attack that included none of his old adversaries.

It was during this latter innings that Ranji, growing bored with scoring so easily, nominated in advance what strokes he would play and where the ball would go – glances to Kelleway's left hand at long leg and then to his right, cuts on either side of Bardsley at third man, cover drives, any stroke he fancied.

His partner was P. G. H. Fender, a comparative newcomer to the Sussex side. In his biography of Fender, Richard Streeton quotes Fender as saying to him: 'It did not last long; he was soon tired of his fun and games, but it was incredible to me at the time and still is. I had always been told he could do anything with a bat if you got him interested.'

Ranji batted most of that summer with his wrist in bandages. He found it harder to concentrate than before and after a few elegant, airy strokes seemed content to lose his wicket. Twice he played for the Gentlemen, making 6 and 55 at Lord's, 24 and 42 at the Oval. At Lord's in the second innings he batted less than an hour; at the Oval he struggled an hour over eight, challenged by the conditions and the bowling.

In all, Ranji batted 28 times in first-class matches. He scored 1,113 runs at an average of 42, putting him sixth to Fry in the national averages. For Sussex he batted eleven times, averaging 50.36. Joe Vine was next, with an average of 32.

Each time it was known Ranji was going to play, large crowds turned up to see him bat. There could only be glimpses in the Jam

Saheb's play of that earlier magnetic Ranji, slight and silken, who made bowlers despair over a whole decade. But to those who had never seen him in his prime, as much as for those who remembered the mastery of the great years, the presence was enough.

At the end of the season A. G. Gardiner wrote in the *Daily News*: 'We have said farewell to cricket. We have said farewell, too, to cricket's king. The game will come again with the spring and the new grass and the burgeoning trees. But the king will come no more. For the Jam Saheb is forty, and, alas, the Jam Saheb is fat. And the temple bells are calling him back to his princely duties amid the sunshine, and the palm trees, and the spicy garlic smells of Nawanagar. No more shall we see him tripping down the pavilion steps, his face wreathed in chubby smiles . . . '

It was Gardiner who coined the phrase 'the prince of a little State, but the king of a great game'. He concluded: 'I think it is undeniable that as a batsman the Indian will live as the supreme exponent of the Englishman's game . . . It is the Jam Saheb's service that, through his genius for the English game, he has familiarised the English people with the idea of the Indian as a man of like affections with ourselves, and with capacities beyond ours in directions supposed to be peculiarly our own . . . He goes back to his own people – to the little State that he recovered so romantically, and governs as a good liberal should govern – and the holiday crowds will see him no more. But his name will live in the hearts of hundreds of thousands of British people, to whom he has given happy days and happy memories.'

'There can be no possible description of his batting,' observed Lord Hawke. 'It must have been seen to be realised.' W. G. Grace, in the speech he made at Ranji's Cambridge banquet, ended up: 'I assure you that you will never see a batsman to beat the Jam Saheb if you live for a hundred years.' *Wisden* remarked: 'From 1895–1912 – with two breaks of four years each – he was the most talked-of man in cricket.'

Ranji did not return immediately to Jamnagar. In the autumn, in a party that included Lord Lamington, Lord Beatty and Lord Londesborough, the Marquis of Bute and Lord George Campbell, he shot with the King at Balmoral. The coloured photograph of the occasion, tattered and faded, still hangs in the gallery at Jamnagar. He spent some weeks at Gilling, recovering from a chest infection, then re-rented his old rooms at Cambridge.

Shortly before sailing for India Ranji spent £30,000 on a riverside house at Staines, Thorncote, belonging to Sir Edward Clarke KC. It would come in more handy than he knew.

EIGHTEEN

War

His serious cricket-playing days over, once and for all, the resourcefulness and ingenuity that Ranji had displayed as a batsman went into the administration of his State. Its growth and development under his eyes were some kind of substitute for the children he never had. Whatever the truth concerning Ranji's alleged engagement to a Rajput princess in his youth, he showed no signs, at any stage of his life, of considering marriage. He liked the company of women – and indeed had a discreet and long-standing relationship with an English girl – but in Jamnagar, officially, he was on his own.

Ranji was greatly helped in the ordering of financial matters by his employment of an old friend, Colonel Berthon, lately of the political service. Berthon was able to introduce proper supervision of income and expenditure as well as modern methods of accounting. Dealings that had been, in former days, haphazardly conducted were put on a business-like footing, and if Ranji's schemes continued to be costly, the State was at least being economically run.

Late in December Ranji had his first State visitor, the Maharajah of Patiala, son of the Maharajah with whom he had stayed on his return from Australia. As usual he threw himself into the most elaborate preparations for his entertainment, incurring once again displeasure from the financial advisers.

Ranji happened to be in Bombay in August when news came through of the declaration of war. Lord Hardinge, then Viceroy, received from the King a telegram which ended: 'Had I stood aside when, in defiance of the pledges to which my Government was a party, the soil of Belgium was violated and her cities laid desolate, when the very life of the French nation was threatened with extinction, I should have sacrificed my honour and given to destruction the liberties of my Empire and of mankind . . . I recall to mind India's gracious message to the British nation of goodwill and fellowship which greeted my return in February 1912 after the solemn ceremony of my Coronation Durbar at Delhi, and I find in this hour of trial a full harvest and a noble fulfilment of the assurance given by you that the destinies of Great Britain and India are indissolubly linked.'

The response of the Indian princes was immediate and generous. Never slow to take up arms on provocation, they identified spontaneously with the British cause on the Western Front. Four years earlier Lord Sydenham, ex-Governor of Bombay, had addressed the princes and chiefs in Durbar at Rajkot, and Ranji, in his reply, had said: 'If ever the need arises for the display of our martial valour we would consider it a high honour and privilege to fight shoulder to shoulder with the British army in maintaining intact this great Empire and its glorious and untarnished name. The Rajputs have still the old fighting spirit burning within their breast, whether they be clad in the sombre raiments of the West or the luxurious silks of the East.'

Within two days of the declaration of war, Ranji had offered the Viceroy all the resources, both of men and material, that the State could provide.

On 31 August a public meeting was convened in Jamnagar and presided over by Ranji. He explained the events that had led up to war and the importance of Indian cooperation. Committees were set up to arrange for donations of money, provisions and equipment.

Germany had counted on Indian reluctance to play an effective part but the Maharajah of Bikaner and other ruling chiefs immediately offered personal service at the head of their armies. Ranji, on behalf of Nawanagar, announced a whole series of contributions. As well as cash donations to various funds they included the services of the Nawanagar State Imperial Service Lancers fully equipped; six large double-poled tents for field hospitals; one ambulance motor car for use in Bombay; the house in Staines, fitted with beds for forty-five, for use as a hospital for officers; every horse and motorcar in the State.

On 16 November Ranji himself left Jamnagar, having handed over control to Berthon. He was initially to be attached to the staff of General Cookson as an Honorary Major but before long word came through that he was to join Field Marshal Sir John French as ADC.

On the ship to England were Inniskilling Dragoon Guards. 'They were a great education to me,' Ranji was to write from France. He was anxious to be of practical value himself but remarked in the same letter, 'I am almost afraid there is a tendency to treat my presence as an encumbrance . . . I fear that my cars are more useful than myself. If, however, I am still regarded as a tin soldier, it is not my fault, and I shall regard myself as unfortunate.'

Soldiering suited Ranji. 'I feel I have missed my vocation,' he wrote. 'I think when I return I shall miss things very much, and I shall never neglect my duty towards my Lancers – provided Government will give them a few serviceable rifles instead of the present firewood sticks.'

Ranji, in common with other Indian princes, was left kicking his heels. 'All the chiefs are complaining. Bikaner is sick of doing nothing,' he wrote. The weather was appalling, and Ranji suffered badly from asthma as well as chilblains. 'We had an inspection by the C-in-C the other day and it was very cold. I felt and looked like a cotton bale with all my warm kit, clothing and overcoats on.'

Altogether Ranji remained on the Western Front just over a year. He did a machine-gun course and had in mind to learn to fly. A number of Indians found conditions so intolerable they discovered reasons to return home. 'I think Maharajah Pratab Singh and I will be the only ones to go right through, if illness, bomb, or bullet does not lay us low,' Ranji wrote to Berthon.

As predicted by Pandit Hareshwar, who foretold safe return but some form of mutilation for Ranji, a bullet did lay him low, but it was a bullet from the gun of a Yorkshire squire, not a German bullet.

During the summer of 1915, on sick leave from France, Ranji took a party of friends up to Crosscliff, near Filey in Yorkshire, for some shooting. Edith Borissow was present, and Dr Heasman, from Sussex; the Maharajah of Rutlam was prevented from attending by toothache.

On the first morning Ranji was hit in the right eye by his neighbour, a notoriously erratic shot, who followed down the line. Edith Borissow, in the butt with Ranji, had only just missed being peppered earlier and it was in protecting her that Ranji received his own wound. Ranji continued to shoot until the end of the drive. 'It may interest you to know,' he wrote to Berthon, 'that after the accident I continued shooting from the left shoulder, and shot ten birds out of twelve shots.'

He was whisked away, blood pouring from his face, to the infirmary at Leeds, having walked three miles to his car. Three days later the decision was made to extract his right eye. By Ranji's express wish the name of the man responsible for his wound, a Mr Fisher, was kept secret. To allay suspicion Ranji invited the man to be his guest the next time he went shooting.

The affair got into the papers and Ranji received a letter of sympathy from the King. Within weeks, with a black patch over his eye, he was shooting again. Few people realised the extent of the damage. But for ever after he wore a glass eye and carried spectacles.

Ranji was anxious to return to the Front, the more so since the number of renegade princes was increasing. For himself he found military life 'a great brotherhoood, a real freemasonry'. In June he had presented the Kathiawar State's fleet of motor ambulances to the King and ten days later his house at Staines was opened by General Sir O'Moore Creagh, late Commander-in-Chief, India, as the Prince of Wales Hospital for Wounded Officers.

These events were matters of some pride to Ranji, who, although present at the bombardment of Neuve Chapelle and frequently accompanying his general up the line, felt that he was really only there on sufferance. In truth, his health made him unfit for trench warfare. He was ill, from bronchitis and asthma, more often than not.

He was especially anxious to return to front-line duties after the
accident. The suffering of the Indian syces in the cold and wind of
the previous winter had horrified him and he wanted to share their
suffering as much as he could.

He was prevented from doing so by the forthcoming marriage
of his younger sister to the eighteen-year-old Maharajah of
Jodhpur. Both Ranji and Sir Pratab Singh, who was Regent of
Jodhpur, had pleaded for the postponement of the wedding until
after the war. For some reason the Viceroy insisted that it go
ahead and that Ranji should return to supervise the arrangements.

It seems improbable that such considerations should have
prevailed, but they did. Before sailing for India in November
Ranji wrote a long letter to Berthon describing his accident and
the loss of his eye. 'Of course I should have loved to have lost it
or any part of my body in France, but such opportunities are
denied us serving princes who are not allowed to take risks,
although I took the opportunity to get right there. One consolation of this unfortunate episode is that I kept absolute control
of myself and behaved in a manner you would like a friend of yours
to behave, and worthy, I hope, of a Rajput, and in a manner my
mother would wish me to act in like circumstances . . . I am perfectly cheerful and resigned, and according to my religious beliefs
(which have given me great consolation) my sins (whatever they
may have been) have been duly atoned for in *this* life by this
punishment.'

Berthon's letters from Jamnagar had been worrying. The
Government was demanding further economies at a time when
the State was contributing everything it could, in both money and
resources, to the war effort. They renewed complaints about the
famine loan and the Delhi Durbar extravagances. Worst of all, the
Government were set on a special inquiry being set up into the
State finances.

Ranji expressed himself, in almost child-like fashion, unable to
understand their attitude. He was able to countenance mild re-
proofs from Berthon himself. 'Your warm friendship has enabled
me to conquer myself of my own weaknesses, and I am not going
to give you further anxiety on account of my propensity for *objets*

d'art.' But he railed against Government supervision or inter-
ference of any kind.

Ranji himself had accepted a drop in income from £2,000 a
month in 1907 to £800 a month after the 1911 famine. But soon
after his expressions of reform to Berthon he was reporting the
purchase of several carriages from Tattersalls: 'They were dirt
cheap, and were for a six in hand. I also bought three Victorias,
a big State carriage for £5, and a State landau.'

He sold some pearls to make up for it.

Despite Ranji's wish for the wedding to be celebrated in keeping
with circumstances it was inevitably a drain on resources already
heavily depleted by contributions to the war. He applied, therefore, for a loan of £15,000.

This he received, though it was granted reluctantly. The wedding went off in fine, Rajput style and Ranji restored his spirits by
shooting over Christmas at Bikaner with such effectiveness that
no one who did not already know realised the extent of his handicap. Before leaving London he had bought from Purdey's two
pairs of guns, one 20-bore, one 16-bore, all stocked cross-eyed,
that is to say, for the right shoulder but left eye. He had ordered
twenty-nine thousand shotgun cartridges to be shipped out from
Tilbury before sailing.

Lord Willingdon, Governor of Bombay, visited Jamnagar early
in 1916. He was able, on this visit, to perform the opening cere-
money of what was to be called Willingdon Crescent, the elegant
and traffic-free centre-piece of Ranji's reconstructed capital. Even
now, over sixty years later, when inevitably cows and bullock
carts have wandered back into the roadways, this part of commercial Jamnagar has an orderly grace rare in Indian cities. One
has only to compare photographs of pre- and post-Ranji Jamnagar
to realise the extent of his improvements.

Ranji took pains to open up vistas and widen alleyways so that
the old buildings, hitherto masked, could be appreciated: the
Jumma Musjid, with its massive walls, domes and minarets, its
sandalwood doors inlaid with mother-of-pearl; the soaring con-
fectionary turrets and humps of the Jain and Kashi Visvanath

temples; the two round lakeside forts, the Lakhota and Khota with their painted narrative chambers; the solid magnificence of the Khambalia Gate.

It is from the Lakhota battlements that the initial concept of Jamnagar can best be realised; a fortified and walled coastal city, floating in calm waters that, at dawn and sunset, turn the same pink as the flamingos that haunt the surrounding countryside. Ranji applied western principles to the treatment of urban problems, but no one could mistake Jamnagar, with its teeming spice markets and brilliant silken bazaars, for anything but Indian.

In his speech of welcome to Lord Willingdon Ranji began by describing to him the conception of his new capital: the removal of the Matwas and their two thousand head of cattle from the temple precincts to a site outside the walls; the aiming of straight roads from the twelve gateways in the city wall into a central circle. He continued: 'The crescent before us thus marks the beginning of a project which aims at making the city habitable and beautiful and nothing has given me greater pleasure than the feeling it will bear the honoured and beloved name of a Governor who has already earned in an uncommon degree the love and gratitude of the princes and people of this Presidency by an exceptionally sympathetic and just administration and who, besides, happens to be my friend of old Cambridge and Sussex days . . .'

Lord Lloyd, visiting Jamnagar some years later, was to state without undue flattery, 'I can sincerely say that in no city in the Bombay Presidency has there been carried out so bold and so well-considered a scheme of town planning as that which we have seen in Jamnagar. I congratulate your Highness on having so skilfully preserved every good characteristic of an Indian town while eliminating from it the grave defects of congestion and bad sanitation which are so often blended with the picturesque. It is a pleasure to see the beauty of Indian handicraft in stone and wood carvings so freely utilised . . .'

1916 was in other ways an unhappy year for Ranji; the Masaheb, to whom he had become increasingly close, died in the spring. Ranji tried to console himself in the Gir Forest, reporting in a letter that there were over 150 lions there.

There were also the usual problems on the financial front. Although Ranji had managed to pay back over half the accumullated loans requested after the famine and the Durbar, he was obliged once more to go cap in hand.

This time the terms offered were such as to make Ranji pause: they were that, as a condition of any loan, Berthon, due shortly for retirement, was to be appointed financial adviser and administrator. This was what Ranji had already considered him to be, but he felt it was one thing for him to do the appointing and quite another to have it imposed upon him.

He wrote, in hurt and protesting tones, to Berthon, with whom he had always enjoyed a warm and companionable relationship. Few letters from government agencies on the subject of money are ever tactfully composed and Ranji, always susceptible to taking offence, was deeply wounded.

In the end both his pride and his pocket were saved by the weather. The monsoon rains were so plentiful that before the loan needed to be finalised, Ranji was able to inform the Governor in person that it was no longer needed. Nevertheless, the humiliation rankled. In any such situation, where the colonial power controls the purse strings and the subject princes are proud, it could hardly be otherwise. The principle apart, Ranji was well aware of Berthon's services. 'Berthon's work furnished the turning point in our prosperity,' he wrote to the Secretary of State for India.

He was helped, too, by another record monsoon in 1917, when forty inches of rain – nearly double the average – fell on Kathiawar. In March of that year Ranji was invested by the Viceroy, Lord Chelmsford, in Delhi with the KCSI, the first of several awards by the British Government. On his way home, at Alwar, he shot a panther from an elephant at three hundred yards.

In 1917, too, the removal of the Viramgam customs line that had been an obstacle to the development of the Nawanagar ports reopened Ranji's interest in them. The Government, for once, approved and within a decade work begun in 1917 on the fine deepwater harbour of Bedi, linking it by lighter and tug to the natural roadstead of Rozi, was to pay huge dividends. Railway sidings and warehouses, docks and piers, canals and approach roads were added as money became available. What had once been a ramshackle and muddy sea-entrance to Kathiawar was turned into a port handsome enough for international shipping lines, such as Clan, Anchor and Hansa, to make use of it.

Before the end of the war the last of the villages had been assessed, the old 'Bhag Batai' system of barter changed into a cash system, with farmers assured of permanent tenancy, rights of transfer and inheritance.

Ranji was offered a post on Sir Douglas Haig's staff but there was no real prospect of his returning to France. His nephew, Lieutenant K. S. Dajiraj, one of three nephews serving overseas, was killed in September on the Western Front, and Savaisinhji, another, who had just received a permanent commission in the Indian Army, was wounded when serving with the 13th Rajputs in East Africa. 'I envy them both,' Ranji wrote, 'Dajiraj and Savaisinhji, one killed, one wounded.'

Instead, a task entirely suited to his organisational talents, Ranji was put in charge of arrangements for a banquet in Delhi to welcome home the three Indian representatives from the Imperial War Cabinet. Three hundred guests were invited, most of them ruling princes, and an occasion of great splendour, attended by the Viceroy and his staff, went off without a hitch.

In the New Year's Honours Ranji was appointed GBE, promoted Lieutenant Colonel and granted a salute of fifteen guns. He was made permanent President of the Princes' Committee, campaigning tirelessly on behalf of Indian troops overseas. 'If India stints at the present moment,' Ranji observed in a speech in Bombay, 'and does not give of her best, we will not deserve to be a nation, and the judgment of history will go against us for ever . . . Shall we stand at the door haggling over the price of our assistance, some sort of exchange for what we give? Shall we be asking for a barter and naming a return for our services?'

That had never been Ranji's way as a cricketer and whatever the slights, imagined or otherwise, he received from the Government, it was not his way now. The Indian contribution, never sufficiently appreciated, was a magnificent one and, in proportion to its resources, no State contributed more than Ranji's own.

Sadly, for Ranji the fruitful years – years in which crops were plentiful, reservoirs began to be constructed, wells dug – were followed by one so bad that it virtually undid all the good. The summer of 1918 resulted in a famine in Jamnagar no less severe than that of 1911. This in turn was succeeded by an influenza epidemic that killed twenty-two thousand in a year.

The irrigation schemes were intensified and speeded up, and in February 1919 the Ganga Sagar tank, on a site seven miles from Jamnagar and with a catchment area of 106 square miles, was opened by the Maharajah of Bikaner, only recently returned from the Versailles Peace Conference. From that time on, whatever hardships the seasons inflicted on Jamnagar, there would never be drought or famine on anything like the same scale.

Railways, particularly to the ports, for some years took priority over roads, but once the war was over Ranji set about linking the main villages and sites of Kathiawar – historical, archaeological, sporting – with Jamnagar. Ranji, his fourteen high-powered State cars still in the hands of the Indian Army, drove about in an ancient two-seater, supervising operations.

There were obligations for Ranji outside the State as well as in it. As one of the four princes co-opted to work on the Montagu-Chelmsford Reforms – British proposals to grant Indians more places in the civil service, which Gandhi described as 'subtle methods of emasculation' – Ranji had to use all his persuasive powers and tact to achieve any semblance of agreement between rulers with more feelings of rivalry towards each other than of friendship. He travelled from State to State urging the princes to unite in protesting the erosion of their privileges. 'It is the conferment and preservation of such rights,' he wrote, 'so dearly cherished by a Rajput or Indian mind, that render possible sacrifices readily and cheerfully made in the service of the Sovereign in times of need.'

Ranji never felt that the services of the Indian princes during the war were recognised appropriately, that is to say by the granting of territory. While Gandhi was proposing, as a means towards *swaraj* (self-rule), non-cooperation and boycott of British goods,

Ranji continued to believe in the enlightened exercise of auto-
cracy under the Crown as being the method most suited for the
betterment of the Indian people. The brutal massacre at Amritsar,
when over four hundred Indians were killed for rioting against
the recently introduced and repressive Rowlatt Act, must have
sorely tried his faith in the British.

Whether Ranji was fighting rearguard actions on behalf of
traditional systems and hereditary wealth – actions with more
opponents among Indians than among the British – or merely
advocating common sense in the management of affairs, his
situation was not easy. Many princes, more at home abroad than
in their own States, ruled carelessly and with scant regard to the
needs of their people; others, conscious of inevitable political
developments, were anxious to be seen to be on the side of demo-
cratisation. Even the communal violence, increasing throughout
British India, failed to bring them to common cause.

Ranji, in committee, may have appeared as the spokesman for
paternalism and privilege, a stickler for protocol and etiquette,
but in his own State he introduced admirable reforms. In his book
The Changing East, J. A. Spender wrote:

> The Jam Saheb is no arbitrary despot. He has a Cabinet of three
> Ministers; his towns have their municipalities; his villages their
> headmen; he has adopted the system of British law; and cases,
> both civil and criminal, are tried by judges with five assessors.
> There is all the apparatus of a modern state, but the ruler keeps
> his hand on every department, and is incessantly moving about
> between his towns and villages, learning the needs of his people,
> hearing their complaints, planning ways of meeting their
> emergencies. His comings and goings are not merely the
> visitations of royalty bestowing smiles and favours; he is Prime
> Minister and Inspector and Chief Engineer and Court of Appeal
> and modern earthly Providence to all the 400,000 and, wherever
> he goes, there is business to do, reports to be considered and
> action to be taken.

Spender, during his visit to Jamnagar, accompanied Ranji on
one of his regular inspections of outlying villages, travelling in

Ranji's personal train and then by Ford car over roads little more than bullock-cart tracks. Ranji held durbar in local court-houses, villagers laying their petitions or complaints with no officials present. 'This is the first rule of these proceedings . . . The Jam Saheb is their father, what he says they will accept, but no one must come between him and them.'

Headmen, cultivators, farmers, merchants, money-lenders, traders, shopkeepers appeared in turn to state their cases. Only when they had done were the officials allowed their say. 'During the whole of the time the villagers, with all their families and bullocks and goats and camels, have sat in a circle about the court-house, the scarlet and orange of the women's dress and the gold embroidered finery of the children lending an indescribable brilliancy to the whole scene . . . Finally, the Jam is garlanded and his friends are garlanded, and the little procession is re-formed and makes off, while the crowd cheer lustily and children sing the State anthem.'

Spender, on another day, drove with Ranji to the oyster-beds. 'The shore is lined with birds of all sorts and hundreds of flamingos, rising suddenly from the flat, make a glorious rose-red cloud against the blue sky.' Most of the fishermen had dyed hair and beards. 'We gravely discuss with them, while we open the oysters, whether it is right to dye . . . There is general agreement that dyeing is a necessity since it is not well that the young should know the age of their elders.'

Today, off the Rozi salt-flats, little has changed. Descendants of the same fishermen sit at their boats, hair and beards dyed every shade between black and pink. Flamingos flush the metallic waters of the marshes and seabirds land and take off continuously from the canals.

'I bear away from Nawanagar,' Spender concluded, 'the impression of a very able, benevolent man doing dutifully the work which has fallen to him and combining new and old in a very interesting way. He and his people are like a great family; they all gather round him and almost any day one may see a large part of his Civil Service playing tennis on the courts behind the palace, while he looks on and criticises their game . . . The relation of the

Government of India to the Ruling Princes is a vastly important subject which will need the most careful consideration, if and when we go forward to a Federal Constitution. The difficulty is to find a general principle which will give the good rulers the freedom which they ought to have to develop their States in their own way and yet prevent the bad from misgoverning or oppressing their subjects.'

NINETEEN

The League of Nations

'More than once it was remarked,' Roland Wild wrote, 'that the Jam Saheb seemed to attain the peak of his enjoyment only when in the company of English guests.' Others found this to be the case, too. Perhaps it was because, with English friends, he could forget for a while his administrative responsibilities and his financial worries. His tastes and his sense of humour had become almost completely anglicised. In the company of visitors from England he could relive experiences on the cricket field and on the moors, memories of Cambridge and London, that he could not share with Indians in the same way. In his own State it was impossible for him to have equals.

He had many visitors, the most regular of whom was Sir Arthur Priestley, who seemed to appreciate Ranji's company and the local oysters equally. The philosopher and poet Rabindranath Tagore was another guest, and their friendship was indication of how easily Ranji adapted to different company.

By 1919 Ranji had completed his shooting lodge at Kileshwar in the Barda Hills. Good roads had been laid through the jungle scrub and sharp rocks Ranji had camped among in the days before he had become Jam Saheb. Today Kileshwar, with its solitary temple and crocodile-filled tank, its priest and handful of villagers, is a deserted place, rarely visited. But in Ranji's day the airy, three-storeyed building, silhouetted against the hills in its formal garden and filled with his Cambridge furniture, was as much a place of entertainment as of rest. Its verandahs looked out over the plain from all levels and in every direction, like bridges on a great yacht. The journey to Kileshwar, even nowadays, is a liver-shaking experience through rough country, but such was its lure for Ranji that any rumour of panther would have him prepare to leave for it, whatever the circumstances. At Kileshwar, too, his mother had frequently stayed before her death. 'Thus Kileshwar embraced,' Wild wrote, 'the varied phases and chapters of his life; the camp where he had dreamed of triumph to come; the evidence of present victory over adversity; the memory of his mother; the thickly covered hills in which he had enjoyed the finest of sport; while near at hand were the sole remaining companions of another life – the cricket groups from Cambridge, the first pictures in his collection of birds . . .'

Not far from Kileshwar, among the Barda foothills, lies Ghoomli, legendary and ruined city, its reputed treasures and ancient temple half-buried by jungle. On the scarcely less ancient temple of Mahadev, which Ranji restored in the vicinity of his shooting lodge, he caused to be erected in the walls a table with the following inscription: 'The Temple of Kileshwar Mahadev, owing to constant and continual changes in the ruling dynasties, like all other ancient shrines in the Province, suffered from neglect and Mahomedan depredations. Owing, however, to the historical antiquity and sanctity of the place it was restored. This denotes a strong landmark in the history of the Province under the aegis of the British Crown, which has enabled a Rajput ruler to successfully restore a Shivi temple with the aid of a Vishnavi engineer and a Mahomedan contractor.'

At Kileshwar Ranji held court under the great banyan tree, enjoying the sunsets. Today there are no longer State papers to be pored over and fewer panthers roam the surrounding woods, but the villagers still come to the temple in the evening and chatter by the tank. The crocodile, like a world-weary clubman, dozes with mouth and eyes open, habitué of an unchanging world. Dismissive of him, shoals of fish flicker for pieces of bread thrown by a priest as burly as a stoker.

Driving back to Jamnagar, away from the blue hills and the pure air, it is impossible not to feel something of Ranji's presence. It was at Kileshwar that he came nearest to finding peace.

In the spring of 1920 Ranji sailed for England. Colonel Berthon had left some time before and Ranji wrote to him from his flat in Hans Mansions in London: 'I found I was getting very jumpy and tired out, and very bronchial. These attacks were beginning to occur more often, and I decided to come here and have a real rest.'

During the summer Ranji achieved his long-nurtured plan of bringing Kathiawar into direct relationship with the Government of India. He had several discussions with Edwin Montagu, to whom he was in due course to erect a statue in Jamnagar. He watched some cricket at Lord's and the Oval and he went down to Hove.

Rather foolishly perhaps, he allowed himself to be persuaded to practise in the nets. 'The King is so keen I should play again, why I don't know,' he wrote. He observed drily to a friend that his real motive was so that he could compile a treatise on the art of batting with one eye.

By early August he felt confident enough to put himself to the test. It was a mistake. He played three times for Sussex, making 16 at Leyton against Essex, 9 and 13 at Leeds against Yorkshire, and 1 at Hastings against Northamptonshire. At Headingley he struggled for forty minutes to make 13 before being caught by Holmes off Rhodes. He was severely restricted in his strokes, trying little on the off side, and in the field he was a passenger.

In his last match he was hit on the elbow and needed an operation, which he chose to have without an anaesthetic. It had been a brave gesture and many were moved by his reappearance. But whatever they had seen in the rotund figure of an Indian prince at the wicket it had not been Ranji.

That summer, in residence at Staines, Ranji had amused himself buying racehorses and jewellery. He spent £20,000 on six horses, shipping them to Bombay. Berthon was no longer in Jamnagar to chide him. In any case his finances, and those of the State, were on a more secure footing than they had ever been. From Cartier Ranji ordered diamond necklaces, emerald puggaree ornaments and emerald and diamond collars. He also bought large paintings, often from the Academy. The least valuable can still be seen at Jamnagar.

Fortunately for him his season as a man of leisure was suddenly interrupted. At short notice, on the recommendation of Edwin Montagu, Ranji was invited to take part, as one of India's three representatives, at the first Assembly of the League of Nations in Geneva. His co-members were Sir William Meyer, Finance Minister of the Government of India during the war, and Sir Ali Imam, a former Dewan to the Nizam of Hyderabad.

Ranji's first move was to ask Colonel Berthon and Charles Fry to accompany him. Any doubts Ranji might have harboured about his suitability for the job quickly vanished. In Geneva, where entertaining was one route to success, he was in his element. 'He took me,' Fry wrote, 'because he said I could speak French and was sure at any rate I was the kind of Englishman who would not be afraid to try. He also knew that if he gave me his points on a subject and we discussed them for a quarter of an hour, I could produce a speech which left none of them out and would if necessary last for an hour.'

Fry remarks on the excellence of Ranji as a speaker – 'one of the best extempore speakers I have heard'. He also describes Ranji's skill in simulation. 'He had cultivated the art of reading out a prepared speech so skilfully that if you did not see he was reading you would have suspected him of speaking without his manuscript or even notes.'

At the Hotel de la Paix, where they were to stay, there was a mix-up over accommodation, the Japanese delegation having spread themselves to the extent of a staff of 170. Once they had got themselves sorted out Ranji started giving parties, his main rival in this respect being the pianist Paderewski, one of the first Premiers of Poland, who had been among the successes of the Paris Peace Conference. Celebrities and performers equally, they got on splendidly.

Fry describes a hair-raising journey back from one of Paderewski's suppers, the chauffeurs having been as well entertained as the guests who were fed on enormous lake trout and Château Yquem. 'We damaged two lamp-posts, and ran over a large heap of stones at the side of the road at an angle of 45 degrees. The road was flat and straight, parallel with the edge of the lake, but the third Indian delegate, Sir Ali Imam, was lost on the way home somewhere up in the mountains and search parties had to be sent out to recover him. One of our party, Colonel Berthon, who always wore a bowler hat, had that hat concertinaed against the roof of the car three times during the drive, each time worse than the last.'

The Indian representatives were under the leadership of Meyer, known in India as Bloody Bill. Fry describes him as being 'small and unobtrusive, with a little white moustache, beady eyes, a parakeet's beak of a nose, and large owlish tortoise-shell spectacles.' He could also, Fry observed, desiccate half a dozen pages of budget at a glance.

Meyer was not without a sense of humour, indulging it to the extent of nominating Ranji to the Finance Committee. Fry had to act as intermediary, which led to him having to call on Meyer at eight-thirty every morning to be briefed. After attending the Committee twice – 'it seemed to sit all day and every day,' Fry wrote – Ranji appointed Fry Substitute Delegate and turned his own attention to more attractive affairs.

Although Ranji may have been most celebrated at the League for the unobtrusive good he did by bringing delegates together over dinner, he was far from a frivolous figure in Geneva. His dinner parties were planned with the idea of familiarising influential world leaders with the problems of India, and in getting restrictions on Indian immigration into the colonies modified. At his table such matters as typhus and cholera in Eastern Europe, the League's relationship with the press, economy in the management of its own affairs, and East–West relations were discussed, and the debates carried into the Chamber.

Ranji considered the League an important forum but a concept inadequately exploited. During the years of Ranji's attendance, 1920–1922, everyone had high hopes of the League as a permanent instrument for settling disputes. The principle of collective security, which was perhaps the most crucial of all the League's aims, and which survives today in the United Nations, failed not through lack of realism in the drafting of its objectives but through the selfishness of its stronger members. The French, comparing the League to a law court without any police, unsuccessfully advocated an international army for its use.

At Geneva in those early days Ranji came into contact with Lord Balfour and Lord Robert Cecil, with Benes, the Czech delegate, and the Frenchmen Viviani and Henri de Jouvenel. If his own specific concerns were to do with internal finances, he had other obligations. Fry describes the following exchange:

' "Charlo, we have got to make a speech."

"What about?"

"Lord Balfour wants me to make a declaration on behalf of the British Empire that, in the opinion of all its delegations, the Corfu question is within the competence of the League."

I said, "When?"

He said, "Now."

"But we can't get it typed."

"Never mind. Write it out large and legible." '

Fry wrote out the speech, which he always claimed turned Mussolini out of Corfu, in a green pencil 'thick as a walking stick'. Ranji delivered the speech on time, and Mussolini, under the watchful eye of the Royal Navy, had to sail out of the harbour he had so recently and so optimistically occupied.

Ranji also took it upon himself to deal with the opium question on behalf of India. He not only defended the eating of it as a necessary sedative in a hot climate, but produced figures to show that Switzerland was one of the main distributors and that Americans consumed more per head than Indians. Moreover, wherever the Americans imported their opium from it was not India.

It was always Ranji's talent to conduct valuable discussions on matters affecting India in general, and Nawanagar in particular, through the medium of civilised social contact. He entertained members of the Secretariat and visiting delegates in a style that softened antipathies and fostered amicable relationships between dignitaries who might otherwise never have met. Although in Indian dress on special occasions, photographs of Ranji generally show him in European clothes, wearing silk waistcoats with black pearl buttons made up from his own fisheries.

Ranjitsinhji's hospitality at Geneva was celebrated [Fry wrote]. When he first arrived in this world of universal politics he was regarded by all other Delegates with awe as the only autocratic sovereign present. . . . But it did not take long for a hundred and twenty or so of the ablest men in the world to discover Ranjitsinhji's ability. In so democratic a collection of humanity it was natural that a ruling prince should be very much admired, but he established his reputation purely on merit, and in the third Assembly was elected one of the Chairmen of Committees, not at all *honoris causa*. The Spanish-speaking bloc offered to get India elected to the Council if we could assure them that Ranjitsinhji would be the Indian representative.

Ranji did his best to offset press cynicism about the League. 'The press can make the League,' he said in a speech. 'The League is in full consonance with the spirit of the East, for the East believes in amity between peoples, and a strong sense of fraternity, of which the more material West has perhaps lost sight. The East is capable of making enormous contributions to the League, but so far the League has completely failed to make known its existence and its purpose, either in the West or the East . . . What is needed is more propaganda and a self-sacrificing spirit among delegates.'

The latter, alas, was never convincingly forthcoming.

Before he left Geneva on this first visit Ranji was invited to join the Permanent Council of the League, but such a responsibility, he felt, would have been too time-consuming. He set off for Staines with a much enhanced reputation, however. 'It might be better if in England this notable man was taken seriously,' Wilson Harris, later to become Editor of the *Spectator*, wrote in the *Daily News*. 'The impression is that India is represented by a notable cricketer. Nothing is further from the truth. The Jam Saheb is before all else a statesman – he is among the dozen most enlightened and sagacious statesmen of the Empire. There may be Western statesmen who have spoken more fearlessly, more convincingly and more hopefully. If there are I have not met them.'

Despite the official demands on Ranji's time in Geneva there were still opportunities for him to increase his store of jewellery and watches. Fabergé objects he bought for himself, but much of the remainder ended up as gifts for departing fellow-delegates.

The Geneva mid-winter climate, with icy mists drifting off the lake, did no good to Ranji's health. It was only later, back in the dry heat of Jamnagar in February, that he began to feel something like his old self.

The anti-climax of his return to first-class cricket had been dissolved by his involvement in the League. There were rumours, too, of an event exactly of the kind to bring out the best, and possibly the worst, in Ranji. For in exactly a year's time the Prince of Wales was due to arrive on a tour of India that was expected to include a stay in Jamnagar.

Heedless of warnings that the Prince's processional itinerary was subject to change, Ranji set out to provide accommodation and entertainment of unprecedented splendour, certainly for Jamnagar. His first act was to turn the Lal Palace, an exotic guest-house not far from his own cricket ground, into a small but luxurious Venetian-style palace for the Prince and his entourage. He laid out lawns and gardens, built drives and approach roads. Then, three weeks before the Prince was due to arrive, it was announced that Kathiawar was no longer on the programme.

Ranji's determination to excel on social occasions at which he was host more than once led him into acts of great extravagance, and this was no exception. The reasons for Jamnagar being excluded, like several other places on the original list, from the Prince's tour were probably perfectly sensible. Riots and disturbances had become commonplace in various Indian provinces. Ranji, however, got it into his head that malicious rumours had been circulated about the unhealthiness of his capital.

The Prince of Wales's loss was the Governor of Bombay's gain, for when Sir George Lloyd arrived in March he was installed in the Lal Palace and entertained in much the same manner as had been intended for the Prince – panther and partridge shoots, banquets, military tournaments, fireworks, gymnastic displays.

In 1921 the Indian princes achieved their own chamber, the Narendra Mandal, largely as a consequence of the recommendations of the Montagu–Chelmsford report. Towards the formation of this Ranji had worked harder than most, though his efforts were not encouraged by some of the most powerful princes of all, such as Gwalior, Baroda, and the Nizam of Hyderabad, each of whom preferred unilateral relationships with the Government. Both the Duke of Connaught, inaugurating the chamber, and Sir George Lloyd, speaking in Jamnagar, were at pains to lend it Government support. 'The sanctity of Treaties is a cardinal article of Imperial Policy,' the Duke said in Delhi. 'His Majesty has reaffirmed his determination ever to maintain unimpaired the privileges, rights, and dignities of the Princes.' And in Jamnagar Sir George Lloyd repeated, on behalf of the Government: 'I desire to assure Your Highness that no one has more at heart the importance of maintaining unimpaired the dignity, interests, and privileges of the Order of Princes.'

But whatever verbal support the Government were able to give to the princes, the princes themselves had many causes for anxiety. The constitutional reform promised to India during the war, and now being demanded with some vehemence by the Indians of British India, threatened to leave the princely States in a curiously anomalous position. The increasing transfer of political power from the civil service and Whitehall into the hands of Indian politicians, caused the Indian princes to consider more carefully than ever before their status and relations with British India.

A year earlier, the Maharajah of Bikaner had received Lord Chelmsford in his State, and in a welcoming speech emphasised his anxieties: 'The deep sympathy of the Ruling Princes with the legitimate aspirations of their fellow countrymen in British India has in the past been voiced in clear and unmistakable terms on several public and private occasions. Nevertheless, the Princes in view of their Treaty relations, in view of their large stake in the country, and in view of the very real identity of interests which exists between the British Government and themselves, cannot look with equanimity on the possibility of the spread of doctrines inimical not only to the interests of good government but of the people themselves – doctrines intended to paralyse constituted authority, which some day are bound directly to affect the Princes' territories also. Nobody desires more ardently than the Princes the peaceful progress of their Motherland to full Nationhood, but that goal can assuredly be reached only by the process of evolution and not by revolution, by constitutional means and by the cooperation of the people with the Government and by these methods alone.'

Not long after this speech, thirty thousand Congress workers were in gaol and Gandhi himself arrested and sentenced to six years' imprisonment for sedition.

It was at Bikaner, shooting, that the Prince of Wales and Ranjitsinhji saw most of each other. Ranji had been a member of the welcoming committee of princes at the Prince of Wales's arrival on board *Renown* in Bombay; and, in Delhi, on the reception of the Prince at the Dewan-i-Am, Ranji had delivered an address to the Prince, speaking after the Maharajahs of Gwalior, Bikaner and Patiala. In the course of that speech he had said: 'A critic might say that we live in troublous times and that your visit has found India in heavy waters; but may it not be that the unpropitious elements now visible are but the froth and foam which ever appear on the surface when progress rides the waves? May we not conceive that the present troubles are but healthy signs of a great forward movement, of a great striving after better things?'

In the jungle, troubles were put aside. It was scarcely surprising that an English prince in India should warm so much to the Indian prince who, in England two decades earlier, had become a legend.

Ranji returned to Geneva in 1922, standing in as Indian representative for the Maharajah of Bikaner at the third Assembly. Largely owing to Ranji's advocacy India was accepted as being one of the eight members of 'chief industrial importance' and therefore entitled to a nominee on the governing body of the International Labour Bureau.

Ranji's other main contribution to this Assembly was his speech on Indian minorities in South Africa. 'I should feel false to my fellow-countrymen in India, and also to my fellow-countrymen in South Africa, were I to neglect this unique opportunity of summoning to the assistance of their aspirations the spiritual power and spiritual blessing of your sympathy.'

In 1923 Ranji, once again with Fry in attendance, was back at the Hotel de la Paix. His speech on the Italo-Greek dispute was received with respect. 'Unless the strong nations, the big brothers, set the example of forbearance,' he said, 'unless they show in their own bodies a willingness to sacrifice their pride of power, then the League of Nations will be a sham; then our hopes will fade, must fade, and the light on the horizon will die, and the familiar and accusing darkness will return . . . India declares that she takes her stand by the new order so far as it lies in her power, and that she accepts the principle and practice of the Covenant without reservation.'

The opium problem was still under discussion and Ranji again spoke: 'India cannot regard as illegitimate the use of opium as a home-made medicine, which is general throughout India. India will not allow the deleterious use of opium for addiction purposes in India so far as stringent laws and efficient administration can prevent it . . . I may further add that opium is a Government monopoly, and speaking on behalf of the Indian States, autonomous or otherwise (such, for instance, as my own) they could not export it without the permission of the Government of India, and could only export it through their agents.'

The committee chaired by Ranji at this Assembly was involved, principally, with reports on the reconstruction of Austria, with health organisations, and with the work of the financial and economic commissions. When it was all over Ranji was happy to return to Staines and a summer of shooting and fishing, and, for the only time in his life, racing. He saw his colours – blue, pink sleeves, black belt – first past the post in the Harewood Handicap and his interest might have continued on his return to India had not his Bombay trainer been involved in the improper running of one of his horses.

The social involvement, colour, country background, expertise, and gambling element might have been expected to make racing a particular passion for Ranji, but it never really became so, and the Bombay incident was merely the *coup de grâce*. Ranji, in all his diversions, preferred physical participation to spectatorship. Jewels rather than race horses stimulated his pride in ownership and it was on the evaluation of precious stones rather than on the breeding and conformation of pedigree yearlings that he chose to exercise his connoisseurship. The friendship Ranji developed this summer with Jacques Cartier led to investments that rarely failed to increase their value many times over. Writing in 1934 Cartier observed: 'He was fond of pearls, rubies, and diamonds, but nothing could rouse his enthusiasm like fine emeralds. The collection he made is today unsurpassed in the world, not perhaps in quantity, but certainly in quality . . . The most important item in the emerald collection is the emerald and diamond necklace, containing 277 carats of first-class emeralds.'

The most remarkable piece of all, 'a really superb realisation of a connoisseur's dream', Cartier describes as consisting of two necklaces of white diamonds connected in the front by a pair of pink square diamonds and containing a centre piece composed of six 'of the finest and rarest diamonds in the world'. Among these was the Ranjitsinhji, a white diamond of 136 carats cut in Amsterdam in 1913 and from the same mine as the Cullinan, part of the British Crown Jewels. 'At no other period in history,' Cartier wrote, 'could such a necklace have come into existence.' The collection has long since been dispersed.

By late November 1923, Ranji was back in Jamnagar. On 4 December he was present to propose the toast at the University Hall, Bombay, when the princes and chiefs of the Bombay Presidency entertained the retiring Governor, Sir George Lloyd, and Lady Lloyd to a farewell banquet. Two hundred and fifty guests were present, including the whole of the nobility of the Presidency, and the University Gardens were festooned with decorations and brilliantly illuminated.

It was an occasion not without awkwardness all the same, for the Jam Saheb and Sir George had differed crucially on the relationship between the Kathiawar States and the Bombay Presidency. The imminent transfer, so long schemed for by Ranji, of Kathiawar political relations from Bombay to Delhi, had not been achieved without the often stated regret and opposition of the retiring Governor.

After the Maharajah of Kolhapur had paid the requisite glowing tributes to the public works inaugurated during Sir George's governorship, it was Ranji's turn. Five years before, Ranji had performed the same task on the retirement of Lloyd's predecessor, Lord Willingdon. Now he began by drawing attention to Lloyd's efforts in reclamation and housing, and most especially to the Sukkur barrage project 'which is going to give Sindh the greatest irrigation works in the world'.

He continued: 'Our associations with Your Excellency's Government have been on the whole happy; there may have been cases of individual disappointments here and there, but we recognise that it is not easy or possible to satisfy everybody. Some of us are going to be transferred to the Central Government leaving others to follow at a later date. I wish it had been possible for all of us to have been transferred jointly with your help, assistance and goodwill. Our eagerness to see the accomplishment of this change is due, not so much to any real or fancied discontent with the condition of our relations with the Presidency, but to the advantages of participation in wider policies of the Government of India, no matter where they are situated. The benefits of this closer union are, to my mind, obvious and, may I add and say, mutual. I am sure this circumstance, I mean this political severance, will never interfere with or diminish our respect and regard for this Presidency and for His Imperial Majesty's Representative in Western India.'

Sir George, in his speech of reply, looked back fondly to the long alliances between the Bombay Presidency and the ruling chiefs. One by one he recalled them, Kolhapur, Rajpipla, Bariya; Chota Udaipur and Idar 'whose name will live for ever linked with that of Sir Pratab Singh, the very mirror and ornament of chivalry'.

He went on: 'But the die is cast, the old order is changed, and tonight we listen to the dying close of an old song . . . And if there are insistent voices which tell me that it is a far cry to Delhi; that the winds of Simla, even if they spangle and uplift, bestow an embrace that is cold and bitter compared with that of our softer and more intimate western breezes; if I often remember that the names of Your Highnesses' friends and foes, which are so well known to us here, will stir no responsible echoes there – can you wonder that I am deeply anxious – even afraid sometimes – for the future of those who have lived under our roof so long that we regard ourselves and them as brothers of one house?'

Sir George turned to Ranji: 'We have differed in one great question of policy, but I can only say that difference of opinion has never done anything but to cement my admiration, respect and warm regard and, if I may say so, affection for Your Highness. It is a lesson which has still to be common in Indian public life that men may differ on the biggest questions of public policy, feel deeply upon them and yet preserve in daily life their friendship and esteem for one another unimpaired.'

There were some who felt Ranji had reason to feel slighted by the retiring Governor's remarks. But reading the full text of both speeches today there seems no substance for such a view. Sir George Lloyd's attitude was understandable; no civil servant likes to see control of any aspect of his department slip away unchallenged. As he stated at the outset of his speech, he was a Celt, and Celts live largely in the past. 'I cannot view without regret the shattering of a great historical tradition.'

For his part, Ranji was delighted that the, in his view, unnecessary intermediary of the Bombay Presidency was ended.

TWENTY

Fishing

As was his habit in his cricketing days Ranji sailed from Bombay in the spring. It was no longer at the Norfolk Hotel, Brighton, where he held court, going up to the county ground in Eaton Road for net practice, but either the Grosvenor Hotel in Victoria, or his house at Staines.

It was during this summer of 1924 that Lord Hawke published his *Recollections and Reminiscences*, an unremarkable volume but one in which a real affection and admiration for Ranji emerges. Whether or not he was justified in stating that Ranji considered standing for Parliament as a Liberal or that 'few men have been more deeply read in Carlyle and Herbert Spencer', Hawke was as generous as it was his nature to be in print: 'He has been very all-round, for he can shoot splendidly, ride "like a native", is an excellent bridge player and the most thoughtful of hosts, besides being a charming companion anywhere and a wonderful judge of the game. But there can be no possible description of his batting. . . . He alone developed new batting strokes, and was also at home on all sorts of wickets.'

Hawke had been Ranji's guest in India on more than one occasion and there is a comical description of an incident on shikar near Kileshwar: 'It was evening and we were facing west. Being warm I had removed my cap. After a rather long wait a panther appeared on the opposite slope of the small ravine, and began to creep stealthily down towards our goat. Suddenly the panther stiffened, and, starting in our direction, simply declined to move for, it seemed, ages. Then, just as were getting bored, and I thought of firing, he dashed up the hill and out of sight. Ranji burst out laughing.

"Why the devil did he do that?" I asked, a bit nettled.

"Why, Martin," said Ranji, "he spotted your bald head, of course." '

By now Ranji was making regular appearances in other people's books. One of his cronies in the old days had been 'Dick' Lilley – Arthur Augustus – the Warwickshire and England wicket-keeper. He was five years older than Ranji and his last match for Warwickshire had been in 1911 but Lilley, an unobtrusively efficient and neat wicket-keeper/batsman, on the lines of Leslie Ames rather than Godfrey Evans, had an England career that lasted far longer than Ranji's, from 1896–1909. He twice toured Australia, in 1901/2 and 1903/4, though was not on Stoddart's tour. In his *Twenty-Four Years of Cricket*, he writes:

> I have already expressed my opinion as to the cricketers who have occupied pre-eminent positions. Dr W. G. Grace, the greatest all-round cricketer of all; Arthur Shrewsbury, the premier professional batsman; Victor Trumper, the greatest batsman Australia has produced; and Clem Hill, unequalled among left-hand players, either in Australia or elsewhere. But as a batsman pure and simple Ranjitsinhji unquestionably was the greatest of all. He stood upon a pinnacle . . . Of all the many brilliant exhibitions I have seen him give, his 154 not out at Old Trafford, in the 1896 Test, stands clearly out to me as the greatest. He seemed to place the ball just where he liked, and the terrible express deliveries of E. Jones were treated with apparent contempt.

Later Lilley discusses Ranji as entertainer and technician:

> Ranjitsinhji was a batsman of unique resource. There is no stroke known to cricketers that he did not execute to perfection, and the ease and style in which all his strokes were made rendered his stay at the wickets a source of the keenest pleasure to all experts, a delight to the spectators, and an education to the student.
>
> In my early days the batsman always 'forced' the ball away

when pitched on the leg-side, or else played it more squarely. But Ranjitsinhji, with a simple flick of the wrist, just slightly altered the course of the ball to very fine leg . . . The Prince so perfected the stroke that he not only made it when the ball was pitched on the leg-side, but even when it was pitched in a line with the leg-stump.

Lilley and Ranji often shot together and Lilley was a frequent visitor to Shillinglee during the summer of 1908. 'The Jam was usually accompanied by two loaders and on one occasion I saw him with three dead pheasants in the air at the same time . . . This happened at Huntingdon. The Jam always used 20-bore guns. He had the best instincts of a sportsman, and whatever I saw him shoot at, he always gave it a sporting chance. He was also a good trap shot, and could kill pigeons in a style quite equal to our best English shots.'

By now fishing was taking first place over all other pleasures in Ranji's heart. As far back as 1912 Lilley was admiring the 'patience and the complete absence of excitement that the landing of so fine a fish [a four-and-a-half-pound trout] might reasonably have aroused . . . This was quite characteristic of the Jam, however, for he was always self-contained, whether fishing, shooting, or on the cricket field.'

The only exception to this, Lilley records, was in the first Test of 1902 against Australia when a mix-up between Ranji and Maclaren resulted in the England captain being run out for nine. Ranji was visibly upset and was bowled by Armstrong soon afterwards. It appears unlikely, though, that Maclaren was a good runner: during the previous winter in Australia, he was run out batting with Hayward in the third Test at Adelaide, and again in the second innings of the fifth Test at Melbourne, batting with Tyldesley.

That summer, 1924, the Ballynahinch estate of thirty thousand acres in Connemara, renowned for its salmon and sea-trout fishing, came on the market. Ranji's acquisition of it, initially on a rental basis, changed his life. More than once, in the ten years before his

death, when political and economic problems in Jamnagar began
to get on top of him, he threatened to give it all up and retire to
Ballynahinch.

In India there was no fishing of the kind Ranji enjoyed; there
were trout-streams in Kashmir, and the Maharajah was a close
friend, but the climate did not suit him. In early days he had gone
there as a guest of the old Maharajah to play cricket. He was out
first ball. When he returned to the pavilion the Maharajah chided
him: 'But, Ranjitsinhji, you have not made duck, surely. I never
make duck.' When the Maharajah's turn to bat came he was soon
bowled. He just picked up the bails and continued batting. Fry
tells the story in his autobiography.

It is Fry to whom we owe the best description of what Ranji
looked for and found at Ballynahinch Castle.

> The Ballynahinch river runs into the sea at Roundstone on the
> west coast not far from Clifden, on the far side of Galway, from
> a chain of loughs, of which four are large ones. A group of blue
> hills called the Pins of Connemara stand up in the distance. The
> short four or five miles of river run through stony, peaty
> ground . . . When the salmon were running, from the middle
> of June to the end of July, the salmon fishing of its kind was
> superb. There is a spot between the upper and lower Bally-
> nahinch loughs called Sna Beg, about some fifty yards of slow
> stream connecting the two pieces of water, where salmon are
> catchable more frequently than anywhere I have known.

Fry describes how Ranji would spend hours and hours trying
to outwit fish at spots where they used to lie, but where no one
else could catch them, 'just as in India he would sit up in a *machan*
every night for a fortnight to bag an unventuresome panther.'

When Ranji first went to Connemara, to his baronial lakeside castle, the Troubles were not long over. He himself was
never harassed, then or later. On his arrival in Dublin he found a
civic reception awaiting him, arranged by President Cosgrave, a
colleague of Geneva days. This was followed by an official dinner
by the Free State Government, reciprocated in due course by
Ranji at the Shelbourne Hotel.

Ranji travelled with his usual large entourage of Indian servants, taking with him an assortment of nephews and nieces, as well as Fry and Colonel Berthon. That first summer he scarcely moved from the river, except to sleep. 'We had some wonderful times together,' Fry wrote, and in his biography Wild observed, presumably quoting Berthon, the *éminence grise* behind his book 'Fishing was the sport he loved above all others. With a light trout rod he was an artist, for his supple wrists came into play, and he could drop a fly on the water as lightly as if it were a piece of thistledown.'

Over the years the people of Connemara had much for which to thank Ranji; not only employment – he used over a hundred men on the estate – but his encouragement of local activities, the breeding of Connemara ponies, light industries, even Church affairs.

For ever after Ballynahinch was the place on earth dearest to Ranji. When he returned to Jamnagar in the autumn he took with him a dessert service, each plate of which contained a different view of castle, lake, river and hills.

Lord Reading, perhaps the most intelligent and wary of the Viceroys during Ranji's time – 'he held the scales of justice so even,' Fry wrote, 'that he himself sat on the tongue of the balance' – was due to arrive in Kathiawar soon after Ranji's return. Kathiawar now dealt directly with the Government in Delhi and Lord Reading's three-day visit was official confirmation of the fact.

Ranji, as usual, went to great lengths to make his overnight stay in Nawanagar memorable. A new road was built to the recently established camp at Samana, electric light and running water installed. Before the evening banquet, the Viceroy unveiled the statue to Lord Montagu that now dominates a central space in the city. 'The greatest friend India has ever had since perhaps Edmund Burke,' Ranji said of his old friend. Lady Reading, too, was pressed into action, opening a women's hospital. The hospital cost £2,000, the entertainment for the Viceregal party £40,000.

Lord Reading, no great sportsman, was enabled to bring down the ritualistic panther, enjoy the sea air at Rozi, and depart well satisfied.

For Ranji, missing the Connemara hills, there was the consolation of economic improvement at home. The port of Bedi was the centre of his activities and, freed from Customs restrictions, it thrived. The money spent on Lord Reading's visit, and on the preparations for the Prince of Wales's visit two years earlier, turned out not to have been entirely wasted, for what had been specially constructed remained a permanent part of the capital. Today, fifty years after Ranji's death, Jamnagar remains a model city of lakes and gardens, of flowering trees and waterways.

Ranji, as at Ballynahinch, did all he could to revive interest in regional crafts; in Jamnagar, this meant the native brocade work, once a speciality of Kathiawar. He himself began to breed Kathi horses.

During the hot weather he spent much time at his seaside bungalow at Balachedi, a twenty-mile drive across narrow causeways raised over paddy fields and salt-marshes. Egrets, white-necked storks, white and black ibis, spoonbills, moorhens, painted snipe take the setting and rising sun on their wings as they circle or dive. What the coastline around Jamnagar may lack in vegetation is made up for by the multitude of sea birds that pick over the estuaries or paddle in the sea-lace of sweeping beaches.

At Balachedi, today a naval school, the air is fresher and saltier than in the Jamnagar palaces and, looking out to sea from this most westerly of India's coasts in the hotter weather, Ranji may have shared some of the relief he felt at Ballynahinch.

He did, in fact, get away to Ireland during the monsoon, returning to India in the autumn with a party of friends – Fry and old 'Skipper' Priestley, the Dudleys and the Tichbornes.

It was during the crisp, dry, winter months, when the climate in India approaches perfection, that Ranji, now fifty-two, was most at ease in Jamnagar. This was the time when he initiated projects, looked into every aspect of the State's administration, and concerned himself personally with the problems of his subjects. In the hot humid season, from April to October, he tried to get away from now on whenever possible, usually to Ballynahinch, leaving the day-to-day running of the State in the hands of the Dewan and his ministers.

15 *(left)* Ranji on the way to his installation as Jam Saheb.

16 *(below)* Ranji, Jam Saheb at last, with Maharajah Sir Pratab Singh of Idar.

17 *(left)* 1907. Ranji, struck down by typhoid, recuperates in Bombay.

18 *(below, left)* Ranji, with cheetah. Until fishing replaced it, shooting was the great passion of his Indian days.

19 *(below)* Ranji, with W. G. Grace in the back seat. Cars were one of Ranji's weaknesses and from Cambridge days onwards no model was safe from him.

20 (*above*) Ranji with Popsey the parrot, his closest companion. Already a certain age when Ranji acquired it at Cambridge, Popsey, blind and balding, outlived him.

21 (*above, right*) Ranji, who himself served on the Western Front, immediately offered the services of his State to the Allied effort. These included squadrons of his own lancers, ambulances, and an officers' hospital at Staines.

22 (*right*) Ranji, on leave, lost an eye out shooting, but not his zest for life.

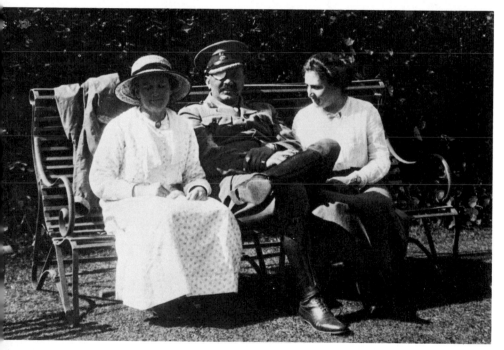

23 (*right*) Jamnagar. One of Ranji's four palaces, but finished only in time to receive the mourners at his funeral.

24 (*below*) The Jam Palace, Ranji's own preferred residence and the palace in which he died.

25 *(left)* Kileshwar, the hunting lodge in the Barda hills, where Ranji came to rest and to hunt panther.

26 *(below)* Ballynahinch Castle, Connemara. The best salmon fishing in the world and the solace of Ranji's last years.

27 *(right)* Group taken at Ajwa during Ranji's visit to Baroda, 1926. Ranji, as in most photographs taken after the loss of his right eye, turns sideways to the camera.

28 *(below)* The Cenotaph. Ranji, at the far end of the front row, with fellow Indian officers, King George V, The Prince of Wales, the Duke of York.

Fry spent much time with Ranji during the winter of 1924/25. The chapters in *Life Worth Living* which he devotes to India give a vivid account of Ranji both at work and at play. At dinner the night before, Ranji would announce that they would be leaving at six the next morning for the Barda Hills. 'We started with the sudden decision characteristic of Ranji, who rarely told anybody what he was going to do till the last moment: he always knew perfectly well days before. Away we went, past the two broad lakes with their ancient round fortresses, and past the high outer walls and the frowning west gate of the city into the sea of plain beyond.'

Fry describes the herds of blackbuck pasted against the hills; the 'gazelle-like' chinkara; the deer. Soon they would pass the deep wells and ruins of Ghoomli, with its rumours of treasure.

> At Kileshwar [Fry wrote] there was an ancient temple a stone's throw outside the garden of the bungalow, surrounded by tall pipal trees, with here and there an aged and expansive banyan tree, under one of which the Jam Saheb used to hold informal audiences of cultivators from the distant villages . . . All round was the wide circle of the wooded hills, complete silence, and a brazen blue sky. The quiet experience of arrival was more than thrilling to one who only knew the woods of Europe and the treeless stretches of the high veldt. Were there not sambur and cheetal somewhere in those mysterious jungles, and panthers sleeping in caves or under shelves where the outcrop of rock showed on the ridges of the round hills? That afternoon a score of white-clad cultivators appeared by magic . . . The Jam Saheb, impassively patriarchal, sat in a camp-chair and heard their case.

It was Ranji's custom, on these regular visits to outlying villages, sometimes to get Fry to sit in with him as the protagonists outlined their troubles. After matters had been disposed of, Ranji's party would set off for the second serious activity of the day, installing themselves in *kotahs* – old two-storied towers (or new ones built especially for the purpose by Ranji) – before nightfall. There, overlooking clearings in which shikaris, goatherds and a tethered goat would be arranged as carefully as if on a stage set, they would settle down with drinks and sandwiches. A carbide arc-light was hung like a moon over the clearing. In due course the goat would begin to bleat.

Sometimes they would wait motionless for hours, the distant honk of sambur the only sound among the gentle rustlings of the jungle. Then, starting up, Ranji would hand Fry his binoculars and point. The panther's eyes would be gleaming like phosphorescent lights in the bushes. They would go out suddenly and Ranji would indicate with his hands that the panther was circling.

On one occasion, when the panther finally entered the clearing and jumped on a boulder to contemplate its prey, Ranji wrote on a small block with a torch pencil, 'It is a lady but you can shoot her if you like.' Fry declined. 'I lowered my rifle on the cushions provided for the very purpose, and Ranji knocked with his knuckles. There was a grey streak and the lady was gone.'

Sometimes, waiting, Fry would snore and Ranji would lean down and pinch his nose. Ranji, Fry noticed, could whisper in the presence of the panthers without any sound of breath.

On that trip, several nights running, there was either no panther or it was a lady. 'Nevertheless, the whole experience was exciting. It is no feat to shoot a panther in the strong artificial moonlight at a distance of twenty yards, but it is intensely interesting to wait while interpreting the mysterious drama of sounds in the jungle at night.'

In due course Fry got his panther, beyond the Barda Hills, near the little village of Moti Gop. It was the first of many.

On the work side there were disagreeable matters to be faced. Summers at Ballynahinch and shooting parties in the winter were all very well when things were running smoothly. But in 1927 Ranji received word from the Government of India that the question of the Viramgam Customs Line – the abolition of which in 1917 had made such difference to his plans for Bedi – was to be reopened. The Government of India, in the wording of their 1917 note, had always reserved their right to reconsider their position if circumstances or 'fiscal interests' required.

Ranji had, at the time, taken them up on this: 'It is out of the question for a Kathiawar State to be in a position to equip and set up a rival port to Bombay or Karachi ... but I hope our acceptance of the conditions will not interfere with a healthy development of our resources to the extent of our natural capacity.'

In the absence of any official comment on this Ranji had spent over £1,000,000 in the intervening decade on the modernisation and extension of the port facilities at Bedi and on communications with it.

Ranji protested strongly against the necessity for any discussion of the matter, preferring it to be settled by arbitration. Lord Birkenhead, Fry's contemporary at Wadham College, Oxford, was Secretary of State for India and it was to him that Ranji appealed. But Birkenhead declined to interfere and despite a further exchange of letters and the appointment by Ranji of Sir Leslie Scott to represent him, the Government of India announced that a conference would be held at Mount Abu at which the Kathiawar State could put their case.

There was little that Ranji could do at Mount Abu other than reject the Government proposals. The decision had already been taken, without reference to the conference, to reimpose the Customs Line. The *Times of India*, in its report, commented: 'A question which is quite as much political as financial has been settled on financial grounds alone, and even then in a way that does little credit to the Finance Department. What the Government of India have done is to take away what they gave, in order to rectify their own miscalculations.'

For the remaining six years of his life Ranji fought bitterly against what he conceived to be a gross injustice to his State, one which cost Nawanagar over £1,000,000 in revenue over the next three years. Fry, later appointed by Sir Leslie Scott as assistant in the formulation of the princes' case to the Butler Commission on constitutional reform in India with particular reference to the States, was witness to Ranji's unceasing efforts over Bedi and the idea of Federation, and the toll it took on him. Praising the work of Sir Leslie Scott and Professor Rushbrook Williams on behalf of the Indian States, Fry observed that when it came to fundamentals 'Ranji was a main source of efficiency'. He concluded: 'I was privileged to see the inner working of a large making of history, and my own small activities in the matter enabled me to see Ranjitsinhji's too little recognised force of character and talent for statesmanship, and also contributed, I should say, materially, to my own enlightenment.' Had Ranji known that in June 1934, after the Viceroy, Lord Willingdon, had finally agreed to arbitration, an agreement would be reached much in line with what he himself had advocated, the last phase of his life would have been much calmer. By the time the long years of expensive litigation and resentment were over and victory assured, Ranji had been dead for fourteen months.

In 1927, the Customs Line was not the only cloud on Ranji's horizon. Violent criticism had been building up in British India against the princely States, largely fomented by the more extreme members of the National Congress. A series of pamphlets, Indian States Series, was launched with the idea of discrediting the princes. The first in the series, devoted to Nawanagar, had as sub-title, 'Indian Princes as their People see them – an inside view of the Administration of the State of Nawanagar of "Prince Ranji" '.

So damaging were the criticisms made in this pamphlet, which was distributed all over India and also sent to British MPs, that the Indian States' Peoples' Conference published a reply, *Nawanagar and its Critics*, being 'a critical examination and review' of the above pamphlet. The twenty-one main criticisms made in the pamphlet were printed on the left-hand side of the page, and the Durbar's detailed answers on the right. The result ran to a booklet of over two hundred pages.

The indictments of the Administration varied from such matters as no freedom of speech, no liberty of the press, no legislation and no representative institutions, to 'tyranny of monopolies, taxation and compulsory labour', from 'unparalleled huge expenses on the person of His Highness' and 'mad waste of public money over friends and entertainment' to 'poverty of education'.

In isolation many of the criticisms seem to contain elements of truth, but when examined in context their formulation appears

specious. The Durbar's refutations were supported by meticulously presented facts and figures, the authority of which was
independently vouched for.

All, that is, except the charges relating to the large sums of
money spent on State guests. Later that year the Viceroy, Lord
Irwin, visited the State and wild rumours circulated – and were
aired in both the Indian and British press – about the extravagance
of the entertainment provided for him.

It is hazardous to pass judgment on such matters from the
standpoint of a western country fifty years later. Lord Irwin's
three-day visit cost something in the region of £25,000, mostly
spent on arrangements at the Samana camp, on banquets, fireworks, and shooting expeditions. That was the way heads of State
entertained in those days and their prestige, so they believed,
related to the magnificence of their hospitality. 'The visit of Lord
Irwin,' Roland Wild wrote, 'showed the Jam Saheb at his best
as a host. The city was transformed, and, after sunset, was like a
page from the *Arabian Nights*. Columns twenty feet high bore
illuminated paintings of Indian mythological heroes; pylons bore
lights and crowns; lawns stretched green where a few months
before there had been rock.'

It was hardly to be expected that Wild, writing a biography
commissioned with the approval of Ranji, would look critically
on such proceedings. Ranji carried Rajput notions of what was
proper in the way of receiving important visitors to the extreme.
The child and the prince, the impresario and the public relations
expert, found equal pleasure in volleys of rockets exploding over
the sky of Jamnagar.

Behind many of the attacks on Ranji was the paper *Saurashtra*, and
behind its editors was a pamphleteer called Abhyankar. In 1919,
when Ranji was General Secretary of the Princes' Conference,
Abhyankar was found to be present in the Conference Hall at
Delhi holding a false ticket. It was Ranji's responsibility to see
that he was removed. From that day on Abhyankar waged an
unremitting campaign whose motivation appeared to be no more
than resentment against the humiliation of that incident.

These attacks, coming on top of the exhausting wrangles with
the Government of India, began to affect even Ranji's equanimity.
His friends began to notice increasing moodiness, often a sadness
close to tears.

The publication in 1931 of *An Atlas of the Progress in Nawanagar
State*, with its charts and tables, provided irrefutable evidence of
what Ranji had achieved in the two decades since his accession:
in wells and new villages, in exports and forest revenue, in
reclamation and industry, in education and medicine, in roads and
railways.

Before returning to Jamnagar to supervise arrangements for Lord
Irwin's visit, Ranji managed to squeeze in some fishing at Ballynahinch and a few weeks in England. His beloved nephew,
Duleepsinhji, was, in 1927, in his third year in the Cambridge
eleven. Duleep had begun the season with a century against
Yorkshire, followed by 254 not out against Middlesex, a record
at that time for the university. Then, much as Ranji had done
thirty years earlier, Duleep caught a chill in the bitter May weather.
He developed pleurisy and was for some weeks near to death.
Ranji arranged for him to be sent to Switzerland. In due course,
after one bad relapse, he began to pick up, but it was June of 1928
before he was ready to play cricket again.

Ranji spent many hours with Duleep during his illness. He was
as protective and concerned now as often, in a jocular way, he had
tended to be hypercritical. From the start of Duleep's career at
Cheltenham, people inevitably used Ranji as a yardstick to judge
him by.

There could, of course, be no real comparison. They were
dissimilar in build, in temperament, and in technique; more
significantly, they played at different stages in the game's development. Yet there was a family likeness in everything they did.
Neville Cardus, stating the irrelevance of the Ranji comparison,
went on: 'Duleepsinhji must be the most promising batsman of
the last two years . . . He cuts sweetly through the slips – his body
falling with lovely curves into the stroke. The main characteristic
of his style is back play; here he is true to the classic tradition . . .

Arm-swing provides, one would say, the main energy of Duleep-sinhji's back-strokes, though some of the bloom of wristwork enters at the last second.'

Duleep, with his more formal training, and his three years as an outstanding schoolboy cricketer in the Cheltenham eleven behind him, was more successful at Cambridge than Ranji had been. Altogether Duleep was four years in the Cambridge eleven, though only playing five innings before his illness in 1927, and he hit five hundreds for the university.

Between Duleep leaving Cheltenham and going up to Cambridge Ranji had insisted that he take a year off. During that time he visited Ballynahinch, stayed at Staines, and spent long enough with Ranji's old friend Dr Heasman at Eastbourne to qualify for Sussex. That Duleep should continue his association with his old county gave Ranji particular pleasure. Worried though he still was over Duleep's health when he returned to India, and careful though he was to mask his pride in his nephew's achievement, he knew in his bones that Duleep was something quite out of the ordinary.

On 17 November Lord Irwin laid the foundation stone in Jamnagar of the hospital that was to bear his own name. In the course of his speech of welcome Ranji, running through the medical history of the State, recalled: 'I inherited a system which was struggling to be popular in the midst of general apathy and ignorance. We had old methods of cure, which consisted of herbs, branding with hot needles and nails and superstitious vows and offerings. Barbers and itinerant priests shared the skill of surgery, and cauterising was freely resorted to when fever developed into delirium, and windows were barred to light and air by special blinds and curtains.'

The new hospital was to contain fifty-six beds, an operating theatre, and rooms for doctors and nurses. Lord Irwin, having performed his task, was whisked off to the Samana camp, 'a sumptuously fitted little township under canvas' as the *Times of India* called it. From here he shuttled between the Barda Hills on panther expeditions and the Vibha Vilas Palace, from where excursions to Rozi were made.

The island of Rozi, four square miles in area, was one of Ranji's most imaginative transformations. In early days it possessed a temple, on the return journey from which Jam Rawal's eldest son lost his life. A lighthouse had been built by Jam Vibhaji on the island, which was connected to the mainland by a mile-long causeway. Charles Kincaid has described how, when serving in Kathiawar during Ranji's first years as Jam Saheb, he accompanied Ranji on one of his evening drives. Ranji, seeing the possibilities of the now uninhabited island as a game covert, had put down vast quantities of captured wild partridge and quail. It was his custom every evening to scatter grain for the birds. 'Very soon the birds got so accustomed to the sound of their benefactor's motor-horn, that directly it was audible they rushed to the edge of the causeway in hundreds . . . On the one occasion that I was privileged to drive with the Jam to feed his birds, he had several times to stop the car altogether, so closely was it besieged by countless quail, partridges and hares.'

Lord Irwin was to reap the reward of these feedings, for the daily bag, by the time he visited Rozi, ran into thousands. Trained Indian keepers protected the game against hawks, rats, foxes and jackals and the rough grass, enriched by the game droppings, paid for the full upkeep of the birds and gamekeepers. Rozi, today, is little changed in appearance, the seabirds screeching over the oyster-coloured waters and the roads running straight as rulers through the salt-pans and scrub. But the shooting parties are no more.

On the second night of his visit a State banquet was held in honour of the Viceroy at the Badminton Hall, in the grounds of the Pratap Vilas Palace. Lord and Lady Irwin sat on chairs of solid gold and ate off gold plate. In proposing the health of his honoured guests Ranji took the opportunity to re-state his views on the problem of the States: 'Our position in the new India that is being evolved needs to be thoroughly safeguarded, and, whatever form the future constitution will assume, our existence as political entities, distinct from, and independent of, the neighbouring parts of British India, will demand an adjustment, which, while recognising and meeting modern conditions, will not ignore history and traditions, and will fully uphold our dynastic prestige, prerogatives, and treaty rights.'

It had become a familiar theme. Ranji went on to refer to the Simla Conference in the previous May: 'May it result in a settlement which will vouchsafe to the States the integrity of their position, and ensure for them a dignified place in the Federated India of the Future.'

Ranji and Lord Irwin had been colleagues in Geneva in 1923 and Ranji recalled their association. He continued with a potted history of Nawanagar and its modest resources: 'Nature is niggardly in her bounties on this side. No high mountains or perennial rivers break the monotony of our soil which lacks the fertility of Gujerat, or even the quality of neighbouring tracts under Gondal and Junagadh. Our water-sheds send out small rivers into the sea, where they discharge a moderate overflow in monsoon months and present a dry aspect for more than half the year . . . Since 1907 I have had ten bad years including four famines.'

There was, too, a brief reference to politics. 'We have tried to move with the times in Jamnagar. I established an Advisory Council some years ago, in which leaders of my people are invited to deliberate and advise on matters of public or general interest. If it be the desire of my subjects to progress on the lines of British India, they will not find me behindhand in an enthusiastic response to their aspirations.'

The Viceroy, in his reply, also alluded to their first meeting in Geneva 'when I in common with the several delegates of the Nations of the world listened with admiration to the speech with which you delighted the Assembly. I had of course long before that worshipped from afar a name that used to appear with almost monotonous regularity at the head of the Sussex batting averages.'

He went on to praise the Jam Saheb's agricultural policy, not only in irrigation but in the granting of tenancy rights to farmers. He remarked on the achievement in transforming 'cramped and insanitary houses and narrow lanes into the fine buildings and the wide thoroughfares through which we drove two days ago.' He quoted Adam Smith's remark that of all baggage man is the most difficult to move; and whereas in olden times rulers, dissatisfied with their surroundings, simply moved their people to new sites, nowadays ancient cities had to be adapted where they stood.

Lord Irwin turned to the future relations of the States with British India. 'You are fortunate in having no communal trouble in Nawanagar and you share this happy position with most of the Indian States . . . It may be that religious animosities are accentuated by struggles for political power.' Lord Irwin went on: 'You desire, and naturally, both to retain the internal autonomy secured to you by your engagements and treaties and at the same time to have a voice in the questions which, owing to the growing complexity of modern conditions, must necessarily affect India as a whole. Although at first sight these two positions may appear difficult of reconciliation I trust that time and a full examination, in consultation with all parties concerned, will lead us to the discovery of the true solution.'

The Viceroy concluded with a reference to his host's sporting spirit and good manners, in circumstances with which they can only with some difficulty have been maintained: 'I appreciate the courtesy which has avoided reference to matters of controversy between the Nawanagar Durbar and my Government. Differences must sometimes occur, but with goodwill on both sides they should seldom be incapable of being brought to a just and reasonable settlement. The generous instinct which has prompted Your Highness to leave these matters on one side during our visit is one with the sportsmanship which has always distinguished you. It made the name of Ranji a household word to generations of cricketers and it still assures Your Highness an affectionate welcome wherever sportsmen are gathered together. Whether you are catching sea trout on the west coast of Ireland or shooting partridges on the west coast of India your chief pleasure lies, I know, in offering good sport to your guests and we shall not soon forget our wonderful shoot at Rozi.'

TWENTY ONE
Duleep

Except for a brief visit to Jamnagar by the MCC team touring India two years earlier, Ranji's only connections with cricket now were through Duleep. By early May of 1928 Duleep was back from Switzerland and gathering strength in the nets at Cambridge. He rejoined the university eleven in a match against the West Indies, making 41, but it was five matches later before he scored his first fifty, against Sussex at Hove. He was still very weak, with little strength in his strokes, especially on the off side. At Lord's, however, he came good, making 52 and 37 in the drawn match against Oxford.

Ranji was in England again that summer, himself much restored by Duleep's return to health. With the university term over Duleep joined the Sussex team at Eastbourne and in his first innings took 121 off the Glamorgan bowlers, following this with 198 at Kettering against Northampton. As the weather warmed up so did strength flow back into Duleep's batting. In two glorious months he hit four more hundreds, against Middlesex, Kent, Somerset and Yorkshire, the last of these on his favourite Saffrons ground at Eastbourne.

Watching and reading about Duleep's exploits was like old times for Ranji. There is a photograph of Ranji at Duleep's bedside the previous winter, Duleep's flesh gone to nothing as he lay propped up on pillows and his eyes huge and stricken in his face. Now all that seemed to be over and Ranji rejoiced. He, too, had need of relaxation, for the Butler Committee was sitting in London and each of its sessions served only to confirm, in Ranji's view and that of most detached observers, its inadequacy and political ineptness.

Ranji made a series of speeches, the most important of them to
the National Liberal Club. In all of them he stressed the loyalty of
the princes and asked only that justice be done to them and their
treaties respected. He emphasised the importance of Indian subjects being treated on non-party lines.

Ranji also undertook a series of visits to further trade relations
between Nawanagar and England, one of his cherished hopes
being the establishment of direct trading between Hull and Bedi.

He spent as much time as he could spare at Ballynahinch. Before
returning to India he dined as a guest of Commander Kenworthy
(later Lord Strabolgi) at the Metropole, the purpose being informal
discussion of Indian affairs between the princes and Opposition
members of the House of Commons, Ramsay MacDonald, George
Lansbury, and Sir Charles Trevelyan among them.

Duleep spent some time at Jamnagar during the winter. In the
Bombay Quadrangular Tournament he made 84 and 38 for the
Hindus against the Parsis, the first match he had ever played in
India.

Ranji was in England – and Ireland – for much of the summer of
1929, so he was close at hand to share in Duleep's triumphs.
Altogether that season Duleep hit five centuries for Sussex and
two double centuries, scoring 2,500 runs. The only disappointment for Ranji was that Duleep failed in his first Test match.
Picked to play against South Africa at Edgbaston he managed only
12 and 1, and was dropped.

Duleep's batting had developed a new power and bloom, fierce
driving now accompanying the delicate glances and late cuts that
revived memories of Ranji.

Such was Duleep's form in June, July and August that, all else
being equal, he would almost certainly have been recalled to the
England side. His replacement, O'Connor, made 0 and 11 at Lord's,
then was dropped in his turn. Instead of Duleep, Woolley was
called back into action, making 83 and 95 not out, and then 154
and 46. Hendren was also dropped after three failures in a row, his
position going to Hammond, who had been injured.

There may have been political undercurrents to Duleep's

subsequent omission. One of the Selectors remarked to Duleep that the South Africans objected to his presence in the England side but Deane, the South African captain, got to hear of this and wrote to Duleep denying it. It was suggested that the South African Government were behind the objection. The rumours left a bitter taste and whatever the truth of the matter Duleep was not picked for the Gentlemen, though easily the leading amateur batsman of the moment. The suspicion grew that had Duleep played a big innings for the Gentlemen it would have been difficult to resist public insistence for his reinstatement.

Duleep was deeply upset. He was being totally supported by Ranji financially and was tempted to return to India and start work. Ranji, disgusted as he was over the situation, persuaded him otherwise. They had their reward the following winter and summer.

One match out of all those Duleep played in 1929 deserves particular mention. Against Kent at Hastings he made 115 in the first innings and 246 in the second. His 115 took him 105 minutes and his was the first century that season completed before lunch. He made his 246 in two instalments, 149 not out in 125 minutes on the second evening and 97 in 70 minutes on the third morning. His innings contained six 6s and forty-five 4s. 'The game was magnetised almost as in the era of his uncle Ranji,' wrote P. F. Warner. 'It is interesting to mention that he has never scored three figures except under two hours at the wicket. His fielding in the slips was wonderful.'

Ranji replied, in answer to a request from the *Evening Standard* for his comments on Duleep: 'You ask whether my nephew, Prince Duleepsinhji, is likely to play for England or for India. Perhaps, if the opportunity is given him, he ought to play for England, because he has learned all his cricket here; and, anyhow, there is no cricket of the very top class to be had in India.'

A. C. Maclaren, entering the debate on Duleep's eligibility, commented: 'Duleep's ability has been proved up to the hilt. If we are going to have the best team playing for England we must include people who come over here and make this country their home.'

In the event Duleep was selected to tour New Zealand that winter with an MCC side under Harold Gilligan. They played five State matches in Australia, Duleep averaging 38 for his ten innings. He played against Bradman and Jackson, and thought Jackson the more interesting. 'Duleep only showed us glimpses of his Eastern skill,' Bradman wrote after watching him score 34 and 37 against New South Wales.

In New Zealand, however, Duleep flourished. He scored 96 against Wellington in his first match, 127 against Nelson in his second, and, in the first Test at Christchurch, 49 and 33 not out. At Wellington, in the second Test, he scored 40 and 56 not out. He made his first Test century at Auckland in the third Test, and 63 in the fourth.

His average in the Tests was 89.50. The New Zealand critics compared him to Victor Trumper.

Ranji, at Jamnagar or in the Chamber of Princes in Delhi all that winter, was kept closely informed of Duleep's achievements. The Australians were due in England in April and Ranji, appointed President of Sussex – to whom he gave a present of £1,000 – in succession to the third Marquess of Abergavenny, was determined to see as much cricket as he could.

It was Duleep, though, who had rekindled his passion for cricket, and during that summer of 1930 Duleep did not disappoint him. In his second innings of the season, against Northamptonshire, the day the new Hove scoreboard was put into action, he scored 333, beating both Ranji's own 285 not out of 1901 as the record score for Sussex and Victor Trumper's 300 not out of 1899, the highest individual score made in Sussex and against the county.

It was the start of a fabulous run: 92 for MCC against the Australians at Lord's, 147 for Sussex against Cambridge, 116 and 102 in the Whitsun match against Middlesex at Lord's. It was during this match that Duleep was sounded out as to whether he would be available to play for England in the first Test match, due to start two weeks later at Trent Bridge. Duleep was fully qualified under the Rules for Test matches framed by the Imperial Cricket

Conference in 1909 and certainly the Australians had no reserva-
tions. The fourth Lord Harris, former Governor of Bombay, who
had doggedly opposed the selection of Ranji as 'a bird of passage',
was still in office at Lord's as Treasurer of MCC, but at the age of
eighty he was not quite the dominating figure of old.

Duleep was chosen for the England side at Nottingham but left
out of the original twelve, agreed generally to be an error. Sutcliffe was unfit for the second Test at Lord's and this time the
mistake was not repeated. England batted first and Duleep, coming
in after the loss of Hobbs and Woolley for 53, made 173 out of 332
in four and three-quarter hours before being caught on the
boundary. He scored 48 in the second innings but England still
lost the match by seven wickets. Bradman hit 254 and with
Woodfull put on 242 in 160 minutes.

About Duleep's century Cardus wrote: 'His late cutting left
even Australian slips standing. His cricket was as though part of
the afternoon's sunshine; it gleams in my mind even as I write
these lines, more than 29 years later.' Bradman later wrote: 'His
drives off Grimmett were so powerful that, fielding at mid-off and
cover where many of them went, I had to bandage my bruised
hand at the tea interval.'

Ranji was in his box to watch his nephew. 'I was at Lord's the
whole day,' he said in an interview, 'and watched every stroke
played with the enthusiasm of a schoolboy. It was only natural
that my greatest interest was centred in Duleep and that I should
feel nervous for him at the beginning. But after he got into his
stride the nervousness disappeared and from then it was nothing
but a sheer delight to see him. Through this innings of Duleep I
have lived over once again all my own cricketing days.'

Ranji was to remark that evening that he was the proudest man
in England. 'I realised one of my life's ambitions today.'

For the rest of that magical summer, wherever he was – at
Staines or Ballynahinch, in Brighton or touring the country making speeches – Ranji was to be uplifted by his nephew's batting.
In the remaining Tests Duleep's scores were 35, 10, 54, 50, 46. In
the Gentlemen v. Players match at Lord's Duleep made 125 and
103 not out, the second time within a month he had made a century

in each innings. He made 185 not out against Essex at Hove a few days later, and followed his 54 in the Old Trafford Test with 188 against Hampshire on the United Services ground at Portsmouth. Altogether that summer Duleep scored 2,562 runs.

Ranji returned from Ballynahinch to give a banquet for the Australians during their match with Sussex. The Australians came to Brighton shortly after the fifth Test. Duleep made only 15 this time, being stumped by Oldfield off Hornibrook who took his wicket seven times in their meetings over the summer. At the Metropole the menus, with the first grouse of the season as the main dish, bore pictures of Ballynahinch.

The Australians, having taken part in the Scarborough Festival, left for home a few days later. Ranji spoke at their farewell dinner. He was never loath to introduce the Indian situation into sporting occasions and this was no exception. Such phrases as 'The princes of India have been very old members of Great Britain's teams; and both on easy and difficult wickets they have tried their best to play with a straight bat for the Empire' must have rung strangely on Australian ears, though similar phrases are not unknown from their own after-dinner speeches.

The Round Table Conference – at which the Mahatma Gandhi, with quite different aspirations for India, appeared in a loin cloth and leading a goat – took place that autumn. Ranji spoke often and at length. 'One thing is certain,' he said, 'if those who have come to this Conference go back to India without the Parliament of Britain making it clear that the minimum constitutional demands of India will be conceded, not only will this Conference have been held in vain, but I am much afraid that such a fiasco would strengthen beyond measure the extremist party in India.'

Ranji was hopeful but wary in his views about the value of the Conference. His wariness was more realistic. The Conference adjourned in a shambles. 'Suspicion and distrust are reigning supreme,' Ranji wrote in a letter.

He hung on at Staines until the new year, though often laid up with either bronchitis or rheumatism. He planned to stay at Jamnagar only until the end of the cold weather, then be back in time for the summer of 1931 at Ballynahinch, for meetings in

London at the resumed Conference, perhaps even to watch Duleep play an innings or two.

He worked hard on the princes' case, undeterred by the divisions in their own ranks. In July he addressed an all-party meeting of MPs at the House of Commons, re-stating his views on federation: 'The princes are in favour of federation but they want safeguards for their States.'

Congress at this time were advocating the boycott of everything British, including the language, and Ranji took pains to try and soften anti-Indian feeling, particularly in the cotton towns of the north-west. 'The princes,' he said, 'are absolutely opposed to the Extremist Party in the Congress and to all this talk of independence. They are determined to remain in the Empire, but at the same time they have no desire to stand in the way of India's ordered progress towards equality within the Empire.'

The continued dissension among the princes distressed him, making him feel all his efforts on their behalf were going to waste. He lobbied MPs, and gave dinner parties at Staines to fellow-delegates and other interested parties from the Commonwealth.

Duleep, alone, did not fail him. He had spent the winter building up his strength in Switzerland and in the softer climate of the South of France, and he had accepted the captaincy of Sussex thirty-two years after his uncle had first taken it on. In May, at the Oval, he hit 162 against Surrey, 112 against Northamptonshire at Northampton, 112 against Leicestershire at Leicester. During the Horsham week, where Surrey and Nottinghamshire were the visitors, Duleep's scores were 20, 59, 97, 109.

In the match before the first and only projected Test match against New Zealand, he took 140 off the Essex bowlers at Chelmsford.

It had been planned that the New Zealanders would play only one Test, at Lord's, but their form so much exceeded expectations that two extra Tests, at the Oval and Old Trafford, were arranged. At Lord's Duleep made 25 and 11, at the Oval 109, at Old Trafford 63.

For Sussex he once again murdered Tich Freeman, this time at Tunbridge Wells, following his Hastings massacre of the year before with 91 and 127. He took another century off Essex at Hove, and made 161 not out at Dudley against Worcestershire. This was the first of four consecutive hundreds, the second of which was his Test hundred at the Oval. For good measure he made 103, his twelfth century of the season, against the New Zealanders in his last match at Hove.

Sussex, after a bad start in a continuously wet summer, finished fourth in the championship, Duleep himself scoring 2,684 runs in first-class matches.

Neville Cardus observed about Duleep, having remarked on an occasional, disfiguring crudeness in an otherwise immaculate innings:

> He is a born batsman, one of the few geniuses cricket knows today; but he has still to make an acquired culture second nature. With Ranjitsinhji we had a different case: Ranji remained from first to last a law unto himself – an Eastern temperament expressing itself in a technique entirely unique and born of that temperament. But Duleepsinhji *has* acquired the orthodox technique of English batsmanship, to which he has lent an exquisite bloom of wrist-play, and a suppleness and swiftness born of sinuous muscle and wonderful eye. Until he has so mastered orthodoxy and rendered a grammar learned on English cricket fields an instinctive thing – until then, he is bound to disturb us, if only at long intervals, by some discordant piece of work.

These curiously critical words were written on the occasion of Duleep's Test century, made in just over two hours, and half of his runs coming from boundaries.

Ranji, delighted as he was at Duleep's success, was able less and less to watch cricket himself. He was rarely well that summer, overwork, recurrent malaria, and increasing problems with his remaining eye forcing him to his bed. Even Ballynahinch could not quite console him for his troubles. When he sailed for India in November 1931 it was some comfort that Duleep was to spend the winter in India with him. India were to play their first Test match at Lord's the following summer and Duleep had been co-opted to

the Selection Committee. Indian cricket, not previously of a consistent enough quality to engage his talent, was in the process of
maturing: C. K. Nayudu, V. M. Merchant, Amar Singh, Mushtaq
Ali, C. S. Nayudu, Mahomed Nissar were among those of great
individual gifts only awaiting the opportunity to make an impact
on international cricket.

In the New Year, while Ranji was hard at work in the Princes'
Chamber, Duleep came up to Delhi to play for the Viceroy's
eleven against the Roshanara Club. Several of the cricketers due
to tour England were playing. Ranji was able to take time off to
watch Duleep score 173 in the second innings and the Nawab of
Pataudi 91.

It was a disappointment for Ranji that the Viceroy could not
see his way to visit Jamnagar for the Silver Jubilee celebrations.
He himself attended the Dwarka Puri temple, where fifty-three
years earlier he had been secretly adopted by Jam Vibhaji as heir,
and once again, to the chanting of Vedas, was bathed in the holy
water of the Ganges.

'In the silver chariot of State,' Roland Wild wrote, 'he rode to
the Palace dressed in the historic costume of a Kshatriya King,
through the thousands of his subjects, preceded by Princes. Every
caste celebrated with a ceremonial dinner, thousands being seated
in the open air and in *shamianas*. The Jam Saheb flung custom to
the winds and visited the feasts of the Untouchables, and when
the headman ran to him with a garland to place at his feet, he
insisted on it being put round his neck. Then he weighed himself,
wearing the full armour of the founder of Nawanagar, against
silver ingots, giving these to the poor.'

Progress towards agreement among the princes on the subject of
federation made no headway, in spite of Ranji's painstaking efforts.
Their interests were too varied, the fears of the greater among them
over questions of status and independence conflicting with the
needs of the lesser.

In May Ranji sailed once again for England. After the bickering
and aggravation of the Chamber, a summer in England might
have been expected to provide change and relaxation. There was

still his garden at Staines and the remoter riverside pleasures of Ballynahinch. But much of his time was taken up with consultations in Whitehall and exhausting visits to the north-west for discussions on direct trade between Kathiawar and the cotton towns.

In an address to one of the Law Society's clubs Ranji concluded: 'I was brought up among the English and have a great affection for them, but I am an Indian at heart, and would not hesitate to advocate the withdrawal of the English from India if I thought it wise. I do not think so, however, and I hope that the firm partnership between the King-Emperor and the princes will continue indefinitely.'

At the end of June India played their first Test match against England, at Lord's, an event which made it unlikely that any Indian-born Indian would ever follow in the footsteps of Ranji and Duleep and play for England. The three-day match had a sensational beginning, Sutcliffe and Holmes being bowled by the burly Nissar for 3 and 6 respectively, and Woolley being run out at 19. England finally won a low-scoring game by 158 runs, but not before India had shown themselves to be a side with a future. England were captained by the Bombay-born D. R. Jardine, by some comfortable way the top scorer in each innings on either side.

Duleep was again captaining Sussex in 1932 and from the start of the season he was in good form. Sussex, too, began to show some of the consistency that was to take them to second place three years running, each time under a different captain. Until they were defeated by the eventual champions, Yorkshire, late in August, they did not lose a match. By that time Duleep was seriously ill.

Duleep hit five hundreds during the season, though one of these was for the South against the North, and another for Gentlemen v. Players at Lord's. He had few failures for the county he led with such unassuming authority and intelligence. In successive innings in June, for example, he made 89 and 30 against Gloucestershire, 116 against Worcestershire, 126 against Surrey, 83 and 91 against Yorkshire, 18 against Warwickshire and 111 against Lancashire. Most of the Sussex side were getting runs, Bowley, Jim Parks, James Langridge, Harry Parks, Tate and Tommy Cook all passing the thousand, and Tate, Jim Langridge and Bert Wensley each taking more than a hundred wickets. The fielding, so often a cause of failure in Ranji's day, rarely let them down. Arthur Gilligan had set an example throughout the 1920s and Sussex since then have generally lived up to the reputation created in those years.

By early August, when Sussex were in with a chance of the championship, Duleep had already received word of his selection for Australia. During the next few weeks Bowley and Wensley were injured and out of the side. Then Duleep himself fell ill. He continued playing for some matches but, a shadow of his true self, managed only one score over 35 in eleven innings.

His doctors forbade him to go on. Ranji, learning only of Duleep's comparative loss of form and ignorant of the gravity of his illness, telegraphed him from Aix-les-Bains not to pay any attention but to see the season through. More than once before, when Duleep had struck a bad patch, Ranji had flippantly wired him to give up the game and concentrate on tennis, preferably against women.

It was a fatal misjudgment on Ranji's part, and one that he came to regret bitterly. His deep love for Duleep was never in doubt but he sometimes chided him in that insensitive fashion parents show to their children. As a result of Ranji's injunction Duleep disregarded his doctor's orders. Ranji's cable, in fact, had been concerned and encouraging, but it also contained the phrase 'think more of the interest of the side than of your reputation.' The cable ended: 'I put your fielding much above most people's batting. Therefore go on. Love and Success.'

Duleep ended his season for Sussex with 83 against Glamorgan at Swansea, and 90 against Somerset at Taunton. That last innings took its toll and it was only with the greatest difficulty that he completed it. He was exhausted and haemorrhaging. 'When I walked off the field,' Duleep wrote later, 'even I did not realise that I would never again step onto a cricket ground as a player. So ended my happy days. I enjoyed my cricket and the many friends I made in the cricket world. I gave my best to the game, and she gave me in return the happiest days of my life.'

On 17 September the *Orontes* sailed for Australia but without Duleep. Captained by Douglas Jardine England, among much ill-feeling over 'body-line', were to win four of the five Tests. The Nawab of Pataudi, like Ranji and Duleep before him, made a hundred in his first Test match against Australia, but after failing in the second Test was dropped for the rest of the series.

Duleep was packed off to a sanatorium in Switzerland. He did not, unfortunately, respond to treatment. By the time the next summer had come he was no better. In a letter resigning from the Sussex captaincy, he wrote: 'I am afraid my playing days are over for at least five years.' In fact, they were over for ever. Over the following months Duleep underwent several operations and convalesced, when he was well enough to travel, on the Cornish coast.

In December 1934 Duleep returned to India for good. There was no longer anything to keep him in England. He devoted himself to State affairs in Jamnagar, and in his spare time did what he could to encourage local cricketers. Vinoo Mankad, one of the greatest all-rounders in the history of cricket, was one of his protégés.

In 1936 Duleep married Princess Jayrajkumari of Rajpipla. After Independence he served as Indian High Commissioner in Australia from 1950–53, in 1954 as Chairman of the Public Services Commission of Saurashtra, and until his death in December 1959 as Chairman of the All-India Council of Sports. About him R. C. Robertson-Glasgow wrote: 'In Duleep's batting, beauty and orthodoxy were perfectly wedded. Lithe, strong of wrists, quick in eye and foot, he had neither cause nor inclination to fear any bowler. In the killing of slow bowling he had no superior, perhaps no equal in England . . . As friend or casual acquaintance, companion or opponent, he is courteous and courageous, interested and interesting; "a very perfect gentle knight".'

Ranji left for India from Victoria on Christmas Eve 1932. Engulfed in a huge overcoat with Astrakhan sleeves and collar he was photographed on the boat train, his parrot Popsey, who had been the most constant companion of his adult life, in a cage beside him.

It was a sad voyage home for Ranji. Duleep's condition, to whose acuteness he felt his own thoughtlessness had contributed, depressed him. He felt, in terms of objectives achieved, that his own mission had been a failure. He arranged to cable comments on the Test matches now under way in Australia to various newspapers but, so far from the scene of action, it was scarcely a responsible commission.

In March Ranji's term as Chancellor of the Princes' Chamber was due to end. He left Jamnagar to attend the annual meeting and to deliver his farewell speech. Repeatedly he had spoken of the feeling of relief that his freedom from office would afford. More and more often he turned his thoughts to Ballynahinch and, fancifully perhaps, to spending the last years of his life in an atmosphere free of Indian politics.

TWENTY TWO

Final Agenda

The Narendra Mandal met in the Council House of the Princes' Chamber, New Delhi, on Monday 20 March 1933, for the first of their two meetings. The Viceroy, Lord Willingdon, presided but the turn-out of princes and ruling chiefs was poor. Forty-five attended on 20 March, representing Kashmir (1), Central India (9), Rajputana (9), Punjab States (6), Western India States (6), Bombay (5), Bihar and Orissa (3), Central Provinces (2), Punjab (2), and United Provinces (2). On 25 March, when the second, more important meeting took place, the Maharajahs of Kashmir, Bhopal, Jaora, Panna and Narsingarh failed to appear, having severed their connection with the Chamber, though not apparently through hostility to Federation.

The eight-point Agenda was dealt with in two parts. On 20 March resolutions were passed of condolence on the death of His Highness the Maharajah of Chatarpur and of welcome to His Highness the Rajah of Bilaspur. Ranji, as Chancellor, next read a statement reviewing the work performed by the Chamber of Princes during the past year. Item 4 was the receipt of the report of Sir Prabhashankar Pattani regarding his work as a representative of India at the last meeting of the League of Nations. All four resolutions were carried unanimously.

The last four items on the agenda were: the statement from the Jam Saheb of Nawanagar regarding the work of the Indian States' Delegation to the Third Round Table Conference; resolutions on matters arising out of the White Paper; a resolution of thanks to His Highness the Chancellor by His Highness the Maharajah of Alwar; and elections.

It was for Ranji, therefore, to open the proceedings on the second morning, 25 March. 'I devoted the whole of my time,' he began, 'during the summer, autumn and early winter of 1932 to a study of the problems of federation. No doubt, like the majority of Your Highnesses, I started on my work with a strong predisposition in favour of federation. The federal form of government seems at first sight well suited to India, providing as it does the means of establishing a joint administration of all-India matters, while reserving to the States and Provinces the control of their local affairs. But it soon became plain to me that the form of federation which His Majesty's Government have in mind for India will differ from all modern federations in one important particular . . . In the case of India, His Majesty's Government are relying upon the Indian States, with their essentially monarchic politics, to contribute the necessary elements of stability and experience. For my own part I feel that it is very unfortunate that the realisation of British India's political ambitions should have been made contingent upon the acceptance of a particular type of federation by the Indian States. I do not see that there is any logical connection between the two matters. I have nothing but the friendliest and most brotherly sentiments for British India and I wish her leaders well. I hope that she will attain her aspirations, but I hope she will do this without involving the States in her own troubles.'

Ranji continued: 'We have to see whether the form of the Constitution is such as to protect the States in the enjoyment of their sovereignity and to secure for them the influence which is their due.' There was a need 'to consider whether the tendencies to which the new Constitution will give rise are such as to preserve in effective form the ancient ideals and institutions of Indian monarchy, upon which the strength and stability of the States and their utility in the new Constitution will alike depend.'

At some considerable length Ranji now began to discuss the merits of these propositions. He quoted in his favour the arguments outlined in a long letter to the *Manchester Guardian* from Dr Berriedale Keith, 'the best known of all modern writers on the Constitutional Law and Government of the Dominions'. Keith's

letter ended: 'The British Government still has the power by a
wise constitution of the legislatures and by using the best elements
of the States to create a form of responsible government which,
with advice and aid from the United Kingdom, may work. But
the idea that it can operate safeguards, defying the Ministry and
Parliament, is a chimera which will utterly disappoint in practice
those unwise enough to accept at their face value the views of the
Secretary of State.'

Some twenty minutes later Ranji, enlarging on the sufferings
endured by the States in the application of policies to themselves
designed primarily for British India, remarked 'economically as
well as politically the monarchial principle will suffer.'

There were several pages of Ranji's speech still to be read, but
at this point the Viceroy interrupted: 'It hardly seems to me to be
a report of the Third Round Table Conference. It seems to me (I
have allowed His Highness the Chancellor the widest possible
latitude in this matter) a personal statement, a statement of the
views of His Highness the Chancellor on the proposed Constitution. I do not wish to criticise, I do not wish to stop His Highness
if he wishes to continue his remarks, but they are purely personal
observations and in no sense a report of the Third Round Table
Conference.'

Ranji, his notes still in his hand, replied: 'Your Excellency, I
will obey Your Excellency's ruling. My first paragraph was an
estimate, as far as I have been able to do it, of the position of
affairs today. If Your Excellency does not wish me to continue
the report and the conclusions . . .'

The Viceroy again broke into Ranji's remarks: 'I am not going
to stop Your Highness if you wish to go on. I am only just stating
the case as I see it from the Chair.'

Ranji continued: 'I am only stating my views on the findings of
the Round Table Conference. May I take it that this be taken as
read?'

H.E. The Viceroy: 'You may do what you like.'

Ranji: 'I will carry out whatever you say.'

H.E. The Viceroy: 'I have already stated that I think your
remarks are going far wider than a report on the Third Round

Table Conference. I would only suggest to you to take what action you feel you should.'

The exchanges continued in this fashion until the Viceroy, plainly wearying of it, said: 'If Your Highness is strongly of the opinion that you are keeping within the terms of the Round Table Conference report I have got nothing more to say. You can continue your speech.'

The sharper tone of the Viceroy's last two remarks seemed suddenly to come home to Ranji. 'No, Sir,' he replied, 'I respect your ruling.' He then sat down.

The Viceroy turned towards him. 'I am sure,' he said, 'we have listened with much interest to what we have heard. With regard to the remarks of His Highness the Chancellor I can only say that, while I have been extremely regretful to cause any inconvenience to His Highness, I do feel that he should have kept entirely within the terms of the report of the Round Table Conference. And from what I have seen – I do not know what Your Highness feels – I think His Highness has been producing his own views, very gloomy views if I may say so, with regard to the future Indian federation, which I do honestly feel should not fall from the lips of the Chancellor of this Chamber which has for four years been endeavouring, supporting and assisting in introducing this all-India federation.'

Ranji, however, had the final say: 'The federation, Sir, which I supported was the federation suggested in the first Round Table Conference. Our representatives went away from that, and I parted company. That, really, Sir, is what I have to say on that point.'

These were the last words of any significance Ranji was to speak in the Chamber. However, his contemporary biographer and subsequent press reports, suggested that in some way Ranji had been prevented from speaking out. Wild, in rather melodramatic fashion, even went so far as to write: 'He did not fight. He seemed to grow older in that moment . . . It was one of his greatest friends who had told him, for the edification of the whole of India, that his fears were of no interest. But more than that, he mourned for the humanity of friends who had stabbed him in the back. Those whom he had helped, sometimes at the expense of his own State, had turned on him. He knew that, and his notorious belief in the goodness of humanity was torpedoed and wrecked.'

Whether or not this represented Ranji's true feelings, it is scarcely a fair account of what took place.

When the speech was reprinted in full three months later – after Ranji's death – it was seen to meander on in much the same way, expressing sincere doubts and a sorrowful divergence of opinion from that of the Viceroy. Yet again, in different words, he reiterated: 'I am not against federation as federation, I want federation for the States only if they can join with safety, complete safety.'

It would have been an even more long-winded and repetitive speech than the one delivered and, irrespective of the merits of the case Ranji argued, it is hard not to recognise that the Viceroy was both indulgent and correct in his assessment of its relevance. On the Minute Paper (Political Department) concerning the proceedings, which was forwarded to Whitehall for the inspection of the Secretary and Under Secretary of State, it was commented: 'The Jam Saheb opened the second day's proceedings with a lengthy criticism of the dangers to the States of the Federal proposals until he was pulled up and rebuked by the Viceroy . . . As to the incident with the late Jam Saheb, the Viceroy seems to have been very long-suffering. The speech – whatever may be thought of the force of the argument used – was very irrelevant to the subject matter, a report on the Third RTC.'

The impression was created that Ranji rose and left the Chamber, a broken man. The events of the next week were to reinforce the view that he had been mortally wounded and had made up his mind to die.

The facts in no way bear this out. There were still three points on the agenda to be dealt with and Ranji was still the Chancellor. Item 6 concerned resolutions on matters arising out of the White Paper and these were dealt with briefly and satisfactorily. Ranji, however, misunderstanding a reference earlier in the day to office procedure made by the Maharajah of Alwar, who commented on the late receipt of documents, took it as a reflection on his administrative efficiency. Ranji used the occasion to offer his colleagues a stinging rebuke of his own: 'If we could only do two things, that is, be punctual and talk less irrelevantly, we should be getting on with our work much better and the office will have some chance of circulating papers in time.'

Ranji spoke again for some time, winding up with formal thanks to the Viceroy: 'Your Excellency, on behalf of the Chamber let me once again thank you for the unfailing sympathy with which you have approached our problems, championed our cause, and appreciated our difficulties.' To this the Viceroy replied, concluding with the wish that 'with all my heart you will be guided in the right way and that your decision will be in the best interests not only of your own Order but of India as a whole.'

It remained for the Maharajah of Alwar to move the resolution of thanks to the retiring Chancellor. In the course of this he remarked: 'While I have had the pleasure of moving three resolutions on previous occasions thanking Chancellors for their work – to no one I personally owe, and I believe this House owes, greater thanks than to His Highness the present Chancellor, for his great industry and untiring labour. His Highness has been the first cricketer who has been elected as Chancellor. He had his eleven, which is the number of the Standing Committee; I am not prepared to say that it worked entirely as a team. There was also a good deal of body-line bowling, but nevertheless His Highness stood his ground and in the interests of our Order has suffered much odium, but at the same time he has also achieved much praise and glory.'

Ranji replied: 'When I undertook the office last year I felt really I was not qualified for this very high position and the reason is this. Your Excellency, Your Hignesses, I am no politician. The politician is one who respectfully has to hide his feelings and to clothe his sentiments in words in exactly the opposite of what he means. I have not got that gift . . . Your Excellency, I would like to give you an assurance that I have the greatest affection and regard for you, and no personal differences of opinion would make the slightest difference in our warm relations towards one another.'

Before the Princes adjourned the Maharajah of Patiala was
elected to succeed Ranji.

Although Ranji had undoubtedly suffered a certain blow to his
self-esteem the subsequent exchanges scarcely suggest it was
irreparable. Ranji had said his say – most of it anyway – and there
was little more for him to do. His public role had come to an end.
Someone else would now have the responsibility of trying to
mobilise the princes into concerted action. Or else they would go
down, pulling in different directions, fading, anachronistic figures
on the screen of the Imperial past.

It was inevitable, and in his heart of hearts Ranji must have
realised it, that the princely States and their rulers would be
overtaken by events in British India. The surge towards democratic government was not going to be deflected by the interests
of hereditary princes, however enlightened. Whatever fears Ranji
entertained, many of his fellow rulers wanted to gamble on the
future and join with the aspirations of the new India, if only to
ensure a measure of survival. It was not Ranji's way. But, whatever
delaying actions could have been mounted, in the long run history
would always have been against a continually sub-divided India.
For Ranji, the British connection, the independence of the States
and their direct relationship with Whitehall, were precious
possessions not lightly to be laid aside.

He was, perhaps, too tired now and too ill – he had made more
than one reference during the day to his 'impaired' health – to be
able to sustain, or have much faith in, notions of progress. Ten
years earlier, in Geneva, he had seen how frail had turned out to
be the notions of brotherly love and collective security which he
had supported so wholeheartedly. It was the law of the jungle
that prevailed.

It was not in the nature of things for there to be ill-feeling between
Lord Willingdon and Ranji. The Maharajahs, one by one, had
said their farewells to Ranji, who appeared to be in a dream, and
left for their States. They were aware, most of them, that things
would not be the same again without their leader and moving
spirit. The events of the day had proved that. Some would find

new and exciting parts to play in a differently constituted society, others would go under.

But the Viceroy was not content to leave it there. He sent word to Ranji that afternoon that he would like to see him. Ranji accepted the invitation and together they talked, as old friends, about the India they shared. Dusk fell. Whether they came any closer in political terms was less relevant than that they parted in friendship. Ranji had no animosity. He had other matters now, more personal and more local, that claimed his attention.

He had, he realised, spent too much time of late on affairs outside his State and too little on Nawanagar. He would put that to rights. And for those months when he could get away for rest and a change of climate, there would always be Connemara, its lakes and rivers, its hedges of wild fuchsia and golden bracken, its mauve-green hills and soft rain.

TWENTY-THREE

The Last Journey

Ranji left for Jamnagar that night. He would have been amazed if he had known the controversy that would develop over the events of that last meeting and of its consequences. Fifteen months after his death, furious letters were to be exchanged in the columns of the *Morning Post* and *The Times*, and the nature of his relationship with Lord Willingdon discussed in leading articles.

For the moment, though, he was exhausted. The dust of Delhi always worried him and a visit there was followed as often or not by an attack of asthma. The train journey to Jamnagar in those days took two days and two nights, and though Ranji had his own private saloon and travelled in considerable comfort it was a tiring business. Many times had he made the journey before on State or shooting visits to neighbouring princes – to Alwar, Jaipur and Jodhpur – and he scarcely bothered to look out of the window. Instead, he did what he always did when he wanted to take his mind off things, he played bridge. The magic cities of Rajasthan slid by on either side of the track – the great camel centre of Bikaner to the west, Alwar, Jaipur and Ajmer to the east. Mostly it was flat desert country, though nearing Gujarat mauve flaps of mountains shielded the lake palaces of Udaipur to the south-east and, closer at hand, the six thousand-feet peak of Guru Sikhar, the highest peak of Mount Abu, rose seemingly sheer from the plain.

Not only was Mount Abu the landmark most familiar to Ranji – he had stayed there often with Sir Pratab Singh – on the last stage of the journey, but it was a place of Hindu pilgrimage. The Dilwara Temples are among the most perfect specimens of Jain architecture in India and the orchid-starred jungles on its slopes house the rarest of birds. The Nakki Talao – a lake scattered with islands – must have reminded Ranji of Connemara. The Lawrence School in the city – an establishment for the children of British soldiers and named after Sir Henry Lawrence, whose wife Honoria is buried in the adjacent cemetery – was run along the same lines as the Rajkumar College of his own youth. Ranji was no stranger to the cricket ground scooped out of the Abu hills.

It was dark when the train entered Gujerat on the second evening. For once the endless rubbers of bridge had failed to do the trick. Ranji remained restless. He went over the proceedings in the Chamber of Princes again and again with his staff. It was not a question of Ranji feeling that he had been muzzled – as the press subsequently tried to make out – but of his testing the force of his own arguments.

The train reached Jamnagar shortly after dawn. It was colder than in Delhi but Ranji, though wearing only the thinnest of silk clothes, insisted, before returning to his palace, on driving out of the capital to inspect some construction work.

Twenty-four hours later, after another sleepless night, he was unable to leave his bed. Attacks of asthma and bronchitis, confining Ranji to his quarters for a few days, were nothing new to the palace staff, but it was soon apparent that this was an attack of unusual severity.

He tossed and turned continually, coughing, and finding it harder and harder to breathe. He began to imagine his secretaries were still in the room, drafting reports. The English doctor who attended him in his last years subsequently described the scene. ‘ “Take them away,” he said. “You know I don’t want them here when I’m ill – let them work downstairs.” ’ ‘Even now,’ Dr Prosser Thomas wrote in an article published in the *Daily Mail* nearly three months later, ‘the memory of those terrible days is so vivid and poignant that any description of them seems almost sacrilegious.’

Far from giving up the ghost and dying out of disillusionment and despair – as was soon to be asserted – Ranji fought tenaciously for life. His luggage was already being prepared for his planned trip to England and Ireland and he was looking forward to it eagerly. Sir Robert Horne had referred glowingly to Ranji in a speech made in the House of Commons the day after Ranji's condition had deteriorated – 'one of the Empire's most loyal citizens' – and the account of it, when it was read out to Ranji, brought a smile of pleasure.

For five days Ranji struggled. 'If I could only sleep,' he said time and again. Hypnotics, Prosser Thomas reported, were useless. Sleep would have been the deciding factor in his illness and nothing could procure it for him.

The terrible coughing continued day and night, accompanied by increasing breathlessness.

His nephew Digvijaysinhji, who had met Ranji on his return from Delhi and who had made a tour of the city with him on that first day – discussing matters that might need attending to during Ranji's absence in Europe – had subsequently left for Bombay to see the young Maharajah of Jaipur off to England. He was now sent for.

On the night of 1 April Ranji's heart began to fail. He embraced in turn those members of his family that were present and at five o'clock in the morning of 2 April he died.

When Digvijaysinhji, alerted by telegram on the train from Bombay, flew in from Ahmedabad at ten o'clock he found the whole city robed in mourning white, the streets silently lined by Ranji's people.

The body, washed in holy water and arrayed in gold, was carried downstairs to lie in state. The mourners, as they passed, laid strips of rich cloth on the body, as is the custom. Shortly before mid-day the procession set out to the burning ghat in the city, Ranji's brother and nephews at its head. When, by sunset, it was all over, and nothing remained of the body, Ranji's eldest nephew Pratapsinhji, who had lit the fire, returned to the palace. Five months later, in the ageless Hindu ritual, he would strew the ashes over the river at that most holy junction of the Ganges and the Jumna.

Tributes to Ranji flowed in from all over the world. His fellow princes made their way to Jamnagar as best they could, but because of the haste with which Hindu cremations are conducted few were able to be present at the funeral pyre. The city, desolate and silent, remained in mourning for six months.

Ranji's passing was no more allowed to take place without controversy than had much of the latter part of his life. On 19 July 1934, the *Morning Post* published under the dramatic heading 'Ranji's Farewell to Life' an article under the New Delhi by-line 'Our Special Correspondent'. This provoked an immediate response but resulted, curiously, in the form of three letters not to the *Morning Post* but to *The Times*. The first letter was from Naoroji Dumasia, author of *Jamnagar and Its Ruler* (1927) and a member of the Legislative Assembly, the second from Roland Wild, author of *Ranji*, and the third from E. F. Hunt, Ranji's own solicitor.

The *Morning Post* despatch, presented under a series of banner headlines 'Tragedy of a Staunch Friend of England', 'Broken Heart After Public Rebuke', 'Ganges Water: A Bare Room: The Will to Die', was editorially introduced, over the photograph of an ill-looking Ranji taken in his Staines garden the year before his death: 'One of the most tragic stories in the history of our Indian Empire – the true story of the death of the late Jam Saheb of Nawanagar, better known as Prince Ranjitsinhji, is the subject of a remarkable despatch from our Special Correspondent.

'Hitherto, the full circumstances, which are described overleaf, have been known only to a few in India, though the Jam Saheb's death, a week after his speech in the Chamber of Princes had been cut short by the Viceroy, has been the subject of much comment and speculation. The facts which we disclose today show that the death of the Jam Saheb was not a coincidence, as has been suggested in certain quarters, but a consequence.'

The article read as follows:

Ranjitsinhji, one of the best Princes India has ever known, one of the greatest cricketers, and one of the best friends England has ever had, died of a broken heart.

During the past year it has been widely suggested that his death within a week of his public rebuke by His Excellency, Lord Willingdon, was a coincidence.

The full and terrible story of the last week of his life proves that his death was no coincidence, but a tragedy of slighted loyalty.

Many will remember the circumstances:

On 25 March 1933, Lord Willingdon presided at the Chamber of Princes. As

Chancellor of the Chamber, the Jam Saheb of Nawanagar reported on the work of the Indian States Delegation at the Round Table Conference. He confessed that later developments and a clearer scrutiny of the Federal scheme had convinced him and other Princes of its dangers.

The Jam Saheb quoted the opinion of Professor Berriedale Keith to the effect that the safeguards proposed by the Secretary of State for India were valueless.

'I confess,' he said, 'that these words cuase me profound disquiet, for they coincide with certain apprehensions arising from our studies as to the difficulty of the Crown retaining in future any effective sovereignty in India.'

Called to Order

By this time Lord Willingdon had heard enough. Exercising his power as Chairman, the Viceroy called the Jam Saheb to order, and stated that he did not see the relevancy of personal opinions to the report of the States' Delegation, and observed that this was no occasion for airing views on the dangers of possible federation. The Jam Saheb replied that he would not proceed further with the reading of his statement. All this is common knowledge, and the speech which the Viceroy cut short was published in full in the *Morning Post* on 28 June 1933.

The Princes were quick to note the rebuke which had been given to their Chancellor, and many regarded it as proof of the British Government's determination to stifle any opposition to their policy. As for the Jam Saheb, he took the Viceroy's action as a public slight.

As Chancellor of the Chamber of Princes and as a loyal friend of England, he had felt that he 'could not evade his duty' to deliver a warning against the dangers of federation, though, as he added in the undelivered part of his speech, 'I should, had I been free to follow my own inclinations, have spoken merely smooth words.'

Feeling himself rebuked by the Power he sought to save, from the moment he left the Chamber he lost all desire to live. Friends who saw him later were horror-struck at the change in his appearance that had taken place in the space of a few hours.

They were never to see him again. A great gentleman to the last, he never uttered a word of reproach, never voiced an unkind comment even to his closest friend, though he did say that he had finished with politics and would never come to Delhi again. But although he gave no expression of his despair, the iron had entered into his soul. One thing alone gave them a hint of what had happened.

Farewell

Before he left Delhi he met all his friends and took leave of them in terms of the deepest affection and emotion. Then he disappeared from their ken. It was only later that they were to know the reason.

On his way home to Nawanagar he made a point of visiting the places he loved best and meeting those of his closest friends whom he had not met in Delhi. They, too, were puzzled by the circumstances and emotion of their meeting.

Reaching his home, his first act was to send for a supply of the holy water of the Ganges and for the removal of the furniture from the principal room of his palace. These were ominous orders. His retainers and servants watched him and carried them out with wondering apprehension, because such orders are only given at the solemn approach of death.

A Pilgrimage

Then began a pilgrimage round Nawanagar. No friends of whom he was fond, no places which had for him happy recollections, no scenes which recalled the great moments of his life were left unvisited. Orders were sent for his favourite perfumes and he permitted himself the use of unusual little luxuries. With great pains he made certain that all his affairs were in order, all his obligations discharged. Slowly the truth dawned: he who was about to die was taking leave of life.

Within a week he was ready to give his last command. A bath of Ganges water was prepared and the room made bare. In the evening it was known that he had a fever. In the morning he was dead. . . .

So passed a great gentleman and one of the best friends that England possessed.

To this, in the columns of *The Times*, Mr Dumasia replied:

THE LATE JAM SAHEB

A CHARGE REFUTED

TO THE EDITOR OF THE TIMES

Sir,—It is extremely painful for an Indian visiting this country to hear and to read the suggestion that death of his Highness the Jam Saheb was hastened, if not actually brought on, by the act of Lord Willingdon in pulling him up in his speech on the federal scheme in the Chamber of Princes. May I be permitted, as an old and intimate friend of the Jam Saheb, to defend the honour of that Prince against the misrepresentation made in this matter, which amounts to a charge of cowardice?

The insinuation is that His Highness so keenly felt the fact that he was not permitted to air a view antagonistic to federation, on an inappropriate occasion, that he crumpled under the blow and deliberately went home to his capital to die. Quite apart from the fact that for some time before that episode the Jam Saheb was in a very bad state of health, and that he was aware of the risks he ran by continuing to do his normal work, it is an insult to his memory to suggest that he was not the man – even when well advanced in years and broken in health – to take any reverse in a sporting spirit. His whole life was an example of struggle and of triumph over adversity. Never before, I think, has it been suggested that he was not a fighter, that he was not prepared to give and to take the hardest of blows. Only after his death was the contemptible suggestion uttered.

In politics as in sport, the late Jam Saheb played the game. The long struggle which he carried on for the rights of his State in developing its port is in itself proof of his ability to stand any knocks and still to persevere. It is a struggle worth recalling, too, because it was at his suggestion that Lord Willingdon agreed to take legal opinion on the issues involved in it – and the recent finding by Lord Dunedin vindicates his wisdom in that respect. Between him and Lord Willingdon there was a deep and abiding friendship, and I have often heard the Jam Saheb speak with the greatest affection of Lord Willingdon. They could differ and oppose each other on occasion as only two friends can do; but it seems to me unthinkable that either of them should have allowed any incident arising between them, however serious or however deep the momentary feeling may have been, to rankle and leave a bitter taste. The Jam Saheb is dead and cannot defend himself. I was his friend, trusted by him on many occasions, and I will not let it be said that I have not tried to defend his memory. I know as a matter of fact that the one great wish of the late Jam Saheb was to see his old friends Lord and Lady Willingdon once more at Jamnagar on the occasion of the jubilee of 25 years of his brilliant rule and the marriage of his heir, the present Jam Saheb Digvijaysinhji, who has formed a lasting friendship with Lord and Lady Willingdon which, in itself, is an irrefutable evidence of the fact that the late Ranji's successor does not believe the absurd story circulated by politicians in England.

It is all the more galling to think that the hideous charge of cowardice has been brought against the Jam Saheb with the obvious motive of attempting to discredit the reform scheme and of bringing Lord Willingdon into disrepute. A time may come when Lord Willingdon will be free to defend himself and to tell how he and the Jam Saheb parted for the last time as good friends, after a tea party given by the latter. But for the moment the man who has brought peace and quiet to India may be content to remain in silence; he can afford to ignore both the petty spite of political opponents and the manoeuvres of those who see in him a serious obstacle to their plans of checking constitutional progress in India. But it behoves those who honour the great Viceroy of India for his character and achievement and who loved the Jam Saheb not to suffer in silence while an infamous story is spread to the discredit of both of them.

Your obedient servant,
NAOROJI DUMASIA.

Roland Wild was not slow to offer corroboration:

THE LATE JAM SAHEB

HIS BIOGRAPHER'S TESTIMONY

TO THE EDITOR OF THE TIMES

Sir,—As one who has been in close touch with the successor of the late Jam Saheb, and with the present régime in Nawanagar, may I offer congratulations to your correspondent, Mr Naoriji Dumasia, for his spirited defence of 'Ranji's' memory which he contributed to your columns on Saturday.

I had the honour to be selected as the official biographer of 'Ranji,' and wish to endorse, in the most emphatic terms, the refutation of the cowardly charges now being made against him. Proof of your correspondent's contention that political motives are behind this campaign of vilification is to be found in the fact that when I protested to the appropriate quarters, giving the true facts of the case as I learnt them from those best in a position to know, I was met by a refusal to reopen the matter. Attempts have frequently been made to make political capital out of the true version of 'Ranji's' illness and death, by deliberate misreading of my words.

Unfortunately, the time has not yet come when a revelation can be made of the Jam Saheb's real feelings after that fateful Delhi meeting, and perhaps only Lord Willingdon will be in a position to give the full facts; but after the most patient research, and with the cooperation of the present Jam Saheb and others in Nawanagar, I am able to deny *in toto* every one of the gestures alleged to have been made by 'Ranji' in preparation for his death. There were incidents and coincidences in plenty to give strength to the theory that he knew the hour of his death, and after careful investigation, I have related these proven facts in the official history; but on the other hand there is abundant evidence to prove that the relations between the Jam Saheb and Lord Willingdon were continued on the same level of confidence, trust, and friendliness to the end.

So many versions of that last meeting have been given that it is essential to separate political bias from fact. Evidently no attempt has been made to perform this feat by ruthless political saboteurs to whom, apparently, not even the good name of a dead man is sacred.

Your obedient servant,
ROLAND G. WILD.

Two days later *The Times* printed the third letter:

THE JAM SAHEB

MISSTATEMENTS REFUTED

PRESENT RULER'S CORRECTIONS

TO THE EDITOR OF THE TIMES

Sir,—I am desired by cable from my client, his Highness the present Maharajah Jam Saheb of Nawanagar, to correct certain misstatements which have obtained circulation in England, and which appear to him calaculated to reflect upon his Highness the late Jam Saheb, and upon his relations with Lord Willingdon; and to ask you the favour of publishing this letter.

It is not the fact that the late Jam Saheb was so deeply affected by the Chamber of Princes incident that he returned home from Delhi after the meeting only to die. Everything points to the contrary. After the meeting of the Chamber he had a lengthy and most cordial conversation with Lord Willingdon, and discussed with him plans for a Viceregal visit to his State in the near future. To the last he looked upon Lord Willingdon as a sincere friend of himself and his State – a feeling which is entertained to the fullest extent by the present Jam Saheb. Nor is it the fact that on his way home from Delhi to Jamnagar the late Jam Saheb made a point of visiting the places he loved best and meeting those of his closest friends whom he had not met in Delhi. He returned direct from Delhi to Jamnagar without visiting any place en route. It is also untrue that on arriving at Jamnagar he began a pilgrimage to the places he loved best, or visited the friends of whom he was fond, in anticipation of his death. As was his usual practice, he visited his sister, but paid no visits to friends. So far from sending for a supply of holy water of the Ganges, he brought a supply of Ganges water with him on every possible occasion, and he did so on this occasion. It was his regular practice, and

no isolated case. The statement that on reaching his home a room was prepared in anticipation of his death is entirely untrue. Nothing of the kind occurred. On his arrival at Jamnagar he drove through the city in an open car to greet and be greeted by his people. It was a chilly morning, and he contracted the chill which ended fatally.

His Highness is deeply distressed by the inaccurate statements which have been, and are being, circulated respecting the events preceding the death of his uncle the late Jam Saheb, and the inferences which they suggest, and trusts that his denial of their truth will put an end to their currency.

Yours truly,
E. F. HUNT.

The *Morning Post* was not, however, satisfied by these rebuttals and on 10 August they returned to the matter.

'RANJI'S FAREWELL TO LIFE'

ATTEMPTED DENIALS

THE REPLY OF OUR CORRESPONDENT

FACTS THAT SPEAK FOR THEMSELVES

BY OUR SPECIAL CORRESPONDENT

Frantic efforts are being made in certain political circles to discredit the account of the death of the late Jam Saheb of Nawanagar, published in the *Morning Post* of 19 July under the heading, 'Ranji's Farewell to Life'.

As was fully expected before the message was written that every attempt would be made to cast reflections on its accuracy, these efforts in themselves are not surprising and leave me quite unimpressed. Those who know something of the political

game in India and England at the present time will know the reasons and, at some future date, it may be necessary to say something more on this point.

But now that the flow of 'denials' seems to have stopped for a day or two, it may be of interest to examine those which have appeared.

They are remarkable for three reasons: their source, their manner, and their irrelevance.

With one exception, which will be dealt with later, no denials have been received by the *Morning Post*. On the other hand, the *Morning Post* received and published on 26 July a letter from Mr C. J. Rush, an intimate friend of Ranji's for 40 years, confirming the accuracy of the story.

The denials have taken the form of letters to the *Times*, which suggest that the authors are less concerned to correct any erroneous impression which might have been given to readers of the *Morning Post*, than to make a certain political impression.

The First Letter

The first letter, from a Mr Naoroji Dumasia, with a glorious lack of logic, accused me of imputing 'cowardice' to the late Jam Saheb. This curious charge I dealt with in a letter to the Editor of the *Morning Post* on 30 July.

The second letter to *The Times* was from Mr Roland G. Wild, and was published on 31 July. Mr Wild stated that he was the official biographer of 'Ranji', and wished 'to endorse in the most emphatic terms Mr Dumasia's refutation of the cowardly charges now being made against him.' As no 'charges', cowardly or otherwise, have ever been made against 'Ranji' in the *Morning Post*, Mr Wild's endorsement was as irrelevant as Mr Dumasia's letter.

But Mr Wild went on to say that 'when I protested to the appropriate quarters, giving the true facts of the case as I learnt them from those best in a position to know, I was met by a refusal to reopen the matter.' Later he writes: 'I am able to deny *in toto* every one of the gestures alleged to have been made by Ranji in preparation for his death.'

Now it is true that Mr Wild wrote to the *Morning Post* on 25 July to say that certain details in the account were untrue and that the *Morning Post* ought to publish the true facts and quote his biography of Ranji 'as the renewed speculation about his death to which your correspondent refers coincides with the arrival of my book in India.' But as the inaccuracies alleged by Mr Wild were trivial and the *Morning Post* had no wish to dwell on a painful subject, Mr Wild's invitation was refused.

This refusal produced a further letter from Mr Wild, dated 27 July, agreeing that the details concerned were 'trivial', but accusing my informants of having 'pirated' the whole story from his book!

The very next day Mr Wild wrote to *The Times*, as stated above, and his letter contained the further statement that 'there is abundant evidence to prove that the relations between the Jam Saheb and Lord Willingdon were continued on the same level of confidence, trust, and friendliness to the end.'

The Next Move

The next move was a letter in the *Times* from a Mr E. F. Hunt, acting for the present Jam Saheb. Mr Hunt laid emphasis on the friendship between Lord Willingdon and the late Jam Saheb 'to the end', and between the present Jam Saheb and Lord Willingdon – the latter friendship being sufficiently obvious. He denied my story in a similar strain. He also wrote: 'It is also untrue that on arriving at Jamnagar he began a pilgrimage to the places he loved best . . .'

All that need be said about both Mr Wild's and Mr Hunt's letter may be taken from Mr Wild's book, of which I have since bought a copy.

The book is called *The Biography of Ranjitsinhji* (Rich and Cowan, Ltd), and, it is important to note, has a Foreword by the present Jam Saheb, who endorses the book. 'The story of his life,' writes the Jam Saheb, 'will no doubt be a surprise to many people. They did not know the depth of feeling, the fervent loyalty . . . that animated him.'

In his preface the author makes a point of acknowledging all the authoritative help received.

Relevant Passages

Here then are some relevant passages from Mr Wild's account of these last days:

'On the only occasion that the Jam Saheb spoke about it, he said: "I accepted His Excellency's dictum." There was the revelation of the depth of his sorrow, which filled his heart more than anger. Many were deceived by his attitude and protested that he was little changed. But even the servants noticed, on his return to Jamnagar, that something was wrong. He played bridge on the train, but it was a brave effort and hardly successful.

'When he arrived back on the morning of the 27th, he was met at the station by Digvijaysinhji . . .

'"The very man I wanted to see," said the Jam Saheb, and proposed immediately a trip round the city. His words were significant, and throughout the whole of the day his conversation, now remembered in every detail, had a tragic meaning.

'"Let us go through our Jamnagar for the last time," he said. But Digvijaysinhji thought he was referring to his forthcoming departure for England . . . But his phrases were ambiguous and when he was asked what he meant he only answered with a smile.

'As he drove round the city he gave final instructions. He told his nephew to build a new market here, a bank there. "Build six new roads," he said, "but don't tarmac the Palace roads until the last . . ."'

'They drove to Bedi, past Rozi Island . . . past Cambridge-gardens reminiscent of youth . . . Sitting in the car at Bedi, he gave final instructions . . . It was as if he knew he would not have another chance of passing on his wishes, as if he were handing over his work at that moment.

'Returning, they spoke about a house for Digvijaysinhji.

'He waved a hand at the Jam Palace. "There is your abode," he said; "I want you to live there. Don't build any more houses and don't live anywhere else." . . . But then he made a curious remark, "But I have not been able to do anything for your brothers," he said, "so give them houses when you can."'

'It was noted that he did not command Digvijaysinhji to live in the Jam Palace. Rather, he pleaded with him. It was as if he had already handed over control . . .'

No need to quote more. Mr Wild's 'official biography', endorsed by the present Jam Saheb, confirms the essentials of the account published in the *Morning Post*.

Every Detail Checked

It is, of course, possible that there may have been slight inaccuracies of detail, but in view of the extraordinary correspondence referrred to above, I may be forgiven for preferring my own sources of information, from which every detail was carefully checked.

On this point, too, it is worth asking Mr Wild why my informants who, he alleges, 'pirated' the account from his book, should have taken only the essentials and got the details wrong.

Somebody (was it Bismark?) once said: 'Nothing is true until it is officially denied,' an observation which every experienced journalist can confirm. Truth is often inconvenient to officials, but it is doubtful if truth has ever been more embarrassing to them than it is in India today.

The account of the death of Ranji is only one small facet of the truth. If there is occasion to write about others, further denials from interested quarters may be confidently expected.

Curiously, even *The Times'* lengthy obituary of Ranji, published on 3 April 1933, did not pass without comment. Sir Leslie Scott KC, one of Ranji's legal advisers over many years, after paying his own homage, added:

May I venture a criticism of two small points in your notice? It is true that the Jam Saheb has had a controversy with the Government of India about Customs dues – upon which, of course, as it is *sub judice* and I have advised him professionally, I can say nothing – but it is not true that 'controversy undoubtedly coloured his more recent attitude towards Federation.' I know that it did not. It is obviously impossible for me to say more: but in justice to the man whom I revered I cannot say less. The other point is, I suspect, a mere matter of words. You say 'he could be uncannily adroit'. If you merely mean to pay a tribute of admiration such as a rather blundering person (like myself) would spontaneously pay to an able diplomat, or a good negotiator, the tribute is well-deserved; but if it means what some may read it as meaning, I say I never knew a man who was straighter than the Jam Saheb.

In conclusion, may I add that no Indian ruler ever recognized more completely than Ranji that it was his duty to govern well – his duty by religion towards his subjects; his duty under the Paramountcy relationship – which in practice meant towards the Viceroy; and his duty of loyalty to the King-Emperor. He was a wise and good ruler, beloved of all his subjects from the humblest to the most prosperous – and very many of the merchant princes of Bombay were his subjects. He had a really fine character as a man; and he was a perfectly delightful companion. Both England and India have lost a great patriot.

The discrepancies of detail were not, in fact, serious and to a certain degree Wild, and by extension, Ranji's successor as Jam Saheb, his nephew Digvijaysinhji, had brought the trouble on their own heads. Wild's biography was not innaccurately quoted and by lending it his authority the new Jam Saheb would certainly have seemed to concur with its account of Ranji's last days.

Even Ranji's own physician, in his article of a year earlier, had finished his description of Ranji's dying with the question: 'But, in the end, did despair come to Ranjitsinhji?'

In fact, as Dr Prosser Thomas made plain in that same article, there was no sense at all in which Ranji could be said to have died 'of a broken heart' or to have made preparations for his death in the way the *Morning Post* suggested. The most charitable explanation for the divergence between Wild's account of Ranji showing Digvijaysinhji round Jamnagar and the denial published in the letter from Hunt is that Digvijaysinhji never finished Wild's book. Or, if he did, the romanticised version of Ranji's farewell to life appealed to him. There is no reason to question the retraction, even if one accepts it as a gesture of friendship to Lord Willingdon.

Of all those present during Ranji's final illness only Dr Prosser Thomas, now living in retirement in Seaford, is in a position to offer first-hand evidence. His own view, expressed to me in 1982 without ambiguity, is quite simple: it is that the strain of Ranji's Chancellorship, the disunity of his fellow princes over federation and the inimical climate of Delhi to one with Ranji's heart and bronchial weaknesses, were undoubtedly contributory factors to the acuteness of the final illness. But there was no medical evidence whatsoever to suggest that Ranji took it upon himself to lie down and die, in bitterness and defeat, in the way outlined. Ranji's date of death may have been forecast by the joshi, and the letter opened after his death confirms it, but the story of his final days at Jamnagar is the tragic one of a man struggling vainly and agonisingly for breath. It was the body not the spirit that failed him.

The Presence of Ranji

There was nowhere Ranji went where he was not loved. There are not many alive now who knew him but all those who are – from palace servants at Jamnagar to ghillies at Ballynahinch – testify to his presence and charm. He was without doubt an immensely attractive personality and though latterly he could be arrogant towards his senior staff and sharp with his immediate family the figure he presented to the world was one of dignified modesty and sparkling good nature. Unlike the gentler and more compromising Duleep, though, he made his authority immediately plain. Touchy, perhaps, where matters of personal pride were concerned, his determination never to be trifled with was rarely at odds with a generous and courteous disposition. If people can be divided into natural hosts and guests Ranji was certainly a host.

In all the places where Ranji lived – Cambridge, Hove, Staines, Shillinglee, Jamnagar, Ballynahinch – something of his now legendary presence remains. But most especially it is at Ballynahinch and Jamnagar that there is tangible evidence.

The castle at Ballynahinch, now a hotel, has a portrait of Ranji in the hall and his old bedroom bears the name 'Maharajah's Room'. Along sides of the lake, numerous piers built by Ranji jut out from the turf margins of the encircling pinewoods. As you look back at the great quartz cone of Benlettery from the stone bridge that divides the lake your eye is caught, not only by the piers and scattered lake islands, but by the huts Ranji built and in which he amused himself at poker while awaiting a salmon.

The Indian prince, always in plus-fours and deer-stalker, is still

remembered at Ballynahinch for his generosity, his involvement
in local affairs, his motorcars, and his birthday. It was Ranji who
introduced the motorcar to Connemara and on his return to India
each autumn he would dispose of that year's purchases to local
worthies: the *Gardai*, a teacher, the local priest.

On his birthday 10 September, he always gave a free day with
full pay for the castle staff and estate workers, himself serving the
ghillies and gamekeepers at a slap-up seven-course lunch.

Not many miles from the wooded oasis of Ballynahinch, the
creamy waters of its river tumbling and frothing under the
austere peaks of Beanna Beóla – the Twelve Bens – stands Kyle-
more Abbey, a vast Victorian castle built on the water's edge by a
Liverpool merchant. It was here that Ranji sent his two nieces
Baba and Bjaniba to school in the twenties, for the abbey was taken
over and turned into a convent after the First World War by
Irish Benedictine nuns exiled from Ypres.

It is strange to think of an Indian prince holding sway over this
remotest of areas, miles and miles of peatbog stretching uninterrupted between the stone flanks of the Connemara hills. Yet,
in a real sense, this has become Ranji country, not only because of
his own love for it but because it complements that other paradise,
the Kileshwar hills. In climate there could scarcely be two more
contrasting areas but in the contours and colours of the landscape,
the stony dispositions of foothills and outcrop, they are mirror-
images of each other. To walk among the Connemara woods and
hills, and along the banks of the teeming rivers, is to realise how
soothing the memory of it all must have been to Ranji sweating it
out in the burning droughts of Kathiawar.

It is, naturally, at Jamnagar that the presence of Ranji remains
most evident. Although the princes have long since been stripped
of their titles and their privy purses – within a score of years all
Ranji's predictions came to be fulfilled, though whether for the
general good or ill is a matter of opinion – in many princely States
the trappings, if not the reality, of power survive. Nawanagar
was never anything but a minnow in the large pond of princely
India but Ranji, by his own prestige and his progressive manage-

ment of industry and agriculture, saw that it counted for far more than its size might have warranted. Fifty years after his death Jamnagar is still recognisably his city. Cattle may wander beside the bazaars or be parked like motorcars outside the arcades of Willingdon Crescent but the job of clearing and cleansing, that was Ranji's first priority when he became ruler has not been undone.

The four main palaces of Jamnagar still remain, externally, much as Ranji left them. They may be the habitat of birds and bats, like the enclosed and highly decorated City Palace, or of pet animals, bucks, antelopes, gazelles, like Ranji's preferred Bhavindra Vilas, or simply shuttered and empty, except for the rare cold weather visitor, like the multi-domed Pratap Vilas Palace, or used as a government guest house like Vibha Vilas Palace; but whatever uses, or disuses, they are put to, they stand within their palace walls – the locked gates attended by Arab guards – as stately and resplendent as ever they did.

The grounds, alas, are scarcely kept up and gradually their handsome outbuildings – stables, garages, badminton and racquet courts – are being disposed of or converted. It is ironic that the huge and magnificently ornate Pratap Vilas Palace, which Ranji himself had built, should have received as its first guests his own mourners.

Within, the palaces reek of desertion, though their long corridors are still swept and a residue of ancient palace servants, a dozen or so in all, emerge sleepily from compounds or pantries to preserve the illusion of occupancy.

It is in Ranji's own room in the Jam Palace – the room in which he died – that the illusion is most devotedly fostered. Nothing here has been disturbed since Ranji's body was carried from it. The bed with its silver headboard is made up, and propped against the pillow lies a portrait of the Jam Saheb in ceremonial dress. On a bedside table Sir Pelham Warner's photograph, inscribed 'To Ranji, the greatest batsman of my time, from his sincere admirer and friend "Plum", December 1912' bears witness to Ranji's farewell season in English cricket. Popsey's cage is there, and many portraits; a row of cricket bats the colour of rich tobacco; old uniforms and turbans.

The heart of the room is not the bed but the locked glass cabinet beside which, on a shelf, stands the romantic alabaster head, in the art nouveau style, of a beautiful young woman. The cabinet itself contains such items as a letter from George V's secretary commiserating on the King's behalf on the loss of Ranji's eye; Ranji's glasses and cigarette case; his medals and Orders; his half-hunter on its gold chain, a miniature silver bat, a lighter; rings and cuff links and pins; pieces of jewellery.

On the highest of the three shelves Ranji's passport, the photograph in Indian dress with turban and eye-glass, lies open: Caste/Rajput; Religion/Hindoo; Indian home/Nawanagar; profession/Ruling Prince; Place and date of birth/ Sarodar 10 Sept 1872; Domicile/Nawanagar; Height 5ft 9; Colour of eyes/dark brown; Colour of hair/Black/grey; Visible distinguishing marks/ Smallpox marks on the face.

On the right of this, the six glass eyes which took their turn in Ranji's face are lodged in two satin-lined cases, marked 'G. Muller, 8 New Oxford Street'. For nearly a third of his life the socket of Ranji's eye had each night to be bathed by his doctor. During his years at Jamnagar, Dr Prosser Thomas later recalled, he had made efforts to establish a clinic in the city. Always, though, Ranji would mischievously summon him from his work to make up a four at bridge. Until the last days the ritual of replacing the eye and washing the eye-socket were the only tasks the doctor was allowed to perform.

There are still two servants alive at Jamnagar who have looked after the Jam Saheb. In their old age they carry out their shadow duties, materialising silently on bare feet, much as if His Highness were still alive. They attend and guard his room as if it were a shrine, allowing nothing to be moved.

For all that, Ranji's room is not a solemn place, simply the bedroom of a much loved and revered ruler who, in his day, happened to be a great cricketer. His trophies and personal effects are all around and though the sun streams through the shutters over the marble corridors outside and the hyenas and peacocks screech, within all is shuttered cool.

'When a person dies who does any one thing better than anyone else in the world,' wrote Hazlitt, discussing the fives player John Cavanagh in his famous essay 'Indian Jugglers', 'it leaves a gap in society.' That was certainly true of Ranji. Elsewhere in the same essay Hazlitt wrote, again about Cavanagh: 'He could not have shown himself in any ground in England, but he would have been immediately surrounded with inquisitive gazers, trying to find out in what part of his frame his unrivalled skill lay' – and that was true of Ranji too.

His effect on people was not confined to cricketers. The sculptor Eric Gill observed in his *Autobiography*, published seven years after Ranji's death:

> And while I am thus writing about the beauty and impressiveness of technical prowess I cannot, for it made an immense difference to my mind, omit the famous name of Ranjitsinhji. Even now, when I want to have a little quiet wallow in the thought of something wholly delightful and perfect, I think of Ranji on the county ground at Hove . . . There were many minor stars, each with his special and beloved technique, but nothing on earth could approach the special quality of Ranji's batting or fielding . . . I only place it on record that such craftsmanship and grace entered into my very soul.

It was Sir Stanley Jackson, Ranji's Cambridge captain, whom the Editor of the 1934 *Wisden* chose to write personally about Ranji. It was not an inspired choice, for Jackson expressed himself stiffly. Nevertheless, the regard and admiration comes through. Jackson makes no bones about not being 'particularly impressed' at coming upon a crowd gathered round a game on Parker's Piece in 1892. In the April of the next year, when Ranji had relays of top-class bowlers, Lockwood, Richardson, J. T. Hearne, Tom Hayward, bowling to him in the nets at Fenner's, Jackson, who had arrived after Ranji and finished his own practice while Ranji was still at it, questioned whether he was not rather overdoing it. Ranji replied: 'I find I am all right for half an hour but I cannot last. I must now master endurance.'

In that one remark by an undergraduate at the very outset of his career lies the clue to much of Ranji's success. Jackson continued: 'Ranji certainly played the game as all would wish to see it played . . . He was happiest when singing the praises of others.' In comparing Ranji and Fry, Jackson observed: 'Ranji played with an ease and grace as though to the manner born; Fry with a skill and technique obviously the product of a wonderful physique, indomitable determination and perseverance, and backed by the brain of a genius and a master of applied science.'

The Editor of *Wisden*, S. J. Southerton, added a postcript of his own. 'So has passed a great cricketer in the history of the game. We may never see his like again, for he burst on the cricket horizon at the start of what has been described as its most brilliant era, when there existed scope for introducing new ideas and methods. To me Ranji was the embodiment of all that a cricketer should be – generous in defeat, modest in success and genuinely enthusiastic regarding the achievements of either colleagues or opponents.

'It is not too much to say that by his extraordinary skill Ranji revolutionised cricket, the effects of his wonderful play on the leg-side being seen day after day down to the present time.'

About Ranji, Jessop wrote: '. . . he was indisputably the greatest genius who ever stepped on to a cricket field, the most brilliant figure in what, I believe, was cricket's most brilliant period.'

Curiously, there are few cricketing memorials to Ranji. In 1934 the small scoreboard near the Secretary's office at Hove was rebuilt in memory of Ranji, and in that same summer the Ranji Trophy, for which the States of India compete, was launched by the Maharajah Bhupindra Singh of Patiala. In its third year Nawanagar, entering for the first time and led by A. F. Wensley of Sussex, won the championship. The team included, besides three Nawanagar princes, L. Amar Singh and Vinoo Mankad.

What Ranji left to cricket was a series of caressive gestures, a range of hitherto undreamed-of strokes whose liquidity became the very music of an English summer. It is in terms of water, perhaps, that his art can best be summarised; patient stillness under high cloud, elusiveness, transparency, mobility. It was said of Ranji that he moved as if he had no bones, a characteristic more generally associated with West Indian cricketers of African negro descent than with Indians. What Ranji did, though, was to master the accepted techniques of batting and then dispense with them. He was the embodiment of free form, architecture without evident structure. Only half a dozen in the history of the game have added something new to it, and Ranji was one of them. His true memorial is in the memory of those who saw him, transmitted down the generations: a shiver of the spine at Hove or Lord's, the air signed with that latest of late cuts, that silkiest of glances. The Indian prince, in all his finery, abroad in an English summer.

An Indian View

This book has dealt with an Indian prince who was an English cricketer. Ranji took virtually no part in the progress of India towards Test status, although the year before he died India played their first Test match in England. Not surprisingly, Ranji's reluctance to involve himself in the development of the game in his own country caused disappointment. In his book *Portrait of Indian Sport* (1959) Anthony de Mello, a leading figure in Indian cricket administration and founder in 1928 of the Board of Control for Cricket in India, devoted the opening chapters to a consideration of Ranji and Duleep. More in sorrow than in anger towards India's great folk-hero, he wrote:

> Ranji did absolutely nothing for Indian sport and sportsmen. To all our requests for aid, encouragement and advice Ranji gave but one answer: 'Duleep and I are English cricketers.' He could not have been more blunt. In short, Ranji was a different man in England and India. That is not to say he was disloyal: far from it – as his work in Nawanagar shows more vividly than could mere words. But when work was done, and the time came for play and relaxation, Ranji's mind did not dwell amongst us in India. It was in England. And it is my understanding of this great and strange man that his heart was in England also.

De Mello continues:

In most other walks of life he was the model Indian Prince. But the Ranji who settled in Jamnagar after the First World War was an altogether different man from the great cricketer who delighted English crowds in earlier years ... It is understandable that when he finally left England to live in India he should leave something behind him. There was talk, too, of an unhappy love affair; and certainly as an Indian Prince Ranji could not have married an English girl. If true, it will take us a step nearer to the explanation why Ranji left his heart somewhere among the green fields of England.

After referring to the 'ironic, bitter parrot, who seemed closer to him than any man' and reaffirming how 'he was in most things kind-hearted, generous and sympathetic', De Mello concludes: 'Towards the end of his life he gave the impression he was dis-illusioned. Always, it seemed, he was waiting for something, waiting with the calm patience of the true Indian, for something which, deep within himself, he knew he would never have. Not in this life, not ever.'

Although de Mello is certainly bitter about Duleep – who though gravely ill in 1932 chose to play until his final collapse for Sussex rather than for India – and about Ranji's influencing of Duleep in this, he acknowledges without reservation the immense prestige Ranji brought to India and Indian cricketers. It was the idea of Ranji, the awareness that it was an Indian who had become the greatest batsman in the world, that contributed more than anything else to the Indian cricketer's realisation of his own possibilities.

De Mello's views, however, stated more than twenty-five years after Ranji's death, make plain an aspect of Ranji's alienation. When Ranji came to prominence there was no such thing as Indian cricket at Test level; like it or not, he was obliged to become an English cricketer. For all the gifts he brought to the game from his own race, his cricket was English-bred. All his serious cricket was played in England. It was inevitable, therefore, that he should, at this most formative period of his life, have made friends with whom he tended to be happier than with those he made later.

It was these attachments that led, more than anything, to strain among his fellow Indians and, ultimately, perhaps, to the sense of disillusionment he experienced in his dealings with the British. Lord Willingdon, the Viceroy, was not simply a figurehead of Empire to Ranji, but an old friend, a past President of MCC, with whom he shared far more pleasures and experiences than with most Indians, of whatever rank.

Ranji never attempted to fuse the English cricketer and the Indian prince. England was his glorious past, not India, which represented a present and future fraught with problems and frustrations.

Duleep was another matter. In due course he served India well, diplomatically perhaps more than as a cricket administrator, but had illness not cut short his career so tragically young he might well have done what the Nawab of Pataudi, only five years his junior, subsequently did – play for both England and India. Historically, it was the just transition.

Career Records – season by season

First-class Cricket

Season	Innings	Not out	Runs	Average	Highest Score
1893	19	2	439	25.82	58
1894	16	4	387	32.25	94
1895	39	3	1,775	49.30	150
1896	55	7	2,780	57.91	171*
1897	48	5	1,940	45.11	260
1897–98 (in Australia)	22	3	1,157	60.89	189
1899	58	8	3,159	63.18	197
1899 (in America)	2	0	125	62.50	68
1900	40	5	3,065	87.57	275
1901	40	5	2,468	70.51	285*
1902	26	2	1,110	46.25	234*
1903	41	7	1,924	56.58	204
1904	34	6	2,077	74.17	207*
1908	28	3	1,138	45.52	200
1912	28	2	1,113	42.80	176
1920	4	0	39	9.75	16
Total	500	62	24,696	56.38	285*

Test Cricket (England v. Australia)

Season	Innings	Not out	Runs	Average	Highest Score
1896	4	1	235	78.33	154*
1897–98 (in Australia)	10	1	457	50.77	175
1899	8	2	278	46.33	93*
1902	4	–	19	4.75	13
Total	26	4	989	44.95	175

Centuries

The following are Ranjitsinhji's seventy-two centuries in first-class cricket:

season

1895	150	Sussex v. MCC at Lord's
	137*	Sussex v. Oxford University, at Hove
	110	Sussex v. Middlesex, at Lord's
	100	Sussex v. Nottinghamshire, at Hove
1896	171*	Sussex v. Oxford University, at Hove
	165	Sussex v. Lancashire, at Hove
	154*	England v. Australia, at Manchester
	146	MCC v. Cambridge University, at Cambridge
	138	Sussex v. Yorkshire, at Bradford
	100	Sussex v. Yorkshire, at Hove
	125*	
	114*	Sussex v. Gloucestershire, at Hove
	107	Sussex v. Somerset, at Hove
	100*	Sussex v. Nottinghamshire, at Hove
1897	260	Sussex v. MCC, at Lord's
	170	Sussex v. Essex, at Hove
	157	MCC v. Lancashire, at Lord's
	149	Sussex v. Hampshire, at Hove
	129*	Sussex v. Middlesex, at Eastbourne
1897–1898	189	A. E. Stoddart's XI v. South Australia, at Adelaide
(in Australia)	175	England v. Australia, at Sydney
	112*	A. E. Stoddart's XI v. New South Wales, at Sydney
1899	197	Sussex v. Surrey, at the Oval
	178	Sussex v. Nottinghamshire, at Hove
	174	Sussex v. Surrey, at Hove
	161	Sussex v. Essex, at Hove
	154	Sussex v. Gloucestershire, at Bristol
	120	Sussex v. Middlesex, at Lord's
	107	Sussex v. Cambridge University, at Eastbourne
	102	Sussex v. Lancashire, at Hove
1900	275	Sussex v. Leicestershire, at Leicester
	222	Sussex v. Somerset, at Hove
	220	Sussex v. Kent, at Hove
	215*	Sussex v. Cambridge University, at Cambridge
	202	Sussex v. Middlesex, at Hove
	192*	Sussex v. Kent, at Tonbridge

	158	Sussex v. Nottinghamshire, at Nottingham
	192*	Sussex v. Kent, at Tonbridge
	158	Sussex v. Nottinghamshire, at Nottingham
	158	A. J. Webbe's XI v. Cambridge University, at Cambridge
	127	Sussex v. Gloucestershire, at Hove
	109	Sussex v. Gloucestershire, at Bristol
	103	Sussex v. Surrey, at Hove
1901	285*	Sussex v. Somerset, at Taunton
	219	Sussex v. Essex, at Hove
	204	Sussex v. Lancashire, at Hove
	170*	Sussex v. Lancashire, at Manchester
	139	Sussex v. Worcestershire, at Worcester
	133	Sussex v. Somerset, at Hove
	115	England v. Yorkshire, at Hastings
	100*	Sussex v. Surrey, at Hove
1902	234*	Sussex v. Surrey, at Hastings
	130	Sussex v. Essex, at Leyton
	135	Sussex v. Surrey, at the Oval
1903	204	Sussex v. Surrey, at the Oval
	162*	Sussex v. Gloucestershire, at Hove
	144*	Sussex v. Lancashire, at Hove
	132	London County v. MCC, at Crystal Palace
	105	Sussex v. Lancashire, at Hove
1904	207*	Sussex v. Lancashire, at Hove
	178*	Sussex v. South Africans, at Hove
	166*	MCC v. Cambridge University, at Lord's
	152	Sussex v. Surrey, at Hove
	148	Sussex v. Yorkshire, at Sheffield
	142	MCC v. Oxford University, at Lord's
	135	Sussex v. Kent, at Tunbridge Wells
	121	Gentlemen v Players, at Lord's
1908	200	Sussex v. Surrey, at the Oval
	153*	Sussex v. Middlesex, at Lord's
	101	England v. MCC Australian Team, at Scarborough
1912	176	Sussex v. Lancashire, at Hove
	128	Sussex v. Kent, at Hove
	125	Sussex v. Australians, at Hove
	101	MCC v. Cambridge University, at Lord's

* Denotes not out.

Other Records

Century on Debut for the County

season

1895   150   Sussex v. MCC (Lord's)

Century in the First Match of a Tour

1897–98   189   A. E. Stoddart's XI v. South Australia (Adelaide)

Century on Debut in Test Cricket

1896   154*   England v. Australia (Manchester)

Century in Each Innings

1896   100 and 125* Sussex v. Yorkshire (Hove)
(on the same day – August 22nd)

Three Centuries in Successive Innings

1896   165   Sussex v. Lancashire (Hove)
         100
         125* Sussex v. Yorkshire (Hove)

1900   127   Sussex v. Gloucestershire (Hove)
         222   Sussex v. Somerset (Hove)
         215* Sussex v. Cambridge University (Cambridge)

Ten or More Centuries in a Season

1900   11 Centuries
1896   10 Centuries

Five Double Centuries in a Season

1900   275   Sussex v. Leicestershire (Leicester)
         222   Sussex v. Somerset (Hove)
         220   Sussex v. Kent (Hove)
         215* Sussex v. Cambridge University (Cambridge)
         202   Sussex v. Middlesex (Hove)

Double Century in Successive Innings

season

1900   222   Sussex v. Somerset (Hove)
         215* Sussex v. Cambridge University (Cambridge)

1901   285* Sussex v. Somerset (Taunton)
         204 Sussex v. Lancashire (Hove)

Thousand Runs in Australia

1897   1,157 runs (average 60.89)

Thousand Runs in a Month

1899   1,037 runs (average 79.76) June
1899   1,011 runs (average 77.76) August
1900   1,059 runs (average 96.27) July

Three Thousand Runs in a Season

1899   3,159 runs (average 63.18)
1900   3,065 runs (average 87.57)

Partnerships Over Two Hundred

1902   344 with W. Newham   7th wkt. v. Essex (Layton)
1899   325 with G. Brann   2nd wkt. v. Surrey (Oval)
1901   298 with E. Killick   3rd wkt. v. Lancashire (Hove)
1901   292 * with C. B. Fry   2nd wkt. v. Somerset (Taunton)
1904   255 with C. B. Fry   3rd wkt. v. Yorkshire (Sheffield)
1899   252 with G. Brann   2nd wkt. v. Gloucestershire (Bristol)

All partnerships were for Sussex.
Partnership of 344 with W. Newham is an England record for the seventh wicket.

* Denotes not out.

Bibliography

Where possible the books I have consulted are mentioned in the text. The only biography to have been published to date, Roland Wild's *Ranjitsinhji*, (Rich & Cowan, 1934) came out only a year after Ranji's death. It was commissioned during Ranji's lifetime and written in close collaboration with Colonel H. W. Berthon who, during most of Ranji's years as Jam Saheb, was his friend and adviser. The book carried a preface by Ranji's nephew and successor, His Highness the Maharajah Jam Saheb Digvijaysinhji of Nawanagar.

As far as the facts of Ranji's life are concerned, Wild's book must be regarded as an authoritative, as well as authorised, version. I have taken it as such and for the chronology of Ranji's life in India I have followed it. Wild, in his turn, relied to some extent on *Jamnagar and its Ruler* by Naoroji Dumasia (Times Press, Bombay, 1927). Neither book deals other than superficially with cricket.

Of particular value to me have been C. B. Fry's *Life Worth Living* (Eyre & Spottiswode, 1939); *Duleep*, edited by Vijay Merchant, Vaisant Raiji, Anandji Dossa and Vithalbhai Jhaveri (Bombay, 1963) and *Ranjitsinhji, Prince of Cricket* by Percy Cross Standing (Arrowsmith, 1903).

The volumes of *Wisden* that cover Ranji's career as a cricketer have, needless to say, been invaluable. Other books consulted include:

Batchelor, Denzil. *C. B. Fry*, Phoenix House, 1951.

Beldham, G. W. and C. B. Fry. *Great Batsmen*, Macmillan, 1905.

Cardus, Neville. *Days in the Sun*, G. Richards, 1924.

The Summer Game, Cayme Press, 1929.

Good Days, Jonathan Cape, 1934.

Gardiner, A. G. *Pillars of Society*, Dent, 1913.

Gordon, Sir Home. *The Background of Cricket*, Arthur Barker, 1939.

Kincaid, Charles. *The Land of 'Ranji' and 'Duleep'*, Blackwood, 1931.

Marshall, John. *Sussex Cricket*, Heinemann, 1959.

Mello, Anthony de. *Portrait of Indian Sport*, Delhi, 1959.

Pouchepadass, Jacques. *The Last Maharajas*, Roli Books, Delhi, 1981.

Pridham, Major C. H. B. *The Charm of Cricket*, Herbert Jenkins, 1949.

Raiji, Vasant. *Ranji, The Legend and the Man*, Raiji, 1963.

Raiji, Vasant (ed.) *Ranji, A Centenary Album*, Seven Star Publications, 1972.

Ranjitsinhji. *The Jubilee Book of Cricket*, Blackwood, 1897.

Ranjitsinhji. *With Stoddart's Team in Australia*, James Bowden, 1898.

Streeton, Richard. *P. G. H. Fender*, Faber 1981.

Swanton, E. W. (ed.) *The World of Cricket*, Michael Joseph, 1966

Thomson, A. A. *Cricket My Happiness*, Museum Press, 1954.

Trevor, Philip. *Cricket & Cricketers*, Chapman & Hall, 1921.

Valette, John de la. *Progress in Nawanagar State*, Bombay, 1932.

Warner, P. F. *Lord's 1787–1945*, Harrap, 1946.

Nawanagar and Its Critics, Times of India Press, 1929.

Index